STONE SAMPLER

STONE SAMPLER

by STUDIO MARMO

Text by Marco Campagna

W. W. NORTON & COMPANY, INC.
NEW YORK • LONDON

First American edition published by W. W. Norton & Company, Inc., 2003

First published in Italy by Absolute Printers under the title STONE BOX

Printed in Italy

Manufacturing by Absolute Printers

Library of Congress Cataloging-in-Publication Data

Campagna, Marco.
Stone sampler / Studio Marmo; text by Marco Campagna.
p.cm.
Includes index.
ISBN 0-393-73118-9 (pbk.)
1. Building stones. I. Studio Marmo (Florence, Italy). II. Title.

TA426.C36 2003
691'.2dc21 2003043018

W. W. Norton & Company, Inc., 500 Fifth Avenue, New York, N.Y. 10110
www.wwnorton.com

W. W. Norton & Company Ltd., Castle House, 75/76 Wells St., London W1T 3QT

0 9 8 7 6 5 4 3 2 1

INTRODUCTION

Since ancient times stone has always been the chief element in building and decoration. The Seven Wonders of the World, and any structure that has survived to modern times and still provokes astonishment and admiration, were realized in stone. The most traditional use of stone is structural, where the stone is not used for its esthetic properties but for its own qualities such as its strength and resistance to wear and tear and to all weathers. Stone is demonstrably the best material for the realization of buildings that defy time: the Pyramids, the Coliseum, castles, cathedrals, and religious buildings all over the world.

Through the years and with technological progress, such as the development of reinforced concrete, the importance of stone as a mere building material has been considerably reduced. Its use as an architectural material has decreased as nowadays round-arch or pillar supports are seldom employed; on the other hand, its use as a purely decorative product has increased. Architects who once employed stone to build buttress walls can use it to beautify the shell of buildings and obtain chromatic and design effects that once were inconceivable, and even achieve the same structural appearance with materials that previously couldn't bear the weight. What is architectural stone? How can we plan to use it when new and ever-different varieties of stone enter the market and new countries become producers? Old quarries are depleted, new quarries are found, and known varieties dramatically change in their characteristics and color. How can you differentiate a piece of marble from a piece of granite? Why are some materials much more expensive than others? We will try to answer these questions in this volume.

CONTENTS

Details of facade of Santa Maria Novella, Florence

V·F·AN·SAL·MCCCCLXX

1. DEFINITION OF NATURAL STONE

It is not easy to come to a clear definition of natural stone. When you dig deep enough into the earth you reach a stratum of stone everywhere, but it doesn't mean you have a quarry useful for architectural purpose. The usual meaning of the term natural stone is: "A portion of rock used as building or decorative material." This book deals only with architectural stone and not with industrial minerals, precious, semiprecious, or ornamental stones, or non-natural materials such as chemical or artificial stones. We are concerned with natural stone that has the characteristics that make it interesting for structural or decorative use. For such a purpose the material should meet the following requirements:

- It must be available in sufficient quantities to be economically convenient;
- The quarry from which it comes must be in a location easily accessible forthe removal of materials (e.g., not under the sea or in the mountains);
- It must be available in blocks that have sufficient dimension to allow the transformation into finished products;
- It must be possible to finish the material by polishing or with thermal or mechanichal treatment to give it pleasant esthetic characteristics;
- Blocks must be in perfect condition and free from defects that could make them unusable;
- The material must have characteristics that make it unique in its genre.

Even if no one of the above points is by itself essential to the exploiting of a natural stone, and there are cases in which one or more of these requirements are not met, their presence enhances the value of the material from a commercial point of view. For example, a material with a color similar to that of other, less expensive varieties has little chance of success compared to a material whose uniqueness justifies a higher price.

The importance of some of these points is decreasing because of the development of new technologies. While in Roman times only outcropping materials could be exploited, today the diamond wire and chain belt allow us to work in tunnels and reach deposits not previously available. Another technological advance that brought deep changes to the market was reinforcement, a technique that permits the reutilization of cracked materials otherwise unsuitable for polishing or even cutting.

As we will see, the classification of stone from a geological point of view differs from the simpler commercial one. While the former is rigorous and relates to the origin of the stone itself, the latter begins from the physical appearance of the materials and proceeds to assimilate the stones that share similar qualities and require analogous processing techniques (for example, those that are cut with diamond blades) despite their geological diversities.

1.1 Geological Classification

Geological classification goes back to Aristotle's division of living and not-living species into three kingdoms: animal, vegetable, and mineral, and each of these is further broken down into more and more specific fields. The first distinction of the mineral kingdom is between minerals and rocks. A mineral is a compound characterized by its own formula and by its ability to crystallize in a specific way. It is improperly called the mixture of usable material and rocks. In common terms, a mineral is the material obtained in the extraction industry as a mixture of exploitable elements and scoriae. In strict terms, it is a compound characterized by its own formula and by its ability to crystallize in a specific way. In contrast, a rock can consist of crystals of the same mineral or of minerals of different chemical compositions. The first possibility is represented by a sample of Bianco Carrara marble, composed of calcium carbonate crystals; the second possibility is represented by granite, which is a compound of quartz and silicates of different composition, crystallized in different crystal structures.
In discussing geology it is appropriate to understand the distinctions between the various branches which deal with natural stone:

- Geochemistry and petrography deal with the formation, alteration, and degradation of rocks and their systematic classification.
- Crystallography and mineralogy are the study of the various ways of crystallization of specific and their physical and chemical properties.

Geology is the science that studies the formation and the structure of the earth's crust and reconstructs the chronological sequence of events that conditioned its evolution. It is common to divide geology into the following branches: general geology, tectonics, geomorphology, stratigraphic geology, and historical geology. General geology studies the mechanisms and the probable causes of the phenomena that occur both inside and outside earth's crust, while tectonics studies its deformations. Geomorphology studies earth's surface shapes and their alterations. Stratigraphic geology examines the materials that comprise the earth's crust in order to describe the areas where they are located, their geographical distribution, and possible correlations, etc. It provides the data that are the basis of historical geology, whose goal is to reconstruct the evolution of the earth's crust, the chronological development of events, and the interdependence of geological processes. Petrography, mineralogy, geochemistry, geophysics, and paleontology are closely related sciences which provide necessary information and knowledge to geology.

As with all artificial schemes imposed on natural phenomena, we cannot give absolute value to any single category: the mineralogical composition and the cooling condition of the rocks vary; furthermore, extremely frequently rocks belong to an intermediate position between two contiguous groups and are therefore difficult to classify.

According to their formation process, rocks are divided into magmatic, sedimentary, and metamorphic.

- Magmatic, also called igneous or eruptive, rocks are formed by the cooling of magma, a mass of melted substance at an extremely high temperature which is present at the various crust levels. These rocks are divided into effusive or volcanic, if the cooling follows a volcanic eruption and therefore occurs outside the earth's crust, and intrusive or plutonic, if the cooling takes place inside the crust.
- Sedimentary rocks originate from the deposit of sediments from the alteration and disaggregation of rocks on the earth's surface and their following lithogenesis at some depth within the earth's crust. As they are constituted of material transported to its final sedimentation place in solid form or in solution, they are divided into detrital or clastic and chemical rocks.
- Metamorphic rocks originate from the mineralogical and structural transformation of preexisting rocks due to magmatic intrusion or to rising temperature and pressure caused by the displacement of the earth's crust. Depending upon the predominance of a particular element, we can divide them into carbonatic, when they predominantly consist of carbonatic minerals (calcite, dolomite, magnesite, etc.), silicatic, when they consist of silicatic materials (feldspars, micas, etc.), and siliceous, when they contain a very high percentage of quartz crystals.

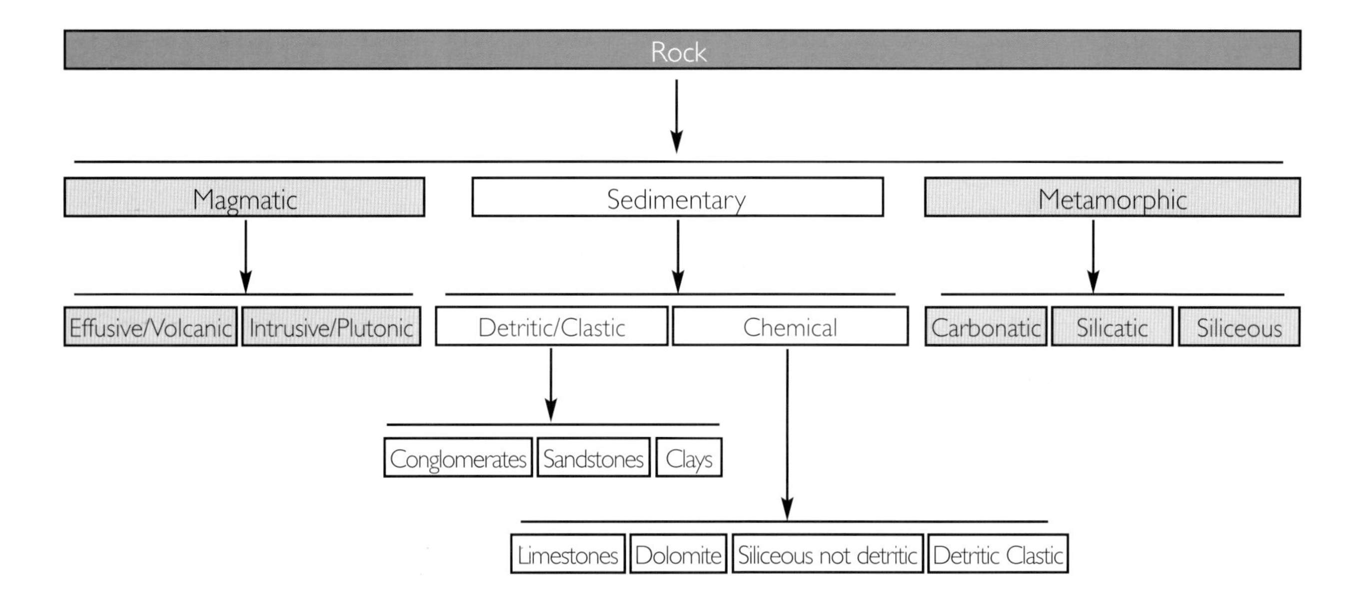

Each group may be further classified according to the different quantity of minerals they contain. The following table helps to trace each natural stone back to the geological groups listed above:

Magmatic Rocks		Sedimentary Rocks		Metamorphic Rocks
Intrusive	Effusive	Clastic	Chemical	
Granite				Granite
				Marble
			Travertine	
			Onyx	
		Limestone		
				Quartzite
	Porphyry			
	Basalt			
	Tuff			
	Trachyte			
		Sandstone		
		Breccia		
				Slate
				Schist
				Gneiss
		Conglomerate		
				Serpentine
		Dolomite		
Serizzo				

1.2 Commercial Classification

Whatever their geological classification, natural stones are, from a commercial point of view, those rocks that can be used for architectonic purposes. The number of different stones available in the market is not fixed and keeps rising. Two factors increase the supply and affect each other: technological development and market demand. The first allows the number and the nature of available stones to increase constantly, as new machinery and tools make impracticable deposits exploitable. Already known stones that are located in unreachable areas become available when new routes are established and transfer costs get lower.

The increasing demand of designers and architects for new products is the other main reason that producers and suppliers send their geologists around the world to discover new material deposits. Once dug out, these stones are tested to establish their technical and esthetic qualities. If they pass these tests it means that they have been deemed interesting enough to face the final test: the market. Actually, the sale will be the final judge of their success in the world markets.

Although materials belonging to all of the three geological groups defined above are used as natural stone, the commercial definition is not so precise as the scientific one. It is likely that classification was originally based on the real typology of the rocks, but with the discovery of new varieties it is reasonable to think that the criterion evolved as follows: "If this is a marble and has to be cut with diamond, and this other material has to be cut with diamond as well, it means that the new one is marble too!" Simplistic, but efficient. This method of classification still exists. It is mainly based on two elements: appearance and processing method.

By appearance we mean the exterior characteristics of rock, such as grain and texture, which, together with veining and color, are the elements used to identify a single material and distinguish it from all the others. The processing method is the set of techniques that allows the transformation from the rough block to the finished product.

This system of classification, despite its simplicity, works rather well from a practical point of view: it is easy to follow because it is based on the experience of the person who uses it, and it is destined to improve and to be refined in practice. Furthermore, when the commercial classification is compared with the scientific one, the differences between them are not so relevant. We can not assume that a stone that is commercially called granite is in fact in that category and shares all of its characteristics. Although a mistake of this kind does not necessarily result in dramatic consequences, an inappropriate use of a particular material might give an unwanted result. For this reason, rigorous tests are mandatory before using a material in extreme conditions. For instance, experience teaches us that travertine, because of its porosity, is inappropriate for exterior use in areas where the temperature drops below freezing point. Humidity trapped in the travertine cavities, following thermal dilatation caused by frost, causes the material to crumble. Thus, where it is likely that the material could be subject to any kind of stress (chemical, mechanical, thermal, etc.), it is useful to consider the technical specifications of the stone. Commercially speaking, natural stones are divided in three macro categories: marble, granite, and stone.

1.2.1 Marble. Marble is a granular aggregate of crystals of calcite or dolomite, with a predominance of the former. In the same marble, crystals usually have a uniform size, but there may be substantial variations between marbles of different quarries. Veined marbles derive their special characteristics from the variation in color and size of the crystals in the different areas of the stone. All marble was originally limestone and pure white in color. Most calcareous stones have been formed by sediments accumulated on the sea bottom. Physical and chemical changes then transformed them into marble. The variations in the stone features are a consequence of the differences in the sediments in the original deposit and of the various subsequent changes. Commercially speaking, the term marble is applied to any calcareous rock capable of being well polished. Therefore, even some materials that from a petrographic point of view do not belong to the marble class are included in this group. This is why it is possible to have substantial differences in aspect, load strength, elasticity, etc. between two marbles in the same group. So, what are the characteristics common to all members of the category? In practice, how can you distinguish a marble from another stone just looking at it from a commercial point of view? You cannot be sure in any case, but marbles generally have a finer grain compared with granites and a more crystalline consistency than the stones. Veining, if present, is generally better amalgamated with the background of the material in comparison with veining in granites, which presents more net changes in color and grain. As it has always been in this field, there are numerous exceptions to the rule and therefore these criteria cannot be applied to materials such as Breccia Multicolore (page 59) or Fossil Brown (page 65), while they can be applied to materials like Bianco Carrara (page 45) or Rosso Laguna (page 61). At this point you can use the criteria of processing: the techniques used to cut blocks or marble and transform them into slabs and the abrasives used for the polishing are different from those used for granites. In addition, marbles are less hard compared with granites, making the cutting of the block in slabs easier and faster. On the other hand, blocks of marble are more often defective and of smaller size than the granite ones. Marble comes in several color combinations, so you can have all the variations in a palette. It is distributed all over the world, but the main producing countries are concentrated in the Mediterranean basin, and the most important are Italy, Greece, Turkey, and Spain. Marble can be subdivided into veined, not veined, and breccias. The last are characterized by ovular inclusions with more or less rounded shape, in a basically uniform material. Further distinctions are usually made with reference to the presence of specific colors, the coarseness of the grain, the presence and the direction of veining, and the country of origin.

1.2.2 Granites. Intrusive magmatic rocks formed mainly by alkaline feldspars and quartz constitute the family of granites. Some authors prefer to locate some granites in the group of metamorphic rocks, because the presence of quartz as a fundamental component, in amounts between 20 and 40 percent, is a feature of this family. Granites are divided in two main groups: veined and not veined.

Veined granites are those in which the minerals form stripes of color different from the background color of the so-called veins that are distributed on the surface of the material giving the appearance of a sinuous movement.

Not-veined materials, in contrast, present the same appearance over the entire surface of the slab. In many cases it is possible to single out, on a base background color, two or three types of crystals whose color and size are slightly different from one another, the combination of which is the characteristic of each material. For example in Rosa Sardo (page 103) there are pink, black, and gray crystals on a white background. Some of the not-veined materials have elongated crystals that draw "dotted" parallel lines so that they show a horizontal pattern. Contiguous pieces of these materials are usually placed with the pattern in the same direction. These materials are called "oriented" (for example, Giallo Topazio page 93). It is possible for the same granite, sawn following different planes, to be both a veined and a not-veined material. Some stones that are usually called granites, because of how they are processed, look like breccias. This is the case with Marinace (page 101), Palladio (page 105), and Jurassic Green (page 99).

1.2.3 Stone. Stone is the broadest category because it includes what is not in the former categories. Some materials in this group might be entitled to an independent category (for example, limestones and travertines), but they are traditionally grouped here. Other materials belong instead to one category or another because of the type of processing they undergo (for example, onyxes can be considered a subgroup of marble, and quarzites a subgroup between marble and granite). The most prominent stone groups are:

Limestone. We have already briefly described this stone in the section on marble, of which it is the geological precursor. The most common color of limestone is beige, with variations that tend to gray and yellow. The grain is generally fine and because this a material of sedimentary origin, it is not unusual to find fossil materials in it, particularly little shells.

Travertine. This is a calcareous material that, due to its easy workability, is traditionally used as a building material. In its most usual form it is cut against the rift, that is, perpendicular to the bedding plane, showing its porosity more clearly. The classical image of travertine is indeed one of a material with very distinct horizontal veining, caused by its several sedimentary strata, studded with little holes formed by the loss of carbon dioxide at the moment of its geological formation. It is common to see these holes filled for esthetic reasons before polishing, which is done with a matte component (cement) to make them uniform with the background, or with a transparent component (epoxy) to give them more prominence.

Sandstone. The name is indicative of both the geological origin and the appearance of this material, which is a compound of quartz cemented with siliceous sand, iron oxide, or calcium carbonate. As a consequence of its formation, the unpolished material has a rough surface, with a rather coarse but only apparently fragile grain.

Quartzite. This is a metamorphic rock that consists of quartz crystals usually so firmly cemented as to form a homogeneous mass. Because the material is almost exclusively quartz, it is generally hard, resilient, and particularly suitable for polishing. It is generally dug out in strata whose surface is unusually smooth.

Onyx. This is crystalline rock characterized by translucency and veining in concentric bands. The transparency is especially evident when onyx is cut into thin pieces. This attribute is frequently exploited in backlit panels.

The following table summarizes the commercial classification of natural stones:

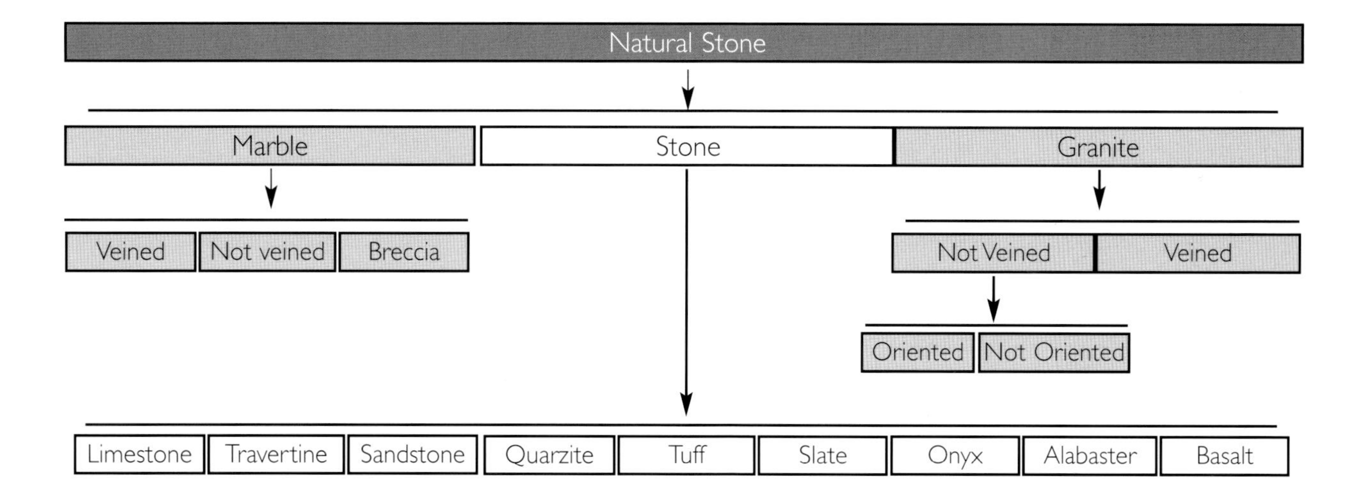

2. NATURAL STONE FEATURES

When stone is employed as a building material, you must consider both its esthetic and technical features. When describing a material, the main characteristics to be considered are color, pattern, and grain. To these three elements, which are always evident when you examine the stone, may be added other considerations such as the classification of the stone or its country of origin, to improve the description.

Color. Color is usually the first and most striking stone quality. The terms used for its description come from daily conversation. When a material is said, for example, to be yellow, this means that the general impression derived from that stone is that yellow predominates. This is not sufficient to pinpoint the material; what in the material is yellow and what other colors are present must be clarified. The main aspects to consider in describing a stone's color are the background color, the secondary color, and the color of the veining. Not all the colors occur with the same frequency, and their rarity is one of the major factors that determines the stone price in the market.

Pattern. Stone pattern is characterized by the presence and distribution of the various components in the rocky mass. It is determined first of all by the absence or presence of veins. In the first case, the material can be described as homogeneous: no dominant pattern is present, and the appearance is uniform in all areas of the stone. A veined material presents another kind of consistency and color in the background pattern of the material. Note that pattern is not predetermined, but rather strongly influenced by the way a material is sawn. If we consider a typical sedimentary stone that has parallel layers of sediments placed horizontally one on the other—e.g., travertine—we notice that sawing this material perpendicularly to the bedding plane (that is, across the rift, or vein-cut), produces a very clear, striped veining (see Travertino Romano Classico, page 77). In contrast, sawing the same block parallel to the bedding plane (that is, along the rift, or fleuri-cut), produces a more open and less clearly defined pattern with a cloudy appearance (see Travertino Romano Classico in Falda, page 77). This result is common with many other veined materials, and also with homogenous material whenever the stone crystal form has a uniform direction. If a homogeneous material like Verde Lavras (page 101) is cut with the rift or against the rift, its pattern changes and acquires an oriented direction as well.

Grain. Grain defines the size and in some cases the crystal shape that constitutes a rock. Although from a commercial point of view there are three types of grain (fine, medium, and coarse), there are no precise indications concerning the range of size each type should include. Two different scales are usually mentioned: one for granite varieties and one for marble and stone. The former denotes a fine or medium grain while the latter denotes a medium or coarse grain. Actually, what is considered fine grain for marble and stone does not exist for granite varieties, and what is considered a coarse grain for granite is normally of no commercial interest for marble and stone. Grain size is generally much less significant than color or pattern if you have to determine a material's esthetic value. However, grain size is important to determine the material's physical and mechanical properties and therefore its final aspect after the application of different surface finishes and its performance in structural contexts. For example, fine-grained marbles often have a much higher compressive strength and hardness than coarse-grained materials. This means that they are more difficult to work with, but they can be used to make a wider range of finished products. Another important factor in considering a material for a project is the range of variation of esthetic features and the presence of defects or blemishes in the stone. Because personal taste is subjective, it is difficult to come to a precise agreement about what is acceptable. Some stone defects often have an effect of esthetic impairment and therefore have to be clearly identified when choosing the material in order to avoid them or to treat them, removing or minimizing their impact on the final product. Other defects affect a stone's technical properties, with a higher probability of reducing the stone's mechanical resistance, so these defects should be avoided during production.

A final important consideration concerning material quality is that of constant esthetic features, the so-called accepted material range. This is subjective too, and it is influenced by the choice of surface finish. If you polish a material you can highlight its minimal defects, while if you bush hammer it you can make them unnoticeable. In case of homogeneous colored or patterned materials, the variation tolerance is very low, and even small alterations may impair their quality. The tolerance is generally higher when the esthetic value of certain materials is based on the pattern or color heterogeneity.

3. ARCHITECTURAL USE OF NATURAL STONE

In nature, stones are shaped like rocks, which you can seldom exploit directly. The first transformation takes place in the quarry, where the stone is separated from the surrounding material using different methods (blasting, diamond-wire sawing, drilling) to make a block that is the first form for trading. Then the stone leaves the country of origin to be processed elsewhere.

What products are available in the market? They can be divided into three groups according to their final use and customization. Standard products are the most elementary ones and can be considered semi-manufactured. Customized products relate to particular needs and are designed for a precise project. Finally, artistic products must satisfy both a definite technical demand and the individual customer's and artist's needs.

3.1 Standard Products

Standard products can be divided in two groups: semi-manufactured products and undiversified products. Products from both groups are commonly in stock in all the warehouses of the different stone industries.

3.1.1 Semi-manufactured Products. This first group includes all those products which need further processing to become a finished item. The listing follows the working process so that strips usually derive from unshaped blocks while slabs derive from blocks. After this stage, strips are transformed into tiles or skirtings.

Block
This is the typical starting element of any process. The ideal block is shaped like a parallelepiped, squared up and with faces as parallel as possible. The extraction techniques and the quarry faults do not often allow this form.
Unshaped block
This is a not-squared-up block, with one, or even no, cut faces. It is usually what remains of a quarry boulder after cutting away the squared-up blocks, or the material which follows the natural quarry fault. These can be more defective than regular blocks.
Slab
A slab is the product of sawing the block and constitutes the starting point for most products. It is possible to saw slabs in any thickness, starting from a minimum of approximately 5mm, but varying according to the material. The usual thicknesses are 2 or 3cm. For thicknesses over 5cm the slab is usually called a solid or massive stone slab.
Strip
A strip is a piece of stone of predetermined width and undetermined or "free" length produced in order to be further cut and transformed into tiles. The usual thicknesses are 0.7 and 1cm, but variations occur depending upon the nature of the material and the required format. As the final sizes are smaller than slabs, strips are obtained by sawing unshaped blocks.

3.1.2 Undiversified Products. The second group includes manufactured products ready for installation.

Tile
Tile is the preeminently modular format, typically used for flooring, especially in interiors. Available in almost all materials, it is the best compromise between quality and price and offers an excellent cladding material with a reduced cost in comparison to that obtained from the cutting of slabs into

customized tiles. The advantages of standardization are moderated by the fact that available formats are limited. The most common formats are 30 x 30cm and 40 x 40cm, though there are larger and not-squared formats. Generally, tiles are polished and ready to install, but different kinds of surface finishing are possible and sometimes rough tiles are installed and later polished on the spot in order to obtain a smooth surface without imperfections.

Skirting

Like strips, skirting is a piece of predetermined width and free length, but it is ready for installation, with one polished and beveled edge.

Free-length flooring

Unlike standard tiles, only one size of free-length flooring is predetermined. The free length produces less waste and therefore costs less.

Landscaping

This category is very large and consists of all stone products used in urban landscaping. The list includes (but it is by no mean complete): cubes or squared or unshaped pavers for flooring, curbs for sidewalks, edgings, traffic islands, gravels, etc. As these items are generally used in large quantities for urban landscaping, they are produced with local materials and different techniques, according to local traditions and the material used. In Carrara, for example, all the sidewalks and curbs are of Bianco Carrara marble, while in Fiorenzuola, the same elements are made of Pietra Serena.

Funerary Art

A separate category must be made for funerary art. There are standard products destined to the funerary art market—mass-produced tombstones of fixed sizes and a few common designs realized with the most popular stones. For a specific mausoleum the necessary pieces are produced following specifications supplied by the client, putting this in the customized product category. Finally, there are items of funerary art realized in stone that can be considered as real works of art. For this reason the category of funerary art will be repeated in each group.

The following scheme summarizes the standard product division:

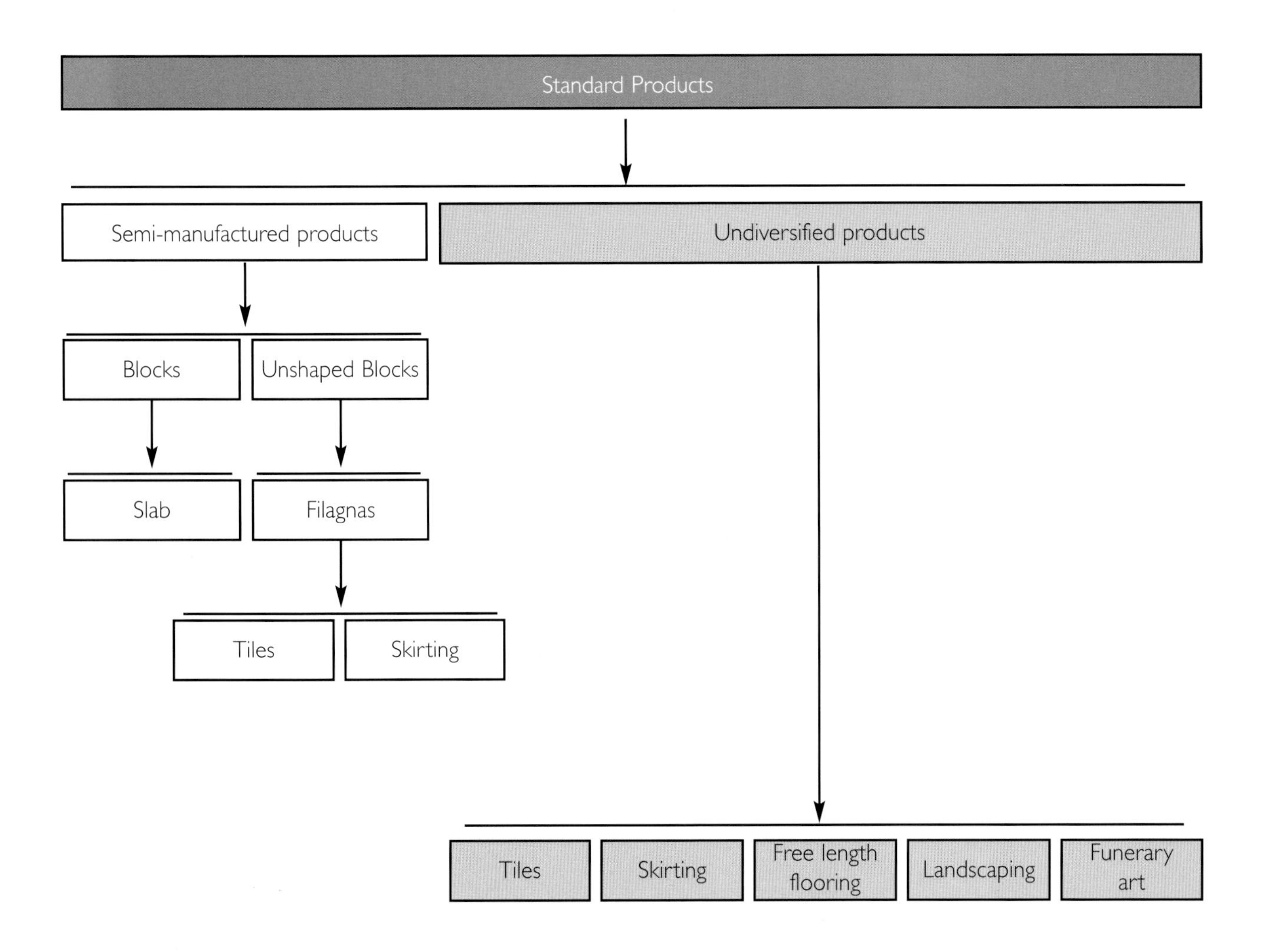

3.2 Customized Products

By the term customized products we mean all those objects that are either new or produced by modifying existing standard products following the request and the project supplied by the client. The applications are left to the designer's imagination and the limitations depend on:

- The availability of the material and the time to find it under the delivery terms imposed by the project;
- The technical specifications for its final use;
- The budget.

Once these elements have been taken into account, the choice is based merely on esthetic criteria. Companies in the stone business usually divide the market into commercial and residential. The commercial market com prises material for offices, shops, hotels, casinos, airports, etc. Most of the stone in these cases is used for internal and external flooring and cladding, and also for vanity tops in hotel bathrooms or columns and arches in prestigious buildings. In the residential market customized stone is used for kitchen countertops and vanity tops, while standard products are often used for the flooring. Some companies specialize in customized funerary art.

3.3 Artistic Products

Artistic products are those in which creativity combined with the technical and chromatic properties of stone transforms it into objects whose beauty is their main quality, though they may have a practical use too. Regardless of the value of the object realized, the market offers a large variety of objects in natural stone. They range from mass-market small objects and knick-knacks, to fine manufactured items that fulfill precise practical needs, to pure art objects that have no practical use and satisfy only the demand of beauty. The boundaries between these categories are not clearly defined; however, in the first group we include ashtrays, paperweights, vases, and the like, where the artistic intent is limited and the attraction comes from the beauty of the stone, whose qualities are highlighted. Because the objects are small in size, we sometimes use stone that is not suitable for other purposes.

The second group combines the artist's creativity and the material features. Examples are inlaid floors where the design is enhanced by the stone color and veining, or mosaics using different types of material as a palette of the necessary shades. Many valuable fireplaces belong to this group because their precious decorati- ve patterns are realized, exploiting the characteristics of the material.

The third group has no other goal but the esthetic one: the material is just a means to realize the author's inspiration. Examples are statues and bas-reliefs, but also the already mentioned objects for common use whose visual impact is more important than their practical use (e.g., a fountain where the water spout is used to enhance its beauty). In some cases funeral monuments may belong to this group.

The material used in the manufacture of artistic products must fulfill precise esthetic requirements and be free from impurities and imperfections that could reduce the value of the realized work.

4. QUARRYING AND PROCESSING TECHNIQUES

The first step in using stone is to obtain the material. Whatever the product, it is useful to have some information concerning the origin of the stone in order to avoid surprises or to have unrealizable expectations.

4.1. Quarries

Natural stone comes from a quarry. However simple this may sound, the problems connected to it are at the origin of many misconceptions.

Nowadays natural stone can be found everywhere in the world, but the countries that supply the majority of the available material in the market are few. The main producers of granite are first of all Brazil and India, then Scandinavia and the countries of southern Africa (Namibia, Zimbabwe, Republic of South Africa, etc.), North America, the Middle East, and China. Sources of marble and stone are mainly countries in the Mediterranean area and, increasingly, Mexico. This does not mean that other countries do not have stone resources, but because of their uninteresting colors, difficulties of extraction, or high transport costs, the quarried material does not reach the international market except in small amounts.

The first market change is because the quarried material is not further transformed in the country of origin, but is transported in blocks to other countries. Italy, for example, is still the most important granite exporter, even though the greatest part of this material is imported from producing countries and only processed locally. This arrangement derives from the historical tradition of natural-stone workmanship in Italy, which then developed into a specific technology. It has for a long time provided a competitive advantage in terms of cost and quality to Italian producers. The beginning of the spread of processing machinery and know-how to countries where the quarries were located has brought an end to Italy's predominance for the low-value-added materials and for those that do not require particularly complicated processing. So, the provenance and the country of origin could be the same for some kinds of stone, but "Made in ..." does not necessarily mean that the material is quarried in that country.

To provide information about some frequently asked questions:

- Quarries seem to be in inaccessible places. This is not always true, but it is clear that the nature of the quarrying operation cannot be effected in the center of a town. Quarries are often situated several hours away from a town center, or, when they are geographically close to it, it is necessary to travel narrow, uneven roads to reach the place where good materials are found. Roads or other infrastructures often may be insufficient or even non-existent, and the material may be in protected areas that would require operating deeply in the ecosystem in order to start or continue extraction. There are quarries on the top of the mountains (as in the case of Sodalite Blue, page 73) and below sea level (for example, Travertino, page 77). Open-pit or tunnel quarries each have particular problems and present reasons for a different material cost. It is not possible to explain briefly the quarry features: each of them has its own story.

- Material colors and features change as time passes. Crème Caramel (page 97), for instance, was named for its brownish yellow color, while now it has a pink tone. In many others materials, however, the color has remained the same through the centuries.
- Quarries of new materials are constantly found. Geologists' research, prospecting, and assay often help us to discover new deposits, but not all of them are valid and have the characteristics to enter the market. However, sometimes a material that at first is not considered a good economic investment can suddenly become popular when its color or characteristics are fashionable.
- Materials may run short for several reasons. For example, the material of a quarry can change its features and color so radically that it becomes a very different material and is therefore sold in the market with a new name. In other cases the material still exists, but its quality has worsened to the point that the producer decides to cease extraction. Finally, the quarry may be just a boulder and the deposit or the vein is effectively depleted.
- It is not completely true that there are unique materials. Actually, it often happens that new deposits are opened close to the main quarry, producing materials analogous to the unique one. Thus, a material may be unique only for a period of time. In addition, there are materials that are practically identical, despite the fact that they come from distant places for example, the original Verde Guatemala and Verde Guatemala from India, or Rosso Santiago from Chile and from Ukraine.
- Some materials are seasonal because in some quarries weather conditions (rain, ice, temperature extremes) make the quarry inaccessible or unworkable for part of the year.
- Blocks from the same quarry and slabs from the same block may not match. Some materials have extreme variations even inside the same block, and the fact that the materials are from the same quarry or from the same shipment does not guarantee their uniformity. In some cases for example, onyx and other stones even consecutive slabs can be totally different.

4.2. Sawing

After the material is obtained, the next step in stone processing is generally sawing. During this process blocks coming from the quarry are transformed into slabs or strips before the surface treatment can be applied. There are three main sawing systems: the diamond wire, the gangsaw, and the diamond disk. These three technologies are employed because they answer different demands, and each of them has advantages and disadvantages.

4.2.1 Diamond wire. The diamond wire is made of a metal cable along which, at regular intervals, are inserted segments containing industrial diamonds. The cable is welded to form a ring and is mounted on a special machine that runs it in a circle at high speed. The lower edge of the cable contacts the stone, and the diamond segments cut it by abrasion. At regular intervals the machine lowers the wire, so that it is always in contact with the block. The feed rate that is the speed with which the wire goes down depends on the hardness of the material and on the length to be cut. The cut time is calculated in hours.

In its simplest form, a single wire merely runs from top to bottom, cutting on a vertical plane, and for this reason it is mainly used to divide big blocks into smaller ones or to square them up before sawing. A more advanced machine, called profiling wire, allows the wire to also move on the horizontal plane during the cut, producing curved cuts, useful to ready pieces for the final cutting process. The most recent technology, called multiwire, places several diamond wires side by side so that a whole block can be cut in a single step. Among the advantages of diamond wires are their speed and their flexibility so that a block can be partially cut, with the rest of the block saved for future cutting. Among the disadvantages are the higher cost per square meter and the inferior thickness tolerance because, though it is improving, this method of cutting is less precise in comparison to other sawing methods.

4.2.2 Gangsaw. This is the oldest sawing system and, despite recent technological improvements, has remained the same in its basic features. It consists of a series of blades placed side by side on a frame that moves back and forth, moving lower as the cutting proceeds. The word "blade" should not evoke the image of a sharp knife cutting the material, because the sawing is done by abrasion. Gangsawing is the usual method of obtaining slabs. There are two methods of gangsawing natural stone: steel-shot gangsawing for granite and diamond gangsawing for marble and stone. There are also some exceptions: particularly hard marbles are cut with special sandy grits.

In steel-shot gangsawing it is not the blade that effectively cuts the material. Its function is to push back and forth a mixture of water, steel grit, and lime in the cutting grooves. The metal grit cuts the material by abrasion, and the lime serves to keep the metallic part suspended in the mixture. The distance between the blades determines the thickness of the slabs. In a typical gangsaw two blocks are cut at the same time. The blocks are previously arranged and if necessary squared up with the diamond wire so that they can lie flat on the trolley. In order to avoid any movement during the cutting, the blocks are cemented down. The cut time ranges from three to five days of continuous sawing. At the end of the sawing the slabs are accurately high-pressure washed one by one to remove any residue of the cutting mixture, which might cause stains on the stone.

In diamond gangsawing toothed blades do the cutting. Because the material cut with this method is softer, the cut time is one working day. Diamond gangsawing is not used for granite because the material is too hard and would wear out the teeth before the sawing is completed.

As in steel-shot gangsawing, the blocks are previously squared up and cemented to a trolley before the sawing starts. When the material is particularly fragile and full of crack lines that could jeopardize the sawing, the external structure of the block is usually reinforced: first the block is boxed in a wooden structure and then this container is filled with resin to strengthen the defective parts. In some sophisticated cases this process is performed in a vacuum in order to allow a better penetration of the resin in the small holes of the block. Among the advantages of the gangsaw are that it is the most precise way to cut slabs and costs the least per square meter.

Among the disadvantages, at least where granite is concerned, is the time needed for sawing. For some fragile materials there is no alternative to gangsawing, however, because diamond wire cutting could break the material, and therefore single-blade gangsaws have been created to square the blocks up.

4.2.3 Diamond disk. Diamond teeth can also be placed on very large disks. If the disk is particularly large, e.g., over 3 meters in diameter, the machine can cut slabs directly from the block. The sawing speed is the highest among the systems we have considered, but so is the cost per square meter. For this reason, this method is mainly used to obtain slabs of over 5cm in thickness. If the disks are smaller and numerous and they are combined with an additional one to perform a horizontal cut, we have the block cutter, the function of which is to cut strips. The block cutter can produce thicknesses of less than 2cm, which would be hard to achieve with other methods.

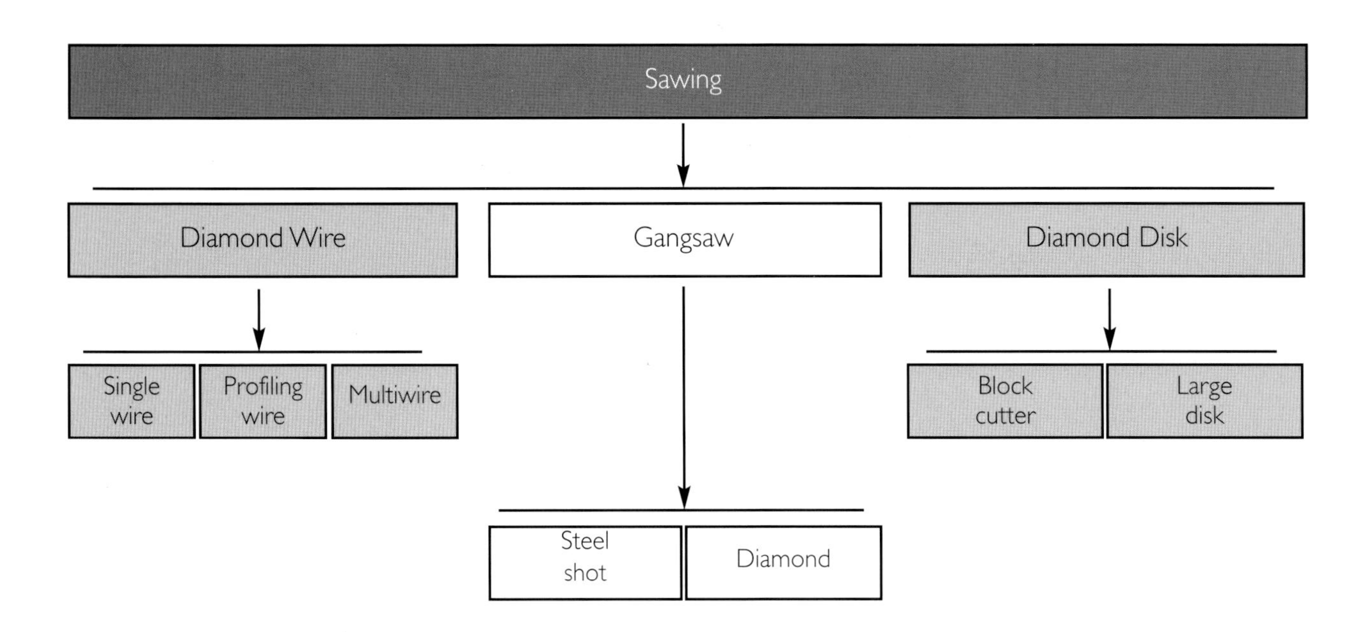

4.3. Surface Finishing

Surface finishing is the treatment that brings out the esthetic features of the material. The ornamental function and also some technical characteristics (e.g., its resistance to wear and to weather conditions or its slipperiness) are strongly influenced by the surface finishing applied to the product. Depending on the treatment, we can divide the finishing into mechanical, impact, and chemical methods.

4.3.1 Mechanical Finishing. In mechanical finishing, the stone is put in contact with an abrasive to reduce the original surface roughness to some extent.

Rough

Though infrequent, sometimes the sawn material or even just-quarried material is ready for installation and needs only to be cut to size. The surface in this case is generally rough, with an uneven face. Rough stone is predominantly used outdoors, where it is appreciated for its non-slip quality. It is often used with slate and with some kinds of sandstone.

Honed

This finishing aims to produce a smooth surface by using abrasives of ever finer grain on the surface, so there is not a single honing but a series of progressive degrees of it. The surface quality of honed stone depends on the last grade of abrasive applied, and therefore the finish gets its name from it (honed 140, honed 200, honed 400, etc.). Honed finish is not reflective and makes the color tones slightly dull, but the treatment preserves the material's natural esthetic characteristics.

Polished

Polishing is the main and the most frequently applied finish. It follows the finest honing and employs polishing abrasives that add brilliance with mirror effect to the stone surface.

4.3.2 Impact Finishing. In impact finishing a strong external force is applied to the stone surface in order to alter and enhance the original surface roughness. Because they produce surface unevenness, these finishes are usually not slippery, but they do get dirty easily.

Brushed

Brushed finish is obtained by applying hard plastic or metal brushes to the stone surface. The heavy action removes the softer part of the stone and wears out the surface, giving it a look similar to that of antique finishing.

Bush hammered

Bush hammering is obtained by hitting the material surface mechanically or by hand with a specific multipointed tool. This method creates a rugged surface full of little grazes at the impact points, and it modifies the color, making it lighter. The surface becomes non-slip. This technique has been replaced by flaming and pressure water finishing because these are faster and less costly.

Tooled

Tooling is similar to bush hammering but it is obtained with a larger, single-pointed steel tool. The chromatic and non-slip effects are similar to those obtained with bush hammering, but tooling can be applied only to a chosen part of the surface, thus leaving some rough areas. The effect it produces is useful in giving stone a medieval character.

Sandblasted

In sandblasting, a high-pressure jet of siliceous sand or carborundum or steel shots is applied to the area to be treated. It produces a smooth abrasion, leaving the material slightly scratched on the surface, but not rugged. The color tones and the veins are a bit dulled.

Flamed

Also called thermal finishing, flaming consists of passing a blowpipe that emits a high-temperature flame over the surface to be treated. The heat acts by blowing the crystals out as they suffer thermal shock, with an effect that is particularly evident in materials composed of minerals with various degrees of expansion, e.g., the vast majority of granites. The surface produced is rough and non-slip, and the color is generally faded, hiding defects and tone variations. Because of oxidation, yellow materials become orange or red.

Water finishing

This process consists of passing a pipe emitting a jet of high-pressure water over the surface to be treated. The effect is the negative of what happens with thermal finishing. While with flaming the hardest part of the material bursts and is removed, in water finishing the softest part is removed. But the result looks the same: the surface is similarly rough. For this reason, water finishing is incorrectly called "water flaming." The colors of the material and the veining pattern are not affected by water finishing and the esthetic effects are comparable even to those obtained by polishing. As water finishing does not induce oxidation, it is the usual finish employed for making yellow materials non-slip.

Antique finishing

Special machinery that looks like industrial washing machines is used to obtain an antique finish. The pieces to be treated are put in the machine with abrasive elements and the cylinder revolves. In a short time the impact of the stone with the abrasives produces an effect similar to aging caused by use and wear. The impact method is not suitable for large pieces, for which brushing or acid washing is the method of choice.

Split

A split finish is obtained by hitting a small block of stone with a metal wedge. If the splitting is performed along the lines of cleavage planes in materials with well-defined parallel layers (e.g., slate), a rather smooth and uniform surface is produced. It is also possible to split other materials, causing a crack that divides the small block in the middle. This is a very stressful finish for the stone, and the surface obtained is extremely rugged. It is not possible to perform it on large pieces that would resist the break.

4.3.3 Chemical Finishing. Chemical finishes are applied to stone in order to produce reactions that transform the material surface, or they are employed together with other types of treatment in order to improve their characteristics. These finishes can also be applied to cut, or even installed, materials.

Acid washed

Acid washing has a corrosive action on the stone. It can be used to obtain different effects depending on the material, the chemical, and finally, the processing time. Finishes can range from simple superficial cleaning of the material to a more definite ruggedness, similar to that achieved by water finishing. Acid washing is sometimes used to obtain an antique finish in place of the impact method. It is possible to acid wash already cut pieces or, with appropriate precautions, already installed ones. Some chemicals produce other results affecting the aspect of the stone but not its roughness. There are "acids" that remove oily or rust spots on the material, others that instead induce oxidation effects and are employed to change the material color.

Epoxy treated

Epoxy treatment is not a finish by itself, because it is difficult to use it separately from polishing. If accurately applied, this method consists of several steps:

- One face is honed to create a smooth surface on which the resin is applied.
- The slab is dried in a special oven to allow the resin to penetrate into the material and set;
- Resin is poured and spread on the slab.
- The slab is put in the oven again to dry the resin. Some plants conduct this operation in a vacuum in order to improve the penetration of the resin into the material.
- When the slab comes out from the oven it is ready for polishing.

This complex process has two main goals: the improvement of the material's esthetic characteristics and its mechanical resistance. The high fluidity of the resin allows it to penetrate the smallest interstices and to fill defects in the material. Thanks to the resin's consolidating action, the material acquires a higher strength and, once polished, its defects are hidden. It is also possible to add colorant to the resin to enhance the chromatic effect. Unlike resin treatment, cement filling, usually applied to travertine, is employed for purely esthetic reasons.

Meshed

In addition to resin treatment, in order to strengthen material it is common to apply a thin net made of fiberglass or plastic on the back side of the most defective marble or stone slabs.

Protective treatment

This category includes all those treatments that are used to protect the material surface from external elements. Among them are hydro- and oil-repellent treatments used to seal kitchen countertops, anti-graffiti treatments to avoid damage caused by vandalism, and products that give a wet appearance to flamed stone. These products are often the final protection given to finished and installed stone.

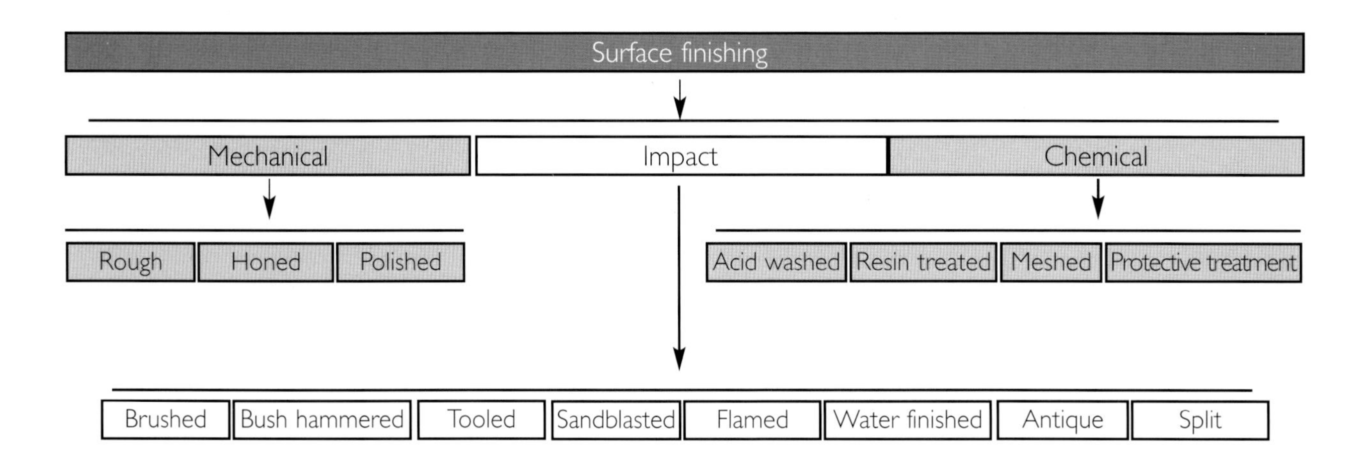

4.4. Manufacturing

Manufacturing is the process by which the material is transformed into the final product. It is the last step before the customized material leaves the factory ready to be installed, and can be divided into three phases: cutting, edging, and anchoring.

4.4.1 Cutting. To obtain a customized product we usually start from the semi-manufactured materials, above all, slabs. These can be easily transformed into a great variety of other objects. The first step towards this goal is cutting, in order to reach the exact dimension of the final piece.

Typical cutting machines usually utilize diamond disks. The most common one is the bridge cutter, which is the most versatile production instrument. Several disks can be placed side-by-side in larger machines, which yield high volumes of typically sized products, e.g., elements for a skyscraper façade.

Limiting the use of these kinds of instruments is the fact that, with them, any curved cut has to be obtained through several distinct linear cuts and then refined, mostly by hand. Recently technology has supplied the market with a water-jet machine that overcomes this limitation and can be employed for even the smallest details. A water jet cuts the material by a high-pressure jet of water mixed with fine abrasive powder, and therefore is not limited to a cut in one direction or by the thickness of disk teeth. While the machine speed is not extremely high, the accuracy of detail and direction are determined by a computer that follows the previously input drawings, so the presence of a worker is not constantly required.

In addition to a cutting machine, it could be useful to employ a drilling one in order to cut out unnecessary pieces of stones (e.g., sink holes).

4.4.2. Edging. Edging is mainly done for esthetic reasons, the type of edging chosen being the most suitable one for the project. It can involve further cutting to remove excess material, if a wedge form is required, or gluing if a thicker detail has to be produced, as for laminated kitchen counter edges; there is even a surface-finishing process for giving the stone edge the same aspect as its face. Special machines are involved in the realization of edge details, most of them using a combination of diamond disks and abrasives, but the most intricate ones are still done by hand.

4.4.3. Anchoring. Anchoring is the last step in the production process and may not be required for certain products (for example, floor tiles), but it is mandatory for exterior cladding where the stone panels have to be hung on the façade somehow. The method of anchoring is determined by the weight, size, and type of stone, generally in combination with holes and grooves. The holes can be placed on the back or on one side of the stone piece or, more rarely, through it. They are made perpendicularly or diagonally to the surface depending on the fixing technique. Alternatively, grooves, called kerfs, are cut, normally on the top and bottom edges of the stone panel, and are used in conjunction with metal anchors on the façade to keep them fixed.

5. THE SAMPLES

Each sample in this volume is accompanied by information that describes the material and defines its main features and technical properties. The samples are also provided in the form of TIFF files on the enclosed CD-ROM.

The technical properties of natural stone are assessed through specific experiments carried out when the material is discovered, even before opening a quarry, in order to determine the material's physical and mechanical characteristics. These results are constantly updated since, as explained earlier, the features of stone change over time. Thus, the data given here must be considered primarily as a ready reference.

If the quantity of material required is large or the stone faces particular stresses, it may be necessary to repeat the tests in order to obtain specific information about the realization of a particular project. These tests are carried out in specialized laboratories and, in order to have results of statistical significance, are performed on several samples of the material to analyze. There are several international institutions that establish rules and values for carrying out testing. In the United States the most important such organization is the American Society for Testing and Materials, known as ASTM International (www.astm.org).

The following information is given for the samples:

Quarrying place. This is the place or the country of origin of the material. As explained earlier, this term refers to the geographical location of the quarry, which is the starting point of the blocks, even if this does correspond to the country from which the final product comes. This information does not change over time.

Availability. This is general information about the greater or lesser ease of finding high-quality material in the market. A notation of scanty availability means that an acceptable material is not easy to find in the market, but it does not mean that the quarry's production is scarce or that the quarry is closed. This is, therefore, the most variable information over time, presenting substantial differences both in the short or long term. We have already noted that some quarries undergo seasonal variations in their production quantity; other quarries can face transitory breaks in production.

Compressive strength and compressive strength after freezing. Tests of compressive strength are carried out by applying an increasing force perpendicularly to the plane of the stone sample in order to measure its load strength. This value must be considered whenever the material is employed for structural purposes (e.g., columns, round arches, plinths, etc.). Additional information is obtained by carrying out the test after freezing cycles—that is, after a series of freeze-and-thaw steps which entail first bringing the samples to a temperature of –10 C°, then heating them to +35 C°, and then testing them for compressive strength. These cycles are repeated several times, with the goal of simulating, in a controlled surrounding and within test-time limits, the variation of material strength caused by a thermal range over 24 hours under real conditions.

Ultimate tensile strength and impact test (also called minimum fall height). Both are defined as modules of rupture and are obtained by specific machines designed to determine the maximum force that needs to be applied before causing the breakage. Depending upon the type of force and the direction it is applied, the tests can determine the tensile strength of the material, that is, its elasticity to traction or the resistance of a stone sample to the stress caused by the fall of a predetermined weight from a set height. The application field of these tests depends on the final intended use of the material tested.

Coefficient of thermal expansion. This test measures dimensional variation of the material after it is heated. The value obtained is the difference between the sample dimension before and after heating. This information is important whenever the material is to be installed in an area subject to a wide thermal range, so the joints and the anchoring are calculated based on this value.

Water absorption. This value defines the material's ability to absorb liquids and it is directly proportional to the material's porosity, that is, to the quantity and the volume of the holes on the material. It is measured by weighing it twice before and after having bathed the sample in water for a predetermined time. It is an im portant datum whenever the material is to be in contact with water, for example on exteriors, in bathrooms, and on kitchen countertops.

Frictional wear test. This test determines the material wear and tear caused by pedestrian traffic on its surface. A machine reproduces the abrasion caused by the impact of shoe soles on the sample and measures the wear after a certain number of contacts. This value is important for areas subject to intense traffic (stations, halls, airports, etc.), and gives information about when maintenance may be necessary to restore the material's original aspect.

Bulk density. Also known as bulk specific gravity or unit weight per volume, this is obtained by dividing weight by the material volume. As this value is directly proportional to the material density, and so varies according to its porosity, this test gives information concerning the compactness of the material.

San Miniato, Florence

STONE SAMPLER
GALLERY

MARBLE

Quarrying location: Italy
Availability: Good
Compressive strength: 1334/kg cm^2
After freezing: 1300/kg cm^2
Ultimate tensile strength: 202/kg cm^2
Coef. thermal expansion: 0,0063 mm/m°C
Water absorption: 0,115%
Impact test / min. fall height: 56 cm
Frictional wear test: 0,58 mm
Bulk density: 2711 kg/m^3

CD file number: 0001

Quarrying location: Italy
Availability: Good
Compressive strength: 1209/kg cm^2
After freezing: 1181/kg cm^2
Ultimate tensile strength: 202/kg cm^2
Coef. thermal expansion: 0,0072 mm/m°C
Water absorption: 0,16%
Impact test / min. fall height: 75 cm
Frictional wear test: 1,12 mm
Bulk density: 2700 kg/m^3

CD file number: 0002

Quarrying location: Italy
Availability: Good
Compressive strength: 1209/kg cm^2
After freezing: 1181/kg cm^2
Ultimate tensile strength: 202/kg cm^2
Coef. thermal expansion: 0,0072 mm/m°C
Water absorption: 0,16%
Impact test / min. fall height: 75 cm
Frictional wear test: 1,12 mm
Bulk density: 2700 kg/m^3

CD file number: 0003

Quarrying location: Italy
Availability: Limited
Compressive strength: 1209/kg cm^2
After freezing: 1181/kg cm^2
Ultimate tensile strength: 202/kg cm^2
Coef. thermal expansion: 0,0072 mm/m°C
Water absorption: 0,16%
Impact test / min. fall height: 75 cm
Frictional wear test: 1,12 mm
Bulk density: 2700 kg/m^3

CD file number: 0004

Bianco Carrara C

Quarrying location: Italy
Availability: Medium
Compressive strength: 1446/kg cm^2
After freezing: 1393/kg cm^2
Ultimate tensile strength: 240/kg cm^2
Coef. thermal expansion: 0,0042 mm/m°C
Water absorption: 0,15%
Impact test / min. fall height: 49 cm
Frictional wear test: 3 mm
Bulk density: 2699 kg/m^3

CD file number: 0005

Bianco Carrara CD

Quarrying location: Italy
Availability: Good
Compressive strength: 1284/kg cm^2
After freezing: 1271/kg cm^2
Ultimate tensile strength: 202/kg cm^2
Coef. thermal expansion: 0,0063 mm/m°C
Water absorption: 0,096%
Impact test / min. fall height: 40 cm
Frictional wear test: 3 mm
Bulk density: 2720 kg/m^3

CD file number: 0006

Bianco Carrara D

Quarrying location: Italy
Availability: Medium
Compressive strength: 1389/kg cm^2
After freezing: 1321/kg cm^2
Ultimate tensile strength: 162/kg cm^2
Coef. thermal expansion: 0,0046 mm/m°C
Water absorption: 0,35%
Impact test / min. fall height: 52 cm
Frictional wear test: –
Bulk density: 2704 kg/m^3

CD file number: 0007

Bianco Bruillé

Quarrying location: Italy
Availability: Medium
Compressive strength: 1389/kg cm^2
After freezing: 1321/kg cm^2
Ultimate tensile strength: 162/kg cm^2
Coef. thermal expansion: 0,0046 mm/m°C
Water absorption: 0,35%
Impact test / min. fall height: 52 cm
Frictional wear test: –
Bulk density: 2704 kg/m^3

CD file number: 0008

Bianco Arni

Quarrying location: Italy
Availability: Medium
Compressive strength: 1426/kg cm^2
After freezing: 1268/kg cm^2
Ultimate tensile strength: 185/kg cm^2
Coef. thermal expansion: 0,0032 mm/m°C
Water absorption: 0,13%
Impact test / min. fall height: 58,8 cm
Frictional wear test: 6,52 mm
Bulk density: 2692 kg/m^3

CD file number: 0009

Bianco Gioia

Quarrying location: Italy
Availability: Limited
Compressive strength: 1287/kg cm^2
After freezing: 1128/kg cm^2
Ultimate tensile strength: 82/kg cm^2
Coef. thermal expansion: 0,0061mm/m°C
Water absorption: 0,20%
Impact test / min. fall height: 82,5cm
Frictional wear test: 5,78 mm
Bulk density: 2961 kg/m^3

CD file number: 0010

Biancospino

Quarrying location: Italy
Availability: Good
Compressive strength: 1118/kg cm^2
After freezing: 1335/kg cm^2
Ultimate tensile strength: 235/kg cm^2
Coef. thermal expansion: 0,0052 mm/m°C
Water absorption: 0,245%
Impact test / min. fall height: 61,3 cm
Frictional wear test: 3,64 mm
Bulk density: 2680 kg/m^3

CD file number: 0011

Bianco Pennsylvania

Quarrying location: Italy
Availability: Medium
Compressive strength: 2060/kg cm^2
After freezing: 1879/kg cm^2
Ultimate tensile strength: 155/kg cm^2
Coef. thermal expansion: 0,0040 mm/m°C
Water absorption: 0,06%
Impact test / min. fall height: 26 cm
Frictional wear test: –
Bulk density: 2670 kg/m^3

CD file number: 0012

Bianco Acquabianca

Quarrying location: Italy
Availability: Good
Compressive strength: 1118/kg cm
After freezing: 1335/kg cm
Ultimate tensile strength: 235/kg cm
Coef. thermal expansion: 0,0052 mm/mC°
Water absorption: 0,245%
Impact test / min. fall height: 61,3 cm
Frictional wear test: 3,64 mm
Bulk density: 2680 kg/m^3

CD file number: 0013

Bianco P

Quarrying location: Italy
Availability: Good
Compressive strength: 1334/kg cm
After freezing: 1300/kg cm
Ultimate tensile strength: 202/kg cm
Coef. thermal expansion: 0,0063 mm/mC°
Water absorption: 0,115%
Impact test / min. fall height: 56 cm
Frictional wear test: 0,58 mm
Bulk density: 2711 kg/m^3

CD file number: 0014

Bianco Venato Gioia

Quarrying location: Italy
Availability: Limited
Compressive strength: 1563/kg cm
After freezing: 1478/kg cm
Ultimate tensile strength: 181/kg cm
Coef. thermal expansion: 0,0045mm/mC°
Water absorption: 0,23%
Impact test / min. fall height: 48 cm
Frictional wear test: –
Bulk density: 2667 kg/m^3

CD file number: 0015

Bianco Perlino

Quarrying location: Italy
Availability: Limited
Compressive strength: 1563/kg cm
After freezing: 1478/kg cm
Ultimate tensile strength: 181/kg cm
Coef. thermal expansion: 0,0045mm/mC°
Water absorption: 0,23%
Impact test / min. fall height: 48 cm
Frictional wear test: –
Bulk density: 2667 kg/m^3

CD file number: 0016

Bianco Carrara Venato

Imperial Danby

Lasa Vena Oro

Palissandro Bianco

Bianco Carrara C
Bianco Carrara CD
Bianco Carrara D
Bianco Bruillé
Bianco Arni
Bianco Gioia
Biancospino
Bianco Pennsylvania
Bianco Acquabianca
Bianco P
Bianco Venato Gioia
Bianco Perlino

Quarrying location: Greece
Availability: Good
Compressive strength: 1563/kg cm^2
After freezing: 1478/kg cm^2
Ultimate tensile strength: 181/kg cm^2
Coef. thermal expansion: 0,0045mm/m°C
Water absorption: 0,23%
Impact test / min. fall height: 48 cm^2
Frictional wear test: –
Bulk density: 2667 kg/m^3

CD file number: 0017

Quarrying location: Greece
Availability: Good
Compressive strength: 1563/kg cm^2
After freezing: 1478/kg cm^2
Ultimate tensile strength: 181/kg cm^2
Coef. thermal expansion: 0,0045mm/m°C
Water absorption: 0,23%
Impact test / min. fall height: 48 cm^2
Frictional wear test: –
Bulk density: 2667 kg/m^3

CD file number: 0018

Quarrying location: Turkey
Availability: Good
Compressive strength: 1563/kg cm^2
After freezing: 1478/kg cm^2
Ultimate tensile strength: 181/kg cm^2
Coef. thermal expansion: 0,0045mm/m°C
Water absorption: 0,23%
Impact test / min. fall height: 48 cm^2
Frictional wear test: –
Bulk density: 2667 kg/m^3

CD file number: 0019

Quarrying location: Indi
Availability: Mediun
Compressive strength: 1563/kg cm
After freezing: 1478/kg cm
Ultimate tensile strength: 181/kg cm
Coef. thermal expansion: 0,0045mm/m°C
Water absorption: 0,23%
Impact test / min. fall height: 48 cm
Frictional wear test: –
Bulk density: 2667 kg/m

CD file number: 0020

Pentelikon

Quarrying location: Greece
Availability: Good
Compressive strength: 1563/kg cm^2
After freezing: 1478/kg cm^2
Ultimate tensile strength: 181/kg cm^2
Coef. thermal expansion: 0,0045mm/m°C
Water absorption: 0,23%
Impact test / min. fall height: 48 cm^2
Frictional wear test: –
Bulk density: 2667 kg/m^3

CD file number: 0021

Bianco Thassos

Quarrying location: Greece
Availability: Good
Compressive strength: 1563/kg cm
After freezing: 1478/kg cm
Ultimate tensile strength: 181/kg cm
Coef. thermal expansion: 0,0045mm/mC°
Water absorption: 0,23%
Impact test / min. fall height: 48 cm
Frictional wear test: –
Bulk density: 2667 kg/m^3

CD file number: 0022

Bianco Royal

Quarrying location: Italy
Availability: Good
Compressive strength: 1280/kg cm
After freezing: 1243/kg cm
Ultimate tensile strength: 125/kg cm
Coef. thermal expansion: 0,0039mm/mC°
Water absorption: 0,21%
Impact test / min. fall height: 36 cm
Frictional wear test: 0,58
Bulk density: 2313 kg/m^3

CD file number: 0023

Boka White

Quarrying location: Ital
Availability: Goo
Compressive strength: 1280/kg cn
After freezing: 1243/kg cn
Ultimate tensile strength: 125/kg cn
Coef. thermal expansion: 0,0039mm/mC
Water absorption: 0,21%
Impact test / min. fall height: 36 cn
Frictional wear test: 0,5
Bulk density: 2313 kg/m

CD file number: 0024

Bianco Sivec

Quarrying location: Greece
Availability: Good
Compressive strength: 1563/kg cm^2
After freezing: 1478/kg cm^2
Ultimate tensile strength: 181/kg cm^2
Coef. thermal expansion: 0,0045mm/m°C
Water absorption: 0,23%
Impact test / min. fall height: 48 cm^2
Frictional wear test: –
Bulk density: 2667 kg/m^3

CD file number: 0025

Crystallina Naxos

Quarrying location: Italy
Availability: Limited
Compressive strength: 1105 cm^2
After freezing: 1082/kg cm^2
Ultimate tensile strength: 146/kg cm^2
Coef. thermal expansion: 0,0067mm/m°C
Water absorption: 0,13%
Impact test / min. fall height: 22,5 cm^2
Frictional wear test: 9,84
Bulk density: 2696 kg/m^3

CD file number: 0026

Calacatta Vagli

Quarrying location: Italy
Availability: Limited
Compressive strength: 1389/kg cm^2
After freezing: 1321/kg cm^2
Ultimate tensile strength: 162/kg cm^2
Coef. thermal expansion: 0,0046mm/m°C
Water absorption: 0,35%
Impact test / min. fall height: 52 cm
Frictional wear test: –
Bulk density: 2704 kg/m^3

CD file number: 0027

Calacatta Vagli Extra

Quarrying location: Ital
Availability: Mediun
Compressive strength: 1118/kg cm
After freezing: 1335/kg cn
Ultimate tensile strength: 235/kg cm
Coef. thermal expansion: 0,0052mm/m°C
Water absorption: 0,24%
Impact test / min. fall height: 61,3 cm
Frictional wear test: 3,6
Bulk density: 2680 kg/m

CD file number: 0028

Calacatta

Quarrying location: Italy
Availability: Medium
Compressive strength: 1389/kg cm^2
After freezing: 1321/kg cm^2
Ultimate tensile strength: 162/kg cm^2
Coef. thermal expansion: 0,0046mm/mC
Water absorption: 0,35%
Impact test / min. fall height: 52 cm
Frictional wear test: –
Bulk density: 2704 kg/m^3

CD file number: 0029

Calacatta Carrara

Quarrying location: Italy
Availability: Limited
Compressive strength: 1389/kg cm^2
After freezing: 1321/kg cm^2
Ultimate tensile strength: 162/kg cm^2
Coef. thermal expansion: 0,0046mm/m°C
Water absorption: 0,35%
Impact test / min. fall height: 52 cm
Frictional wear test: –
Bulk density: 2704 kg/m^3

CD file number: 0030

Calacatta Arni

Quarrying location: Italy
Availability: Scarse
Compressive strength: 1389/kg cm^2
After freezing: 1321/kg cm^2
Ultimate tensile strength: 162/kg cm^2
Coef. thermal expansion: 0,0046mm/m°C
Water absorption: 0,35%
Impact test / min. fall height: 52 cm
Frictional wear test: –
Bulk density: 2704 kg/m^3

CD file number: 0031

Calacatta Cremo

Quarrying location: Ital
Availability: Medium
Compressive strength: 1389/kg cm
After freezing: 1321/kg cm
Ultimate tensile strength: 162/kg cm
Coef. thermal expansion: 0,0046mm/m°C
Water absorption: 0,35%
Impact test / min. fall height: 52 cn
Frictional wear test: –
Bulk density: 2704 kg/m

CD file number: 0032

Pentelikon

Bianco Thassos

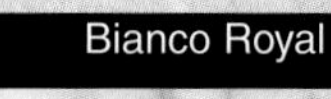
Bianco Royal

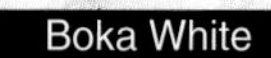
Boka White

Bianco Sivec

Crystallina Naxos

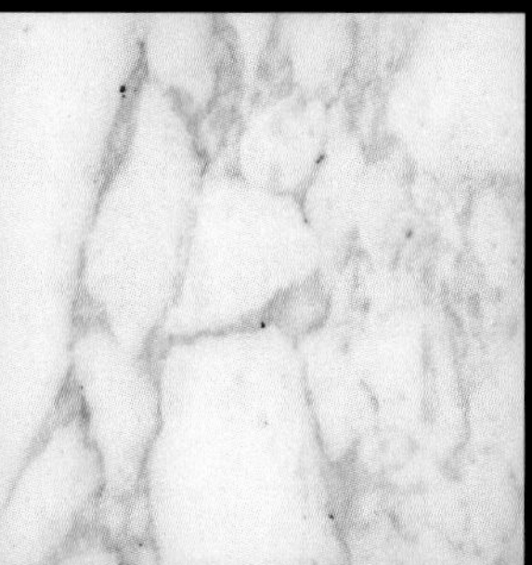
Calacatta Vagli

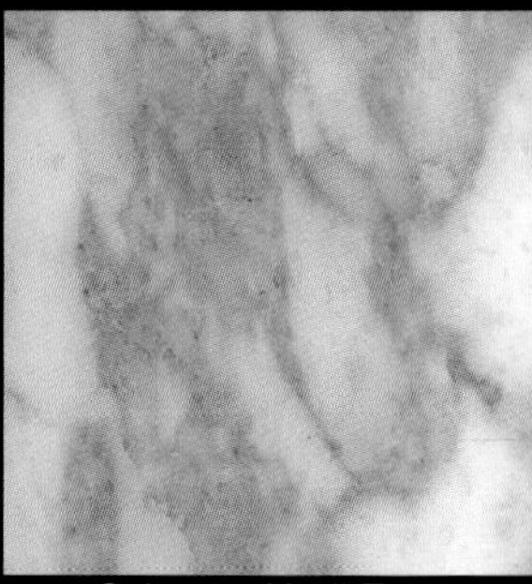
Calacatta Vagli Extra

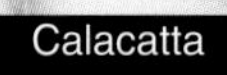
Calacatta

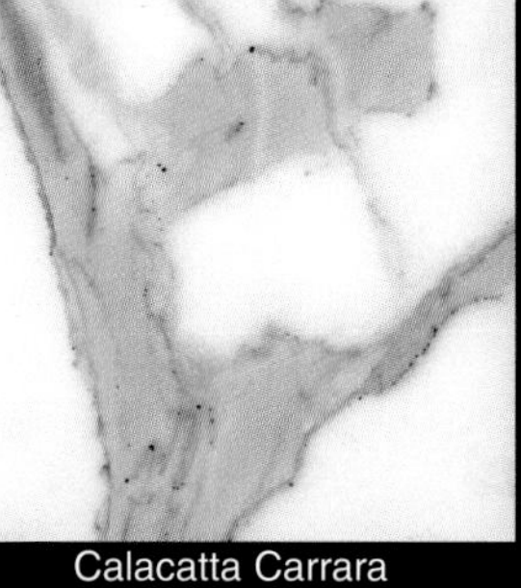
Calacatta Carrara

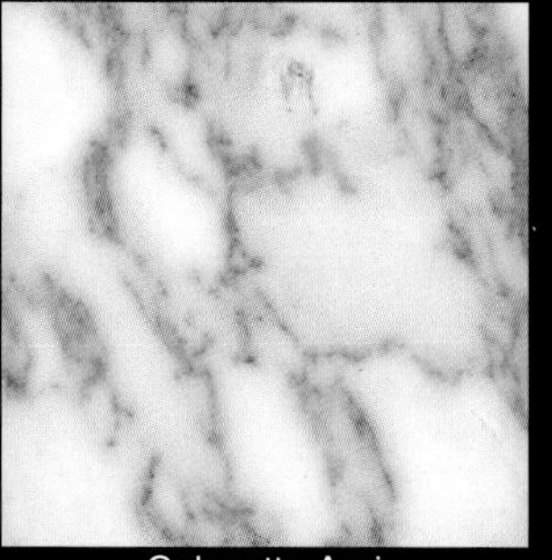
Calacatta Arni

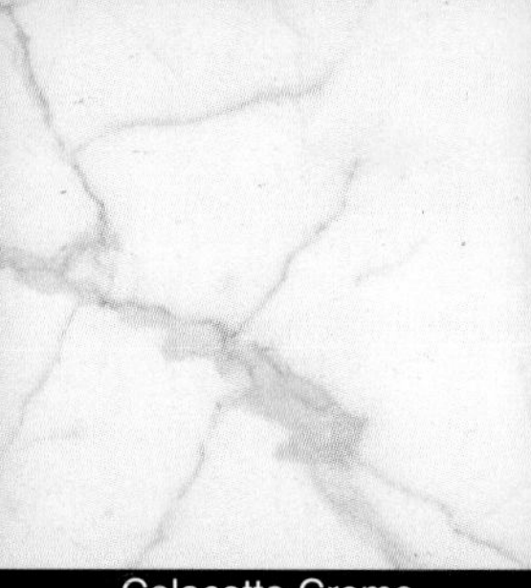
Calacatta Cremo

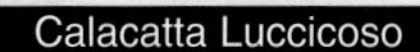
Calacatta Luccicoso

Calacatta Oro

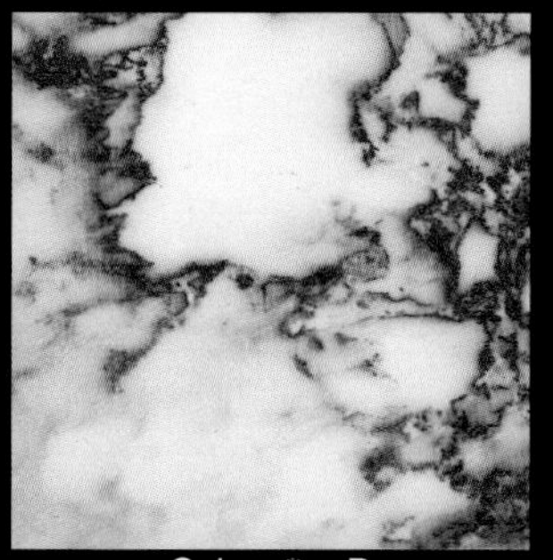
Calacatta P

Calacatta Sponda

Quarrying location: Italy
Availability: Medium
Compressive strength: 1334/kg cm^2
After freezing: 1214/kg cm^2
Ultimate tensile strength: 239/kg cm^2
Coef. thermal expansion: 0,0064mm/m°C
Water absorption: 0,12%
Impact test / min. fall height: 48,8 cm
Frictional wear test: 5,79
Bulk density: 2702 kg/m^3

CD file number: 0033

Quarrying location: Italy
Availability: Medium
Compressive strength: 1334/kg cm^2
After freezing: 1214/kg cm^2
Ultimate tensile strength: 239/kg cm^2
Coef. thermal expansion: 0,0064mm/m°C
Water absorption: 0,12%
Impact test / min. fall height: 48,8 cm
Frictional wear test: 5,79
Bulk density: 2702 kg/m^3

CD file number: 0034

Quarrying location: Italy
Availability: Medium
Compressive strength: 1334/kg cm^2
After freezing: 1214/kg cm^2
Ultimate tensile strength: 239/kg cm^2
Coef. thermal expansion: 0,0064mm/m°C
Water absorption: 0,12%
Impact test / min. fall height: 48,8 cm
Frictional wear test: 5,79
Bulk density: 2702 kg/m^3

CD file number: 0035

Quarrying location: Italy
Availability: Medium
Compressive strength: 1334/kg cm^2
After freezing: 1214/kg cm^2
Ultimate tensile strength: 239/kg cm^2
Coef. thermal expansion: 0,0064mm/m°C
Water absorption: 0,12%
Impact test / min. fall height: 48,8 cm
Frictional wear test: 5,79
Bulk density: 2702 kg/m^3

CD file number: 0036

Statuario Classico

Quarrying location: Italy
Availability: Medium
Compressive strength: 1359/kg cm^2
After freezing: 1290/kg cm^2
Ultimate tensile strength: 239/kg cm^2
Coef. thermal expansion: 0,0061mm/m°C
Water absorption: 0,14%
Impact test / min. fall height: 42,5 cm
Frictional wear test: 3,70
Bulk density: 2699 kg/m^3

CD file number: 0037

Statuario Michelangelo

Quarrying location: Italy
Availability: Medium
Compressive strength: 1359/kg cm^2
After freezing: 1290/kg cm^2
Ultimate tensile strength: 239/kg cm^2
Coef. thermal expansion: 0,0061mm/m°C
Water absorption: 0,14%
Impact test / min. fall height: 42,5 cm
Frictional wear test: 3,70
Bulk density: 2699 kg/m^3

CD file number: 0038

Statuario Vena Grossa

Quarrying location: Italy
Availability: Medium
Compressive strength: 1359/kg cm^2
After freezing: 1290/kg cm^2
Ultimate tensile strength: 239/kg cm^2
Coef. thermal expansion: 0,0061mm/m°C
Water absorption: 0,14%
Impact test / min. fall height: 42,5 cm
Frictional wear test: 3,70
Bulk density: 2699 kg/m^3

CD file number: 0039

Statuario Vena Fine

Quarrying location: Italy
Availability: Medium
Compressive strength: 1389/kg cm^2
After freezing: 1321/kg cm^2
Ultimate tensile strength: 162/kg cm^2
Coef. thermal expansion: 0,0046mm/m°C
Water absorption: 0,35%
Impact test / min. fall height: 52 cm
Frictional wear test: –
Bulk density: 2701 kg/m^3

CD file number: 0040

Arabescato Classico

Quarrying location: Italy
Availability: Medium
Compressive strength: 1359/kg cm^2
After freezing: 1290/kg cm^2
Ultimate tensile strength: 239/kg cm^2
Coef. thermal expansion: 0,0061mm/m°C
Water absorption: 0,14%
Impact test / min. fall height: 42,5 cm
Frictional wear test: 3,70
Bulk density: 2699 kg/m^3

CD file number: 0041

Arabescato Corchia

Quarrying location: Italy
Availability: Medium
Compressive strength: 1411/kg cm^2
After freezing: 1189/kg cm^2
Ultimate tensile strength: 225/kg cm^2
Coef. thermal expansion: 0,0043mm/m°C
Water absorption: 0,14%
Impact test / min. fall height: 62,5 cm
Frictional wear test: 5,21
Bulk density: 2682 kg/m^3

CD file number: 0042

Arabescato Carcariana

Quarrying location: Italy
Availability: Medium
Compressive strength: 1389/kg cm^2
After freezing: 1321/kg cm^2
Ultimate tensile strength: 162/kg cm^2
Coef. thermal expansion: 0,0046mm/m°C
Water absorption: 0,35%
Impact test / min. fall height: 52 cm
Frictional wear test: –
Bulk density: 2701 kg/m^3

CD file number: 0043

Arabescato Cervaiole

Quarrying location: Italy
Availability: Medium
Compressive strength: 1472/kg cm^2
After freezing: 1352/kg cm^2
Ultimate tensile strength: 102/kg cm^2
Coef. thermal expansion: 0,0041mm/m°C
Water absorption: 0,54%
Impact test / min. fall height: 41 cm
Frictional wear test: 0,44
Bulk density: 2714 kg/m^3

CD file number: 0044

Arabescato Piana

Quarrying location: Italy
Availability: Medium
Compressive strength: 1577/kg cm^2
After freezing: 1549/kg cm^2
Ultimate tensile strength: 202/kg cm^2
Coef. thermal expansion: 0,0080mm/m°C
Water absorption: 0,13%
Impact test / min. fall height: 78,8 cm
Frictional wear test: 3,73
Bulk density: 2638 kg/m^3

CD file number: 0045

Arabescato Faniello

Quarrying location: Italy
Availability: Medium
Compressive strength: 1118/kg cm^2
After freezing: 1335/kg cm
Ultimate tensile strength: 235/kg cm^2
Coef. thermal expansion: 0,0052mm/m°C
Water absorption: 0,24%
Impact test / min. fall height: 61,3 cm^2
Frictional wear test: 3,64
Bulk density: 2680kg/m^3

CD file number: 0046

Arabescato Trambiserra

Quarrying location: India
Availability: Good
Compressive strength: 1334/kg cm
After freezing: 1300/kg cm
Ultimate tensile strength: 202/kg cm
Coef. thermal expansion: 0,0063 mm/mC°
Water absorption: 0,115%
Impact test / min. fall height: 56 cm
Frictional wear test: 0,58 mm
Bulk density: 2711 kg/cm

CD file number: 0047

Arabescato Vagli

Quarrying location: Brazil
Availability: Medium
Compressive strength: 1563/kg cm^2
After freezing: 1478/kg cm^2
Ultimate tensile strength: 181/kg cm^2
Coef. thermal expansion: 0,0045mm/m°C
Water absorption: 0,23%
Impact test / min. fall height: 48 cm^2
Frictional wear test: –
Bulk density: 2667 kg/m^3

CD file number: 0048

Arabescato Arni

Paonazzo

Ambajy White

Pinta Verde

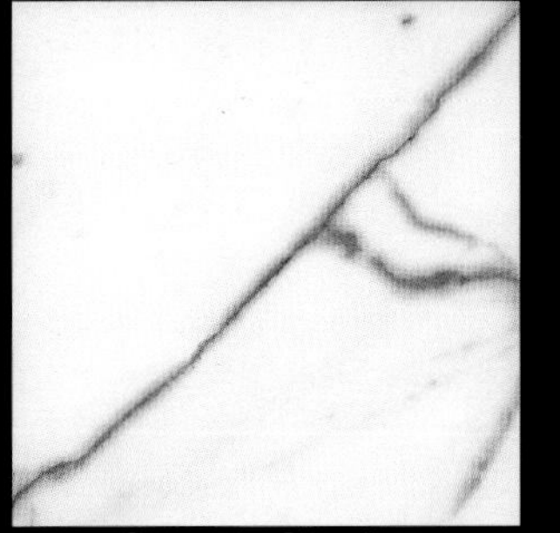
Statuario Classico

Statuario Michelangelo

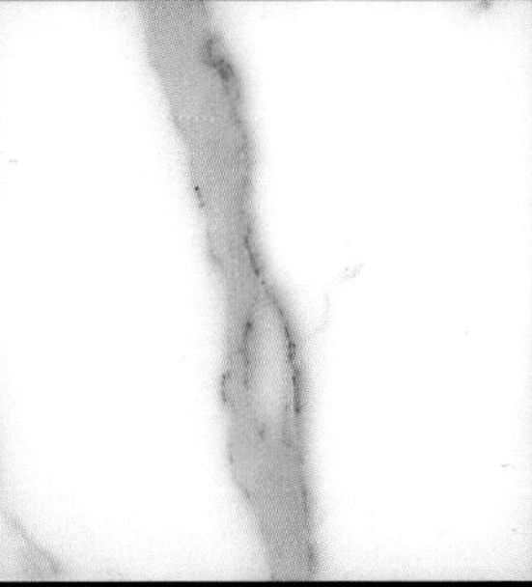
Statuario Vena Grossa

Statuario Vena Fine

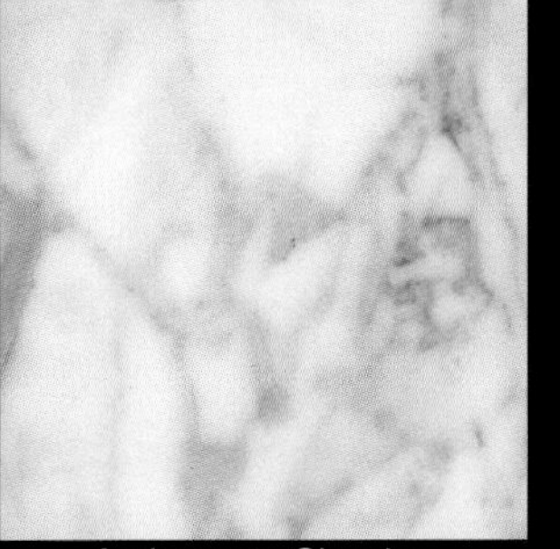
Arabescato Classico

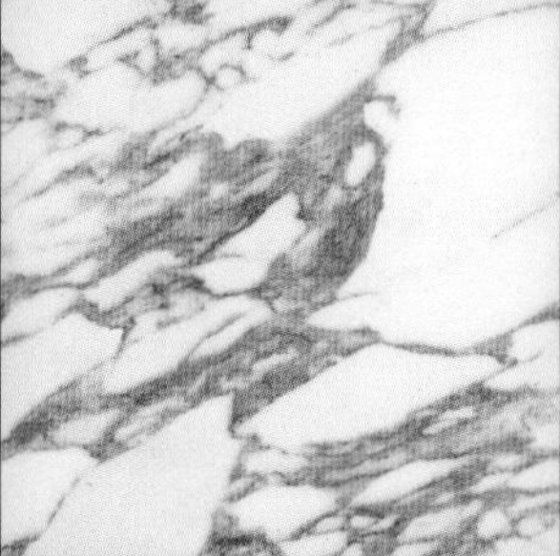
Arabescato Corchia

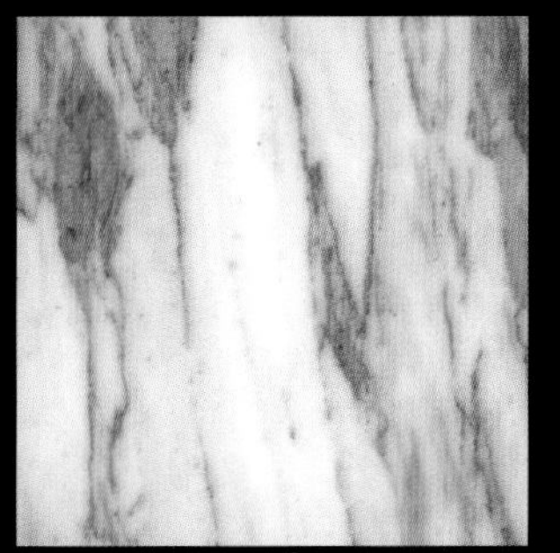
Arabescato Carcariana

Arabescato Cervaiole

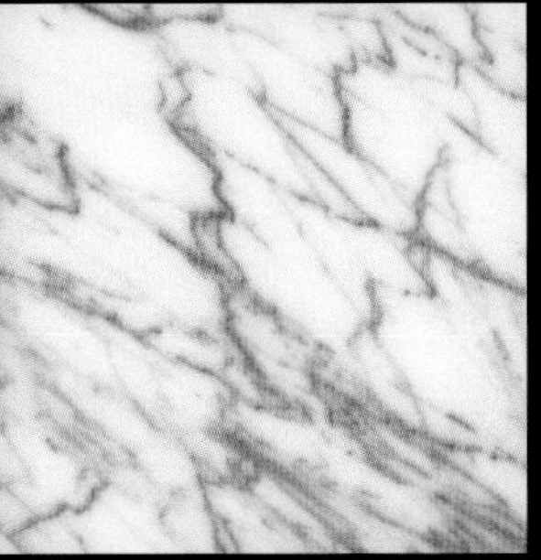
Arabescato Piana

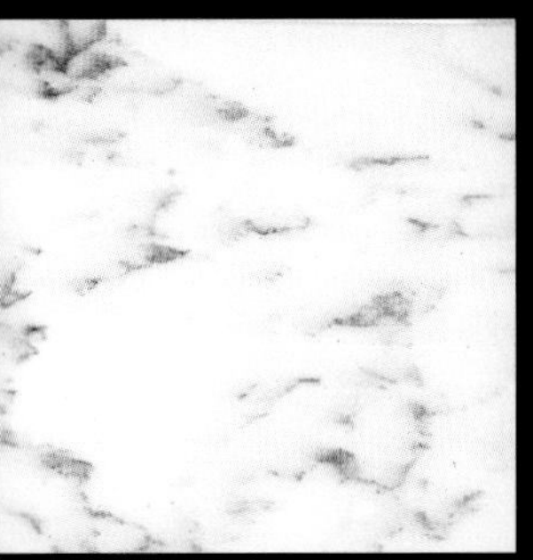
Arabescato Faniello

Arabescato Trambiserra

Arabescato Vagli

Arabescato Arni

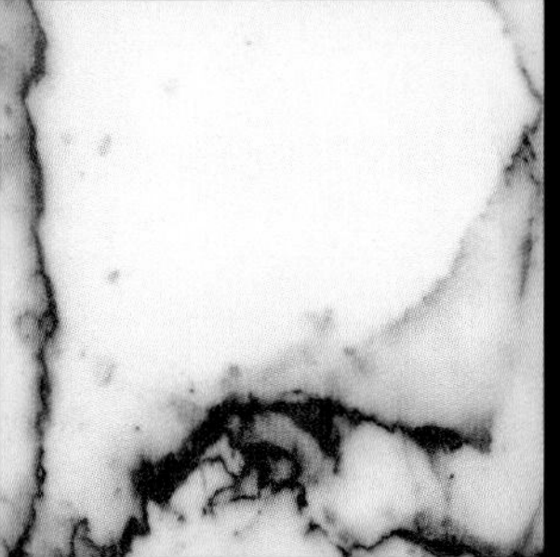
Paonazzo

Ambajy White

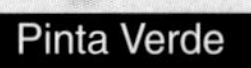
Pinta Verde

Quarrying location: Italy
Availability: Medium
Compressive strength: 1811/kg cm^2
After freezing: 317/kg cm^2
Ultimate tensile strength: 218/kg cm^2
Coef. thermal expansion: 0,0033mm/m°C
Water absorption: 0,17%
Impact test / min. fall height: 37 cm
Frictional wear test: 0,97
Bulk density: 2710 kg/m^3

CD file number: 0049

Quarrying location: Italy
Availability: Medium
Compressive strength: 1811/kg cm^2
After freezing: 317/kg cm^2
Ultimate tensile strength: 218/kg cm^2
Coef. thermal expansion: 0,0033mm/m°C
Water absorption: 0,17%
Impact test / min. fall height: 37 cm
Frictional wear test: 0,97
Bulk density: 2710 kg/m^3

CD file number: 0050

Quarrying location: Italy
Availability: Medium
Compressive strength: 1811/kg cm^2
After freezing: 317/kg cm^2
Ultimate tensile strength: 218/kg cm^2
Coef. thermal expansion: 0,0033mm/m°C
Water absorption: 0,17%
Impact test / min. fall height: 37 cm
Frictional wear test: 0,97
Bulk density: 2710 kg/m^3

CD file number: 0051

Quarrying location: Italy
Availability: Medium
Compressive strength: 1811/kg cm^2
After freezing: 317/kg cm^2
Ultimate tensile strength: 218/kg cm^2
Coef. thermal expansion: 0,0033mm/m°C
Water absorption: 0,17%
Impact test / min. fall height: 37 cm
Frictional wear test: 0,97
Bulk density: 2710 kg/m^3

CD file number: 0052

Botticino Classico

Quarrying location: Italy
Availability: Medium
Compressive strength: 1610/kg cm^2
After freezing: 1454/kg cm^2
Ultimate tensile strength: 165/kg cm^2
Coef. thermal expansion: 0,0039mm/m°C
Water absorption: 0,40%
Impact test / min. fall height: 34cm
Frictional wear test: –
Bulk density: 2669 kg/m^3

CD file number: 0053

Botticino Semiclassico

Quarrying location: Italy
Availability: Medium
Compressive strength: 1610/kg cm^2
After freezing: 1454/kg cm^2
Ultimate tensile strength: 165/kg cm^2
Coef. thermal expansion: 0,0039mm/m°C
Water absorption: 0,40%
Impact test / min. fall height: 34cm
Frictional wear test: –
Bulk density: 2669 kg/m^3

CD file number: 0054

Botticino Fiorito

Quarrying location: Italy
Availability: Medium
Compressive strength: 1610/kg cm^2
After freezing: 1454/kg cm^2
Ultimate tensile strength: 165/kg cm^2
Coef. thermal expansion: 0,0039mm/m°C
Water absorption: 0,40%
Impact test / min. fall height: 34cm
Frictional wear test: –
Bulk density: 2669 kg/m^3

CD file number: 0055

Botticino Royale

Quarrying location: Greece
Availability: Medium
Compressive strength: 2680/kg cm^2
After freezing: 2540/kg cm^2
Ultimate tensile strength: 165/kg cm^2
Coef. thermal expansion: 0,0060mm/m°C
Water absorption: 0,30%
Impact test / min. fall height: 35cm
Frictional wear test: –
Bulk density: 2715 kg/m^3

CD file number: 0056

Breccia Sarda

Quarrying location: Spain
Availability: Good
Compressive strength: 1854/kg cm^2
After freezing: 1775/kg cm^2
Ultimate tensile strength: 171/kg cm^2
Coef. thermal expansion: 0,0043mm/m°C
Water absorption: 0,20%
Impact test / min. fall height: 31cm
Frictional wear test: –
Bulk density: 2669 kg/m^3

CD file number: 0057

Breccia Sarda Chiara

Quarrying location: Greece
Availability: Good
Compressive strength: 1854/kg cm^2
After freezing: 1775/kg cm^2
Ultimate tensile strength: 171/kg cm^2
Coef. thermal expansion: 0,0043mm/m°C
Water absorption: 0,20%
Impact test / min. fall height: 31cm
Frictional wear test: –
Bulk density: 2669 kg/m^3

CD file number: 0058

Daino Reale

Quarrying location: Turkey
Availability: Good
Compressive strength: 1610/kg cm^2
After freezing: 1454/kg cm^2
Ultimate tensile strength: 165/kg cm^2
Coef. thermal expansion: 0,0039mm/m°C
Water absorption: 0,40%
Impact test / min. fall height: 34cm
Frictional wear test: –
Bulk density: 2669 kg/m^3

CD file number: 0059

French Vanilla

Quarrying location: Turkey
Availability: Good
Compressive strength: 2060/kg cm^2
After freezing: 1879/kg cm^2
Ultimate tensile strength: 155/kg cm^2
Coef. thermal expansion: 0,0040 mm/m°C
Water absorption: 0,06%
Impact test / min. fall height: 26 cm
Frictional wear test: –
Bulk density: 2670 kg/m^3

CD file number: 0060

Crema Marfil

Quarrying location: Italy
Availability: Medium
Compressive strength: 1118/kg cm^2
After freezing: 1335/kg cm
Ultimate tensile strength: 235/kg cm^2
Coef. thermal expansion: 0,0052mm/m°C
Water absorption: 0,24%
Impact test / min. fall height: 61,3 cm^2
Frictional wear test: 3,64
Bulk density: 2680 kg/m^3

CD file number: 0061

Cremo Supremo

Quarrying location: Italy
Availability: Medium
Compressive strength: 1854/kg cm^2
After freezing: 1775/kg cm^2
Ultimate tensile strength: 171/kg cm^2
Coef. thermal expansion: 0,0043mm/m°C
Water absorption: 0,20%
Impact test / min. fall height: 31cm
Frictional wear test: –
Bulk density: 2669 kg/m^3

CD file number: 0062

Crema Nuova

Quarrying location: Egypt
Availability: Good
Compressive strength: 1854/kg cm^2
After freezing: 1775/kg cm^2
Ultimate tensile strength: 171/kg cm^2
Coef. thermal expansion: 0,0043mm/m°C
Water absorption: 0,20%
Impact test / min. fall height: 31cm
Frictional wear test: –
Bulk density: 2669 kg/m^3

CD file number: 0063

Cremo Bello

Quarrying location: Italy
Availability: Medium
Compressive strength: 2060/kg cm^2
After freezing: 1879/kg cm^2
Ultimate tensile strength: 155/kg cm^2
Coef. thermal expansion: 0,0040mm/m°C
Water absorption: 0,06%
Impact test / min. fall height: 26cm
Frictional wear test: –
Bulk density: 2670 kg/m^3

CD file number: 0064

Cremo Delicato

Cremo Sicilia

Galala

Biancone

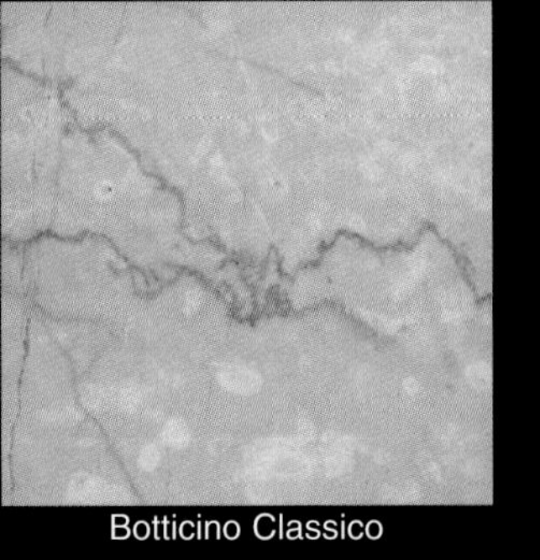
Botticino Classico

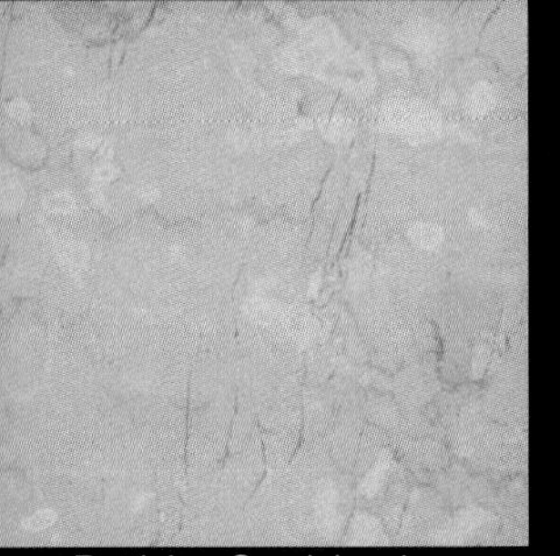
Botticino Semiclassico

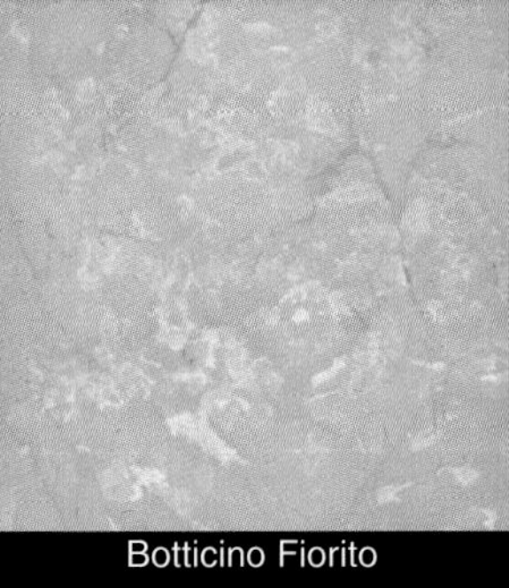
Botticino Fiorito

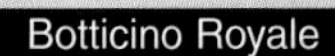
Botticino Royale

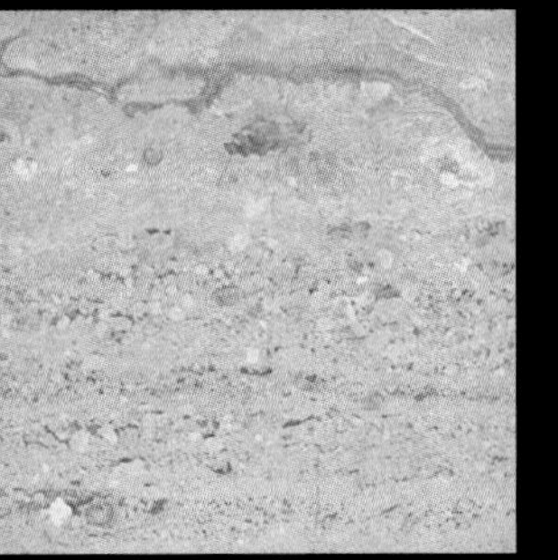
Breccia Sarda

Breccia Sarda Chiara

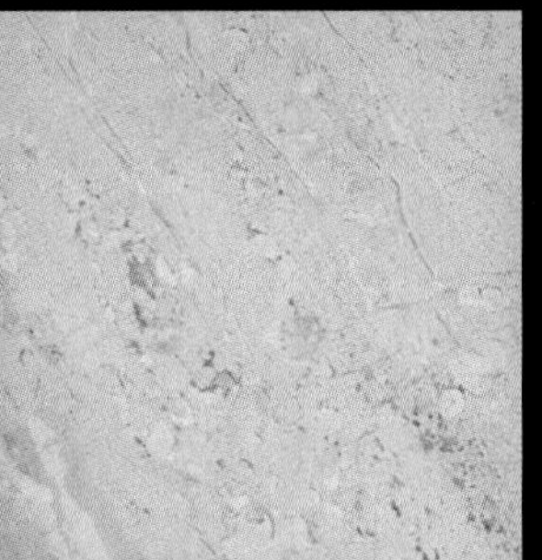
Daino Reale

French Vanilla

Crema Marfil

Cremo Supremo

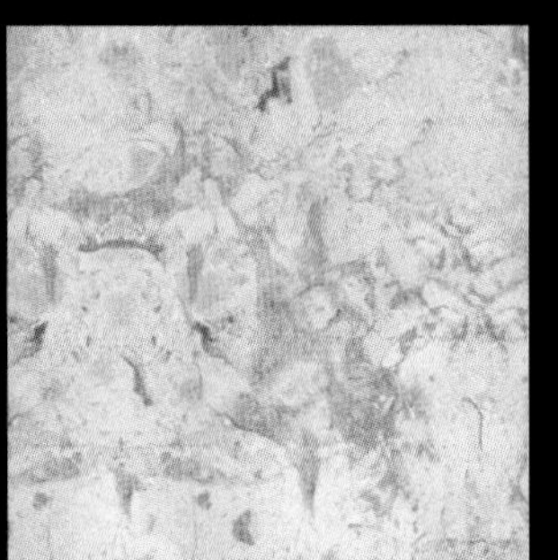
Crema Nuova

Cremo Bello

Cremo Delicato

Cremo Sicilia

Galala

Biancone

Quarrying location: Italy
Availability: Medium
Compressive strength: 2275/kg cm^2
After freezing: 2224/kg cm^2
Ultimate tensile strength: 224/kg cm^2
Coef. thermal expansion: 0,0043mm/m°C
Water absorption: 0,20%
Impact test / min. fall height: 23cm
Frictional wear test: –
Bulk density: 2665 kg/m^3

CD file number: 0065

Quarrying location: Italy
Availability: Medium
Compressive strength: 2275/kg cm^2
After freezing: 2224/kg cm^2
Ultimate tensile strength: 224/kg cm^2
Coef. thermal expansion: 0,0043mm/m°C
Water absorption: 0,20%
Impact test / min. fall height: 23cm
Frictional wear test: –
Bulk density: 2665 kg/m^3

CD file number: 0066

Quarrying location: Italy
Availability: Good
Compressive strength: 1854/kg cm^2
After freezing: 1775/kg cm^2
Ultimate tensile strength: 171/kg cm^2
Coef. thermal expansion: 0,0043mm/m°C
Water absorption: 0,20%
Impact test / min. fall height: 31cm
Frictional wear test: –
Bulk density: 2669 kg/m^3

CD file number: 0067

Quarrying location: Italy
Availability: Good
Compressive strength: 1854/kg cm^2
After freezing: 1775/kg cm^2
Ultimate tensile strength: 171/kg cm^2
Coef. thermal expansion: 0,0043mm/m°C
Water absorption: 0,20%
Impact test / min. fall height: 31cm
Frictional wear test: –
Bulk density: 2669 kg/m^3

CD file number: 0068

Serpegginate

Quarrying location: Germany
Availability: Good
Compressive strength: 1610/kg cm^2
After freezing: 1454/kg cm^2
Ultimate tensile strength: 165/kg cm^2
Coef. thermal expansion: 0,0039mm/m°C
Water absorption: 0,40%
Impact test / min. fall height: 34cm
Frictional wear test: –
Bulk density: 2669 kg/m^3

CD file number: 0069

Serpegginate KF

Quarrying location: Germany
Availability: Medium
Compressive strength: 1610/kg cm^2
After freezing: 1454/kg cm^2
Ultimate tensile strength: 165/kg cm^2
Coef. thermal expansion: 0,0039mm/m°C
Water absorption: 0,40%
Impact test / min. fall height: 34cm
Frictional wear test: –
Bulk density: 2669 kg/m^3

CD file number: 0070

Trani Classico

Quarrying location: Germany
Availability: Good
Compressive strength: 1610/kg cm^2
After freezing: 1454/kg cm^2
Ultimate tensile strength: 165/kg cm^2
Coef. thermal expansion: 0,0039mm/m°C
Water absorption: 0,40%
Impact test / min. fall height: 34cm
Frictional wear test: –
Bulk density: 2669 kg/m^3

CD file number: 0071

Trani Fiorito

Quarrying location: France
Availability: Medium
Compressive strength: 1853/kg cm^2
After freezing: 1792/kg cm^2
Ultimate tensile strength: 155/kg cm^2
Coef. thermal expansion: 0,0042mm/m°C
Water absorption: 0,40%
Impact test / min. fall height: 35cm
Frictional wear test: –
Bulk density: 2659 kg/m^3

CD file number: 0072

Iura Gelb Chiaro

Quarrying location: Namibia
Availability: Limited
Compressive strength: 2680/kg cm^2
After freezing: 2540/kg cm^2
Ultimate tensile strength: 165/kg cm^2
Coef. thermal expansion: 0,0060mm/m°C
Water absorption: 0,30%
Impact test / min. fall height: 34cm
Frictional wear test: –
Bulk density: 2715 kg/m^3

CD file number: 0073

Iura Gelb Scuro

Quarrying location: Egypt
Availability: Medium
Compressive strength: 1610/kg cm^2
After freezing: 1454/kg cm^2
Ultimate tensile strength: 165/kg cm^2
Coef. thermal expansion: 0,0039mm/m°C
Water absorption: 0,40%
Impact test / min. fall height: 34cm
Frictional wear test: –
Bulk density: 2669 kg/m^3

CD file number: 0074

Iura Grau

Quarrying location: Italy
Availability: Medium
Compressive strength: 1854/kg cm^2
After freezing: 1775/kg cm^2
Ultimate tensile strength: 171/kg cm^2
Coef. thermal expansion: 0,0043mm/m°C
Water absorption: 0,20%
Impact test / min. fall height: 31cm
Frictional wear test: –
Bulk density: 2669 kg/m^3

CD file number: 0075

Napoleon Gran Melange

Quarrying location: Egypt
Availability: Medium
Compressive strength: 1610/kg cm^2
After freezing: 1454/kg cm^2
Ultimate tensile strength: 165/kg cm^2
Coef. thermal expansion: 0,0039mm/m°C
Water absorption: 0,40%
Impact test / min. fall height: 34cm
Frictional wear test: –
Bulk density: 2669 kg/m^3

CD file number: 0076

Karibib

Quarrying location: Italy
Availability: Medium
Compressive strength: 1854/kg cm^2
After freezing: 1775/kg cm^2
Ultimate tensile strength: 171/kg cm^2
Coef. thermal expansion: 0,0043mm/m°C
Water absorption: 0,20%
Impact test / min. fall height: 31cm
Frictional wear test: –
Bulk density: 2669 kg/m^3

CD file number: 0077

Yellow Dream

Quarrying location: Italy
Availability: Medium
Compressive strength: 1854/kg cm^2
After freezing: 1775/kg cm^2
Ultimate tensile strength: 171/kg cm^2
Coef. thermal expansion: 0,0043mm/m°C
Water absorption: 0,20%
Impact test / min. fall height: 31cm
Frictional wear test: –
Bulk density: 2669 kg/m^3

CD file number: 0078

Bronzetto

Quarrying location: Italy
Availability: Medium
Compressive strength: 1610/kg cm^2
After freezing: 1454/kg cm^2
Ultimate tensile strength: 165/kg cm^2
Coef. thermal expansion: 0,0039mm/m°C
Water absorption: 0,40%
Impact test / min. fall height: 34cm
Frictional wear test: –
Bulk density: 2669 kg/m^3

CD file number: 0079

Filetto Hasana

Quarrying location: Egypt
Availability: Medium
Compressive strength: 1854/kg cm^2
After freezing: 1775/kg cm^2
Ultimate tensile strength: 171/kg cm^2
Coef. thermal expansion: 0,0043mm/m°C
Water absorption: 0,20%
Impact test / min. fall height: 31cm
Frictional wear test: –
Bulk density: 2669 kg/m^3

CD file number: 0080

Filettato America

Filetto Rosso

Perla Classico

Sinai Pearl

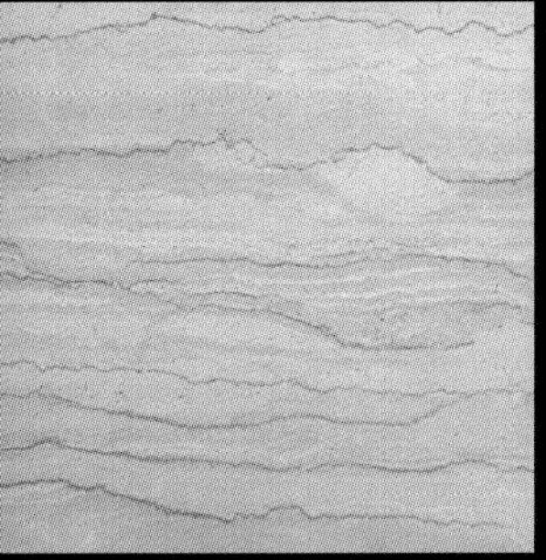

Serpegginate

Serpegginate KF

Trani Classico

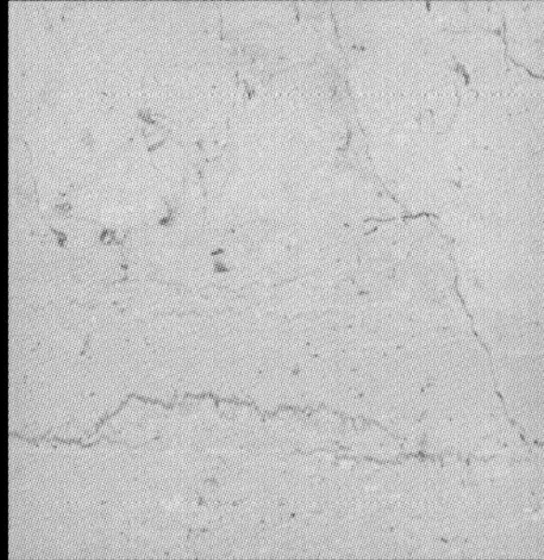

Trani Fiorito

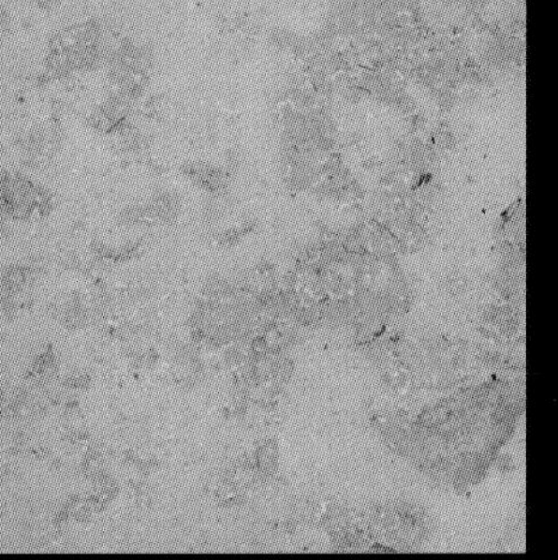

Iura Gelb Chiaro

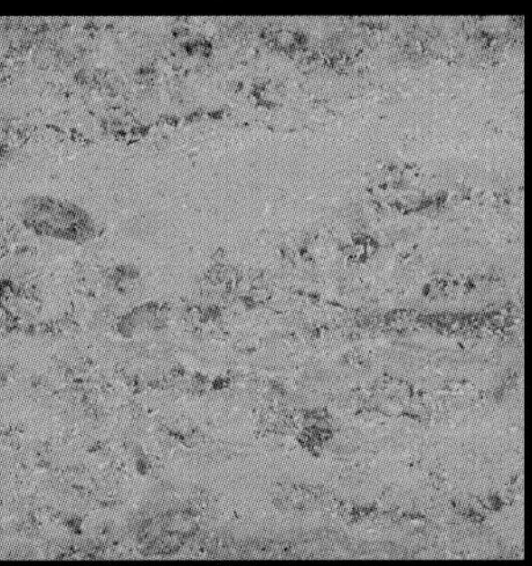

Iura Gelb Scuro

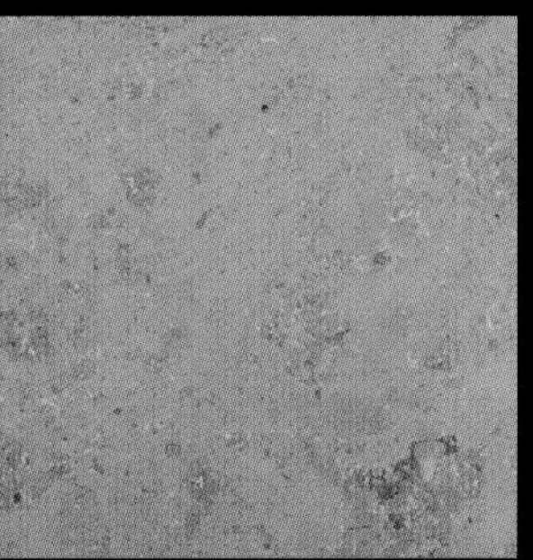

Iura Grau

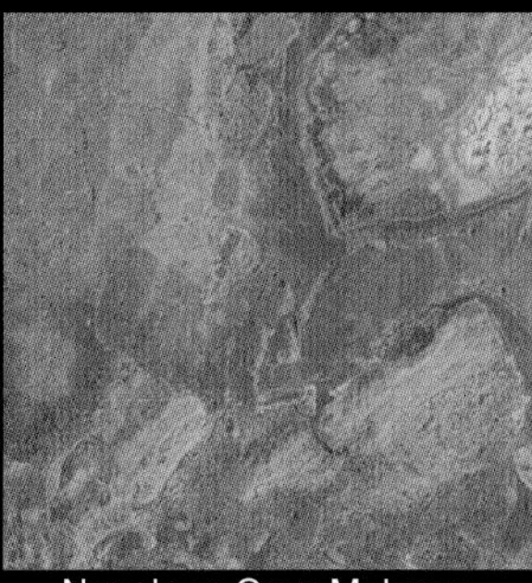

Napoleon Gran Melange

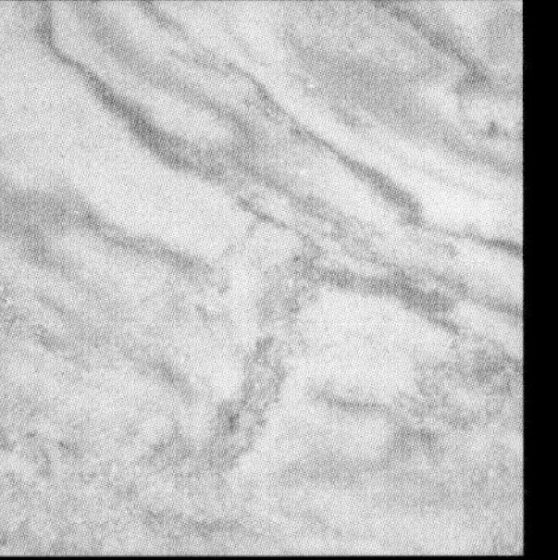

Karibib

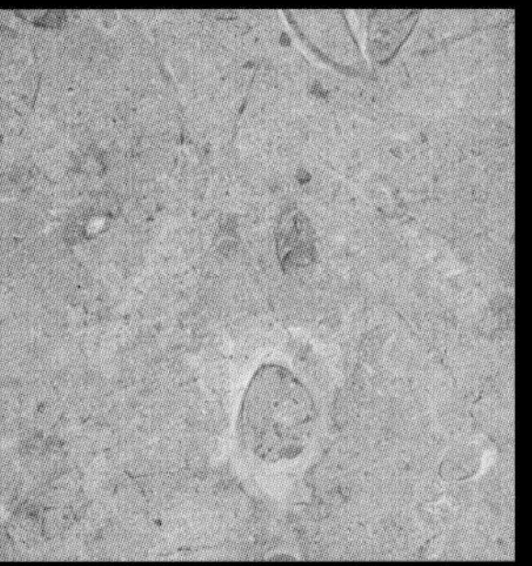

Yellow Dream

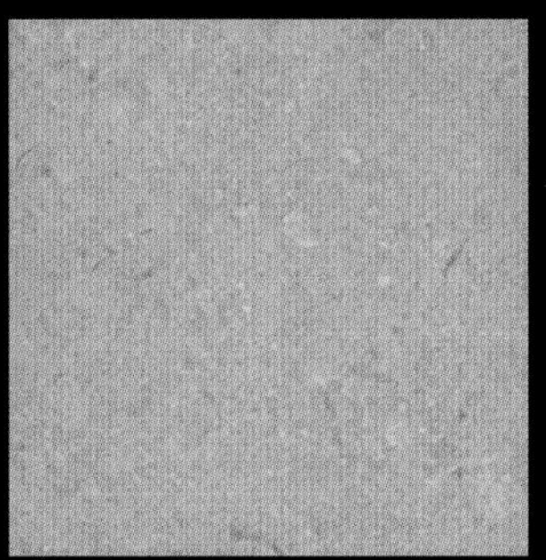

Bronzetto

Filetto Hasana

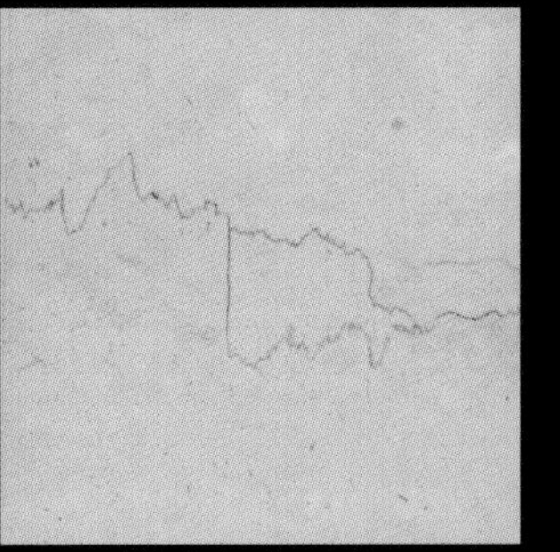

Filettato America

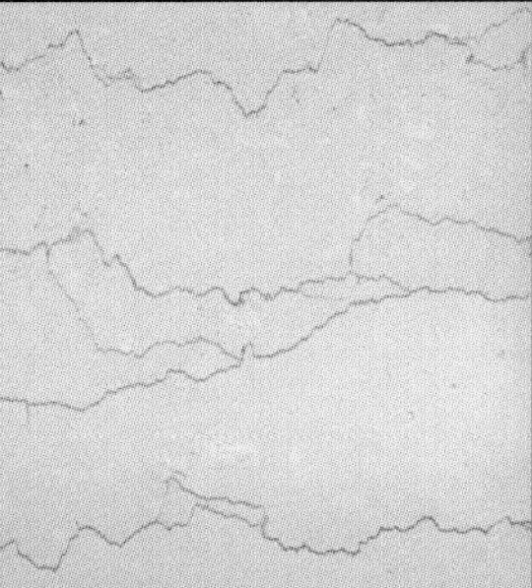

Filetto Rosso

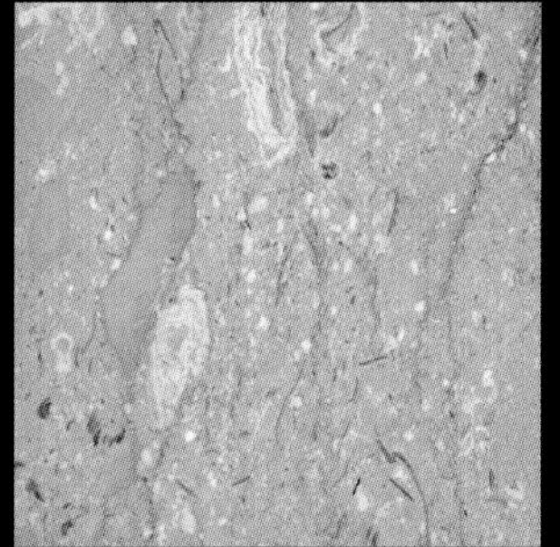

Perla Classico

Sinai Pearl

Quarrying location: Italy
Availability: Medium
Compressive strength: 1853/kg cm^2
After freezing: 1792/kg cm^2
Ultimate tensile strength: 155/kg cm^2
Coef. thermal expansion: 0,0042mm/m°C
Water absorption: 0,40%
Impact test / min. fall height: 35cm
Frictional wear test: –
Bulk density: 2659 kg/m^3

CD file number: 0081

Quarrying location: Italy
Availability: Good
Compressive strength: 1610/kg cm^2
After freezing: 1454/kg cm^2
Ultimate tensile strength: 165/kg cm^2
Coef. thermal expansion: 0,0039mm/m°C
Water absorption: 0,40%
Impact test / min. fall height: 34cm
Frictional wear test: –
Bulk density: 2669 kg/m^3

CD file number: 0082

Quarrying location: Italy
Availability: Good
Compressive strength: 1610/kg cm^2
After freezing: 1454/kg cm^2
Ultimate tensile strength: 165/kg cm^2
Coef. thermal expansion: 0,0039mm/m°C
Water absorption: 0,40%
Impact test / min. fall height: 34cm
Frictional wear test: –
Bulk density: 2669 kg/m^3

CD file number: 0083

Quarrying location: Ital
Availability: Good
Compressive strength: 1660/kg cm
After freezing: 1550/kg cm
Ultimate tensile strength: 130/kg cm
Coef. thermal expansion: -
Water absorption: 0,40%
Impact test / min. fall height: 32cm
Frictional wear test: 0,9
Bulk density: 2738 kg/m

CD file number: 0084

Aurisina Fiorita

Quarrying location: Italy
Availability: Good
Compressive strength: 1610/kg cm^2
After freezing: 1454/kg cm^2
Ultimate tensile strength: 165/kg cm^2
Coef. thermal expansion: 0,0039mm/m°C
Water absorption: 0,40%
Impact test / min. fall height: 34cm
Frictional wear test: –
Bulk density: 2669 kg/m^3

CD file number: 0085

Perlato Royal

Quarrying location: Indonesia
Availability: Good
Compressive strength: 1610/kg cm^2
After freezing: 1454/kg cm^2
Ultimate tensile strength: 165/kg cm^2
Coef. thermal expansion: 0,0039mm/m°C
Water absorption: 0,40%
Impact test / min. fall height: 34cm
Frictional wear test: –
Bulk density: 2669 kg/m^3

CD file number: 0086

Perlato Sicilia

Quarrying location: Italy
Availability: Medium
Compressive strength: 1854/kg cm^2
After freezing: 1775/kg cm^2
Ultimate tensile strength: 171/kg cm^2
Coef. thermal expansion: 0,0043mm/m°C
Water absorption: 0,20%
Impact test / min. fall height: 31cm
Frictional wear test: –
Bulk density: 2669 kg/m^3

CD file number: 0087

Perlatino

Quarrying location: Italy
Availability: Medium
Compressive strength: 2275/kg cm
After freezing: 2224/kg cm
Ultimate tensile strength: 224/kg cm
Coef. thermal expansion: 0,0043mm/m°C
Water absorption: 0,20%
Impact test / min. fall height: 23cm
Frictional wear test: -
Bulk density: 2665 kg/m

CD file number: 0088

Perlato Svevo

Quarrying location: Italy
Availability: Medium
Compressive strength: 2275/kg cm^2
After freezing: 2224/kg cm^2
Ultimate tensile strength: 224/kg cm^2
Coef. thermal expansion: 0,0043mm/m°C
Water absorption: 0,20%
Impact test / min. fall height: 23cm
Frictional wear test: –
Bulk density: 2665 kg/m^3

CD file number: 0089

Perlatino Indonesia

Quarrying location: Italy
Availability: Limited
Compressive strength: 1853/kg cm^2
After freezing: 1792/kg cm^2
Ultimate tensile strength: 155/kg cm^2
Coef. thermal expansion: 0,0042mm/m°C
Water absorption: 0,40%
Impact test / min. fall height: 35cm
Frictional wear test: –
Bulk density: 2659 kg/m^3

CD file number: 0090

Pink America

Quarrying location: Egypt
Availability: Medium
Compressive strength: 1610/kg cm^2
After freezing: 1454/kg cm^2
Ultimate tensile strength: 165/kg cm^2
Coef. thermal expansion: 0,0039mm/m°C
Water absorption: 0,40%
Impact test / min. fall height: 34cm
Frictional wear test: –
Bulk density: 2669 kg/m^3

CD file number: 0091

Silvabella

Quarrying location: Egyp
Availability: Medium
Compressive strength: 1610/kg cm
After freezing: 1454/kg cm
Ultimate tensile strength: 165/kg cm
Coef. thermal expansion: 0,0039mm/m°C
Water absorption: 0,40%
Impact test / min. fall height: 34cm
Frictional wear test: -
Bulk density: 2669 kg/m

CD file number: 0092

Visone

Quarrying location: Italy
Availability: Limited
Compressive strength: 832/kg cm^2
After freezing: 289/kg cm^2
Ultimate tensile strength: 107/kg cm^2
Coef. thermal expansion: 0,0038mm/m°C
Water absorption: 0,29%
Impact test / min. fall height: 31 cm
Frictional wear test: –
Bulk density: 2715 kg/m^3

CD file number: 0093

Spuma di Mare

Quarrying location: Italy
Availability: Limited
Compressive strength: 832/kg cm^2
After freezing: 289/kg cm^2
Ultimate tensile strength: 107/kg cm^2
Coef. thermal expansion: 0,0038mm/m°C
Water absorption: 0,29%
Impact test / min. fall height: 31 cm
Frictional wear test: –
Bulk density: 2715 kg/m^3

CD file number: 0094

Golden Cream

Quarrying location: Italy
Availability: Limited
Compressive strength: 832/kg cm^2
After freezing: 289/kg cm^2
Ultimate tensile strength: 107/kg cm^2
Coef. thermal expansion: 0,0038mm/m°C
Water absorption: 0,29%
Impact test / min. fall height: 31 cm
Frictional wear test: –
Bulk density: 2715 kg/m^3

CD file number: 0095

Sunny

Quarrying location: Egyp
Availability: Medium
Compressive strength: 832/kg cm
After freezing: 289/kg cm
Ultimate tensile strength: 107/kg cm
Coef. thermal expansion: 0,0038mm/m°C
Water absorption: 0,29%
Impact test / min. fall height: 31 cm
Frictional wear test: -
Bulk density: 2715 kg/m

CD file number: 0096

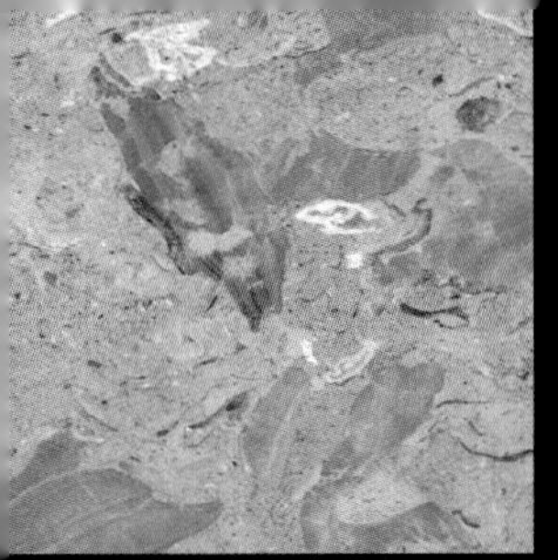

Aurisina Fiorita

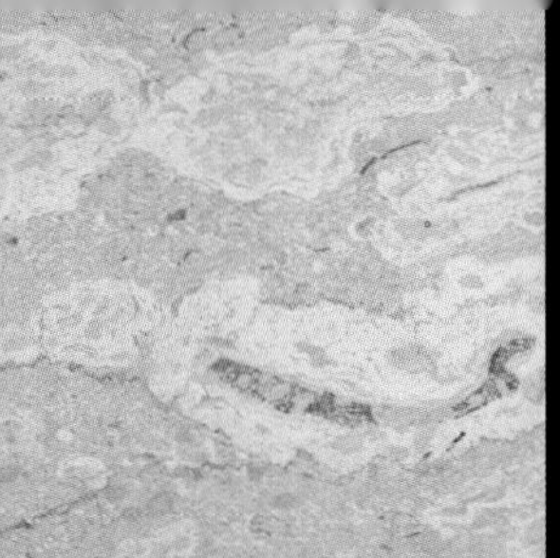

Perlato Royal

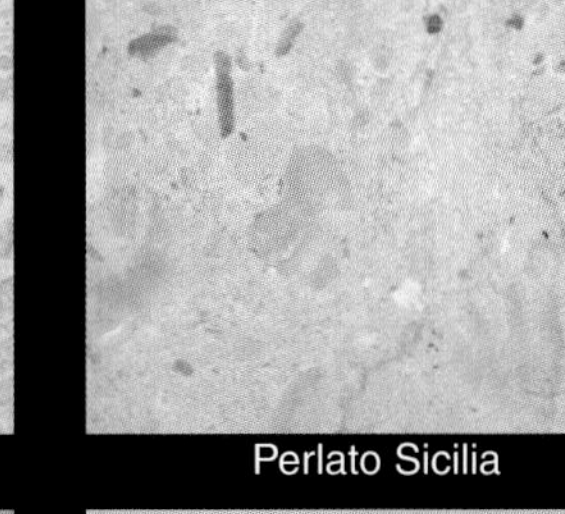

Perlato Sicilia

Perlatino

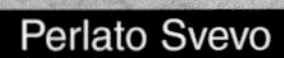

Perlato Svevo

Perlatino Indonesia

Pink America

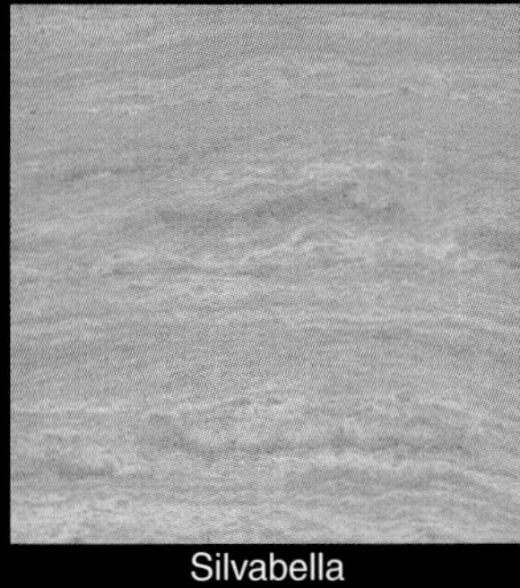

Silvabella

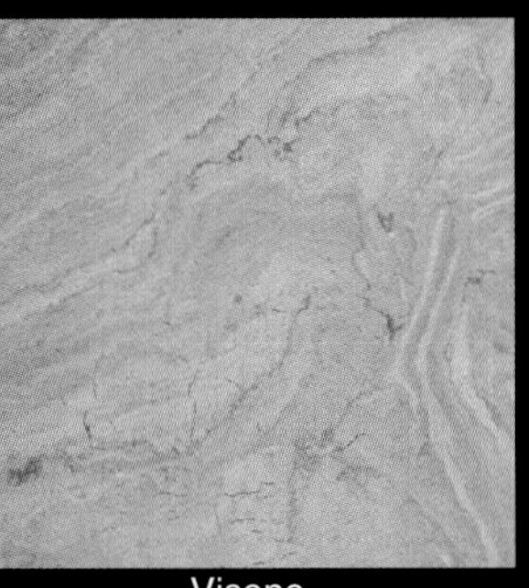

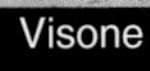

Visone

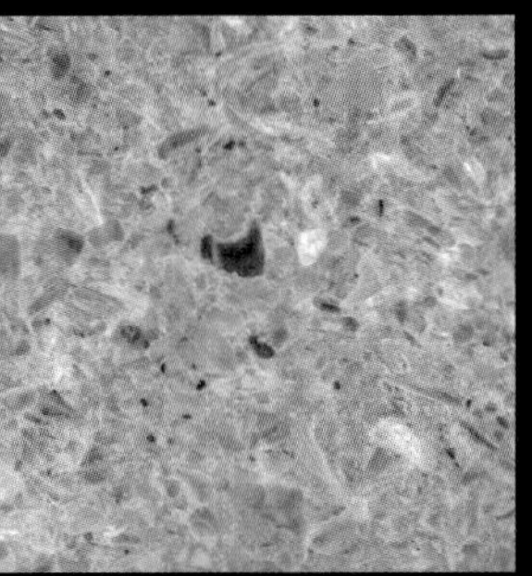

Spuma di Mare

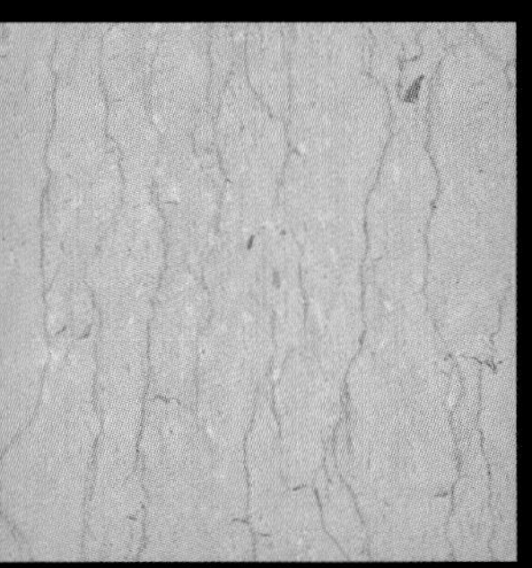

Golden Cream

Sunny

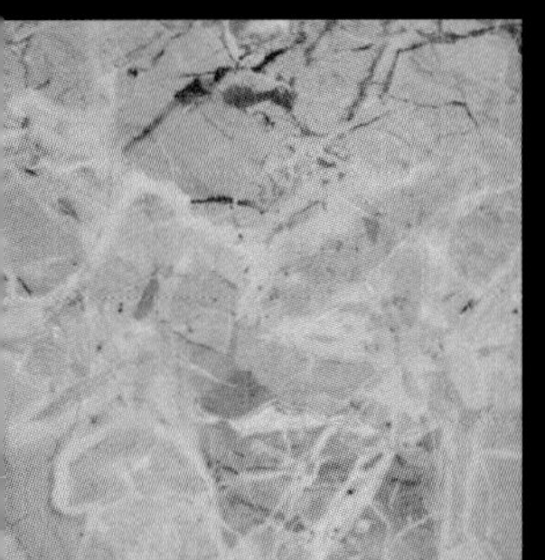

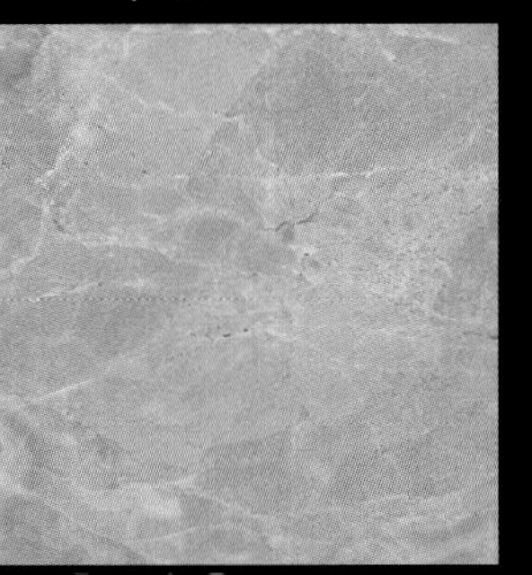

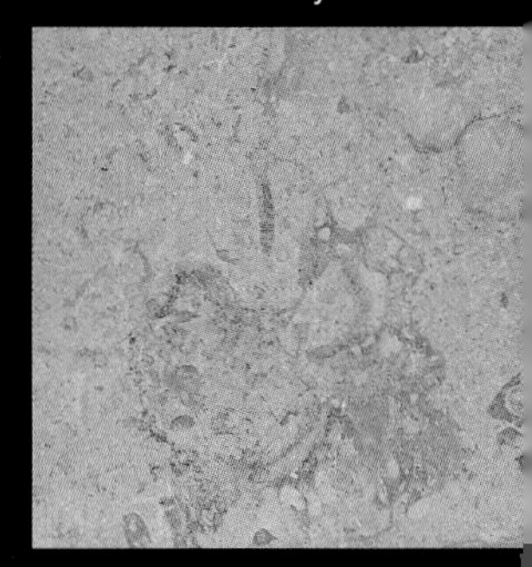

- Quarrying location: Turkey
- Availability: Good
- Compressive strength: 974/kg cm^2
- After freezing: –
- Ultimate tensile strength: 134/kg cm^2
- Coef. thermal expansion: –
- Water absorption: 0,05%
- Impact test / min. fall height: 50 cm
- Frictional wear test: –
- Bulk density: 2730 kg/m^3

CD file number: 0097

- Quarrying location: Italy
- Availability: Medium
- Compressive strength: 1805kg cm^2
- After freezing: 1727/kg cm^2
- Ultimate tensile strength: 139/kg cm^2
- Coef. thermal expansion: 0,0045mm/m°C
- Water absorption: 0,12%
- Impact test / min. fall height: 29 cm
- Frictional wear test: –
- Bulk density: 2686 kg/m^3

CD file number: 0098

- Quarrying location: Portugal
- Availability: Good
- Compressive strength: 974/kg cm^2
- After freezing: –
- Ultimate tensile strength: 134/kg cm^2
- Coef. thermal expansion: –
- Water absorption: 0,05%
- Impact test / min. fall height: 50 cm
- Frictional wear test: 8 mm
- Bulk density: 2730 kg/m^3

CD file number: 0099

- Quarrying location: Italy
- Availability: Medium
- Compressive strength: 1805kg cm^2
- After freezing: 1727/kg cm^2
- Ultimate tensile strength: 139/kg cm^2
- Coef. thermal expansion: 0,0045mm/m°C
- Water absorption: 0,12%
- Impact test / min. fall height: 29 cm
- Frictional wear test: –
- Bulk density: 2686 kg/m^3

CD file number: 0100

Rosa Bellissimo

- Quarrying location: Italy
- Availability: Scarse
- Compressive strength: 832/kg cm^2
- After freezing: 289/kg cm^2
- Ultimate tensile strength: 107/kg cm^2
- Coef. thermal expansion: 0,0038mm/m°C
- Water absorption: 0,29%
- Impact test / min. fall height: 31 cm
- Frictional wear test: –
- Bulk density: 2715 kg/m^3

CD file number: 0101

Chiampo Rosa

- Quarrying location: Italy
- Availability: Scarse
- Compressive strength: 832/kg cm^2
- After freezing: 289/kg cm^2
- Ultimate tensile strength: 107/kg cm^2
- Coef. thermal expansion: 0,0038mm/m°C
- Water absorption: 0,29%
- Impact test / min. fall height: 31 cm
- Frictional wear test: –
- Bulk density: 2715 kg/m^3

CD file number: 0102

Fior di Rosa

- Quarrying location: Portugal
- Availability: Medium
- Compressive strength: 1805kg cm^2
- After freezing: 1727/kg cm^2
- Ultimate tensile strength: 139/kg cm^2
- Coef. thermal expansion: 0,0045mm/m°C
- Water absorption: 0,12%
- Impact test / min. fall height: 29 cm
- Frictional wear test: –
- Bulk density: 2686 kg/m^3

CD file number: 0103

Rosa San Marco

- Quarrying location: Turkey
- Availability: Medium
- Compressive strength: 832/kg cm^2
- After freezing: 289/kg cm^2
- Ultimate tensile strength: 107/kg cm^2
- Coef. thermal expansion: 0,0038mm/m°C
- Water absorption: 0,29%
- Impact test / min. fall height: 31 cm
- Frictional wear test: –
- Bulk density: 2715 kg/m^3

CD file number: 0104

Rosa Sicilia

- Quarrying location: Italy
- Availability: Limited
- Compressive strength: 832/kg cm^2
- After freezing: 289/kg cm^2
- Ultimate tensile strength: 107/kg cm^2
- Coef. thermal expansion: 0,0038mm/m°C
- Water absorption: 0,29%
- Impact test / min. fall height: 31 cm
- Frictional wear test: –
- Bulk density: 2715 kg/m^3

CD file number: 0105

Liberty

- Quarrying location: Turkey
- Availability: Good
- Compressive strength: 1805kg cm^2
- After freezing: 1727/kg cm^2
- Ultimate tensile strength: 139/kg cm^2
- Coef. thermal expansion: 0,0045mm/m°C
- Water absorption: 0,12%
- Impact test / min. fall height: 29 cm
- Frictional wear test: –
- Bulk density: 2686 kg/m^3

CD file number: 0106

Rosa Atlantide

- Quarrying location: Namibia
- Availability: Good
- Compressive strength: 974/kg cm^2
- After freezing: –
- Ultimate tensile strength: 134/kg cm^2
- Coef. thermal expansion: –
- Water absorption: 0,05%
- Impact test / min. fall height: 50 cm
- Frictional wear test: 8 mm
- Bulk density: 2730 kg/m^3

CD file number: 0107

Rosa Tea

- Quarrying location: Norway
- Availability: Medium
- Compressive strength: 1960/kg cm^2
- After freezing: –
- Ultimate tensile strength: 75/kg cm^2
- Coef. thermal expansion: 0,0030mm/m°C
- Water absorption: 0,10%
- Impact test / min. fall height: –
- Frictional wear test: –
- Bulk density: 2600 kg/m^3

CD file number: 0108

Arabescato Orobico Rosa

- Quarrying location: Greece
- Availability: Limited
- Compressive strength: 974/kg cm^2
- After freezing: –
- Ultimate tensile strength: 134/kg cm^2
- Coef. thermal expansion: –
- Water absorption: 0,05%
- Impact test / min. fall height: 50 cm
- Frictional wear test: –
- Bulk density: 2730 kg/m^3

CD file number: 0109

Rosalia

- Quarrying location: Portugal
- Availability: Good
- Compressive strength: 974/kg cm^2
- After freezing: –
- Ultimate tensile strength: 134/kg cm^2
- Coef. thermal expansion: –
- Water absorption: 0,05%
- Impact test / min. fall height: 50 cm
- Frictional wear test: –
- Bulk density: 2730 kg/m^3

CD file number: 0110

Rosa West

- Quarrying location: Portugal
- Availability: Good
- Compressive strength: 974/kg cm^2
- After freezing: –
- Ultimate tensile strength: 134/kg cm^2
- Coef. thermal expansion: –
- Water absorption: 0,05%
- Impact test / min. fall height: 50 cm
- Frictional wear test: –
- Bulk density: 2730 kg/m^3

CD file number: 0111

Rosa Norvegia

- Quarrying location: Portugal
- Availability: Good
- Compressive strength: 974/kg cm^2
- After freezing: –
- Ultimate tensile strength: 134/kg cm^2
- Coef. thermal expansion: –
- Water absorption: 0,05%
- Impact test / min. fall height: 50 cm
- Frictional wear test: –
- Bulk density: 2730 kg/m^3

CD file number: 0112

Rosa Egeo

Rosa Aurora

Rosa Portogallo

Rosa Portogallo Venato

Rosa Bellissimo

Chiampo Rosa

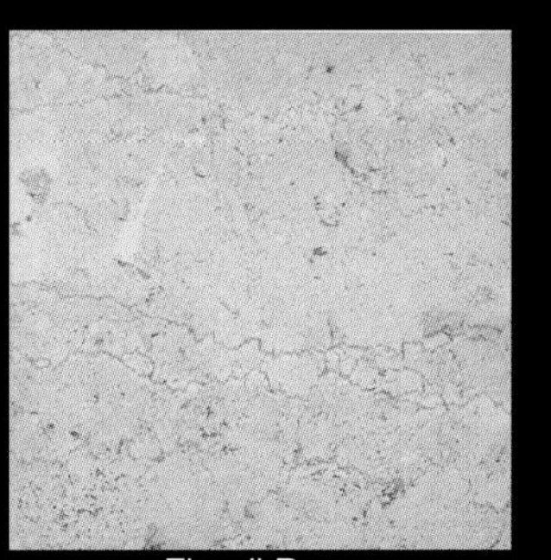

Fior di Rosa

Rosa San Marco

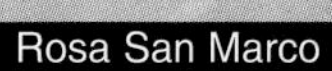

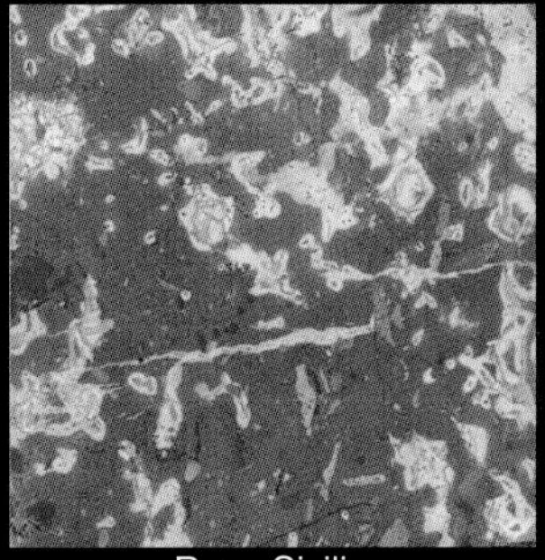

Rosa Sicilia

Liberty

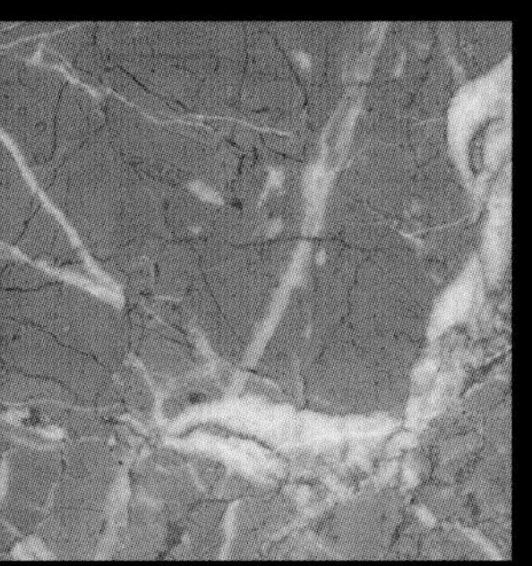

Rosa Atlantide

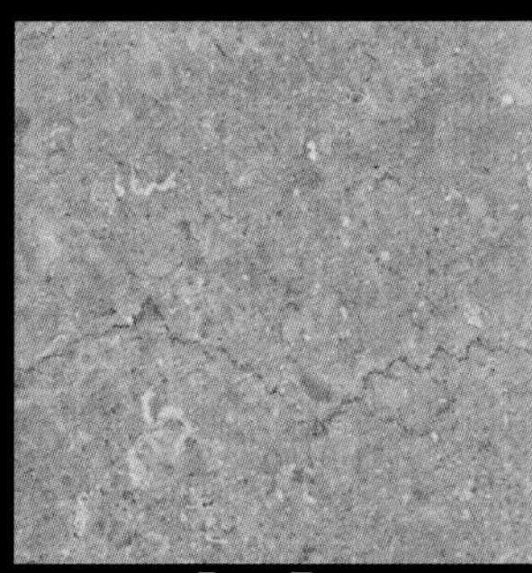

Rosa Tea

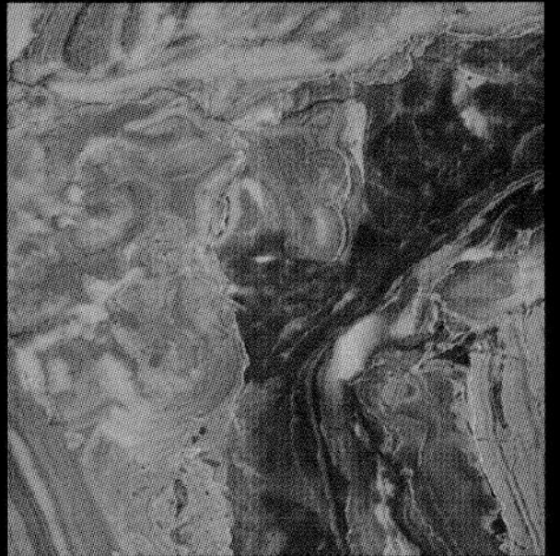

Arabescato Orobico Rosa

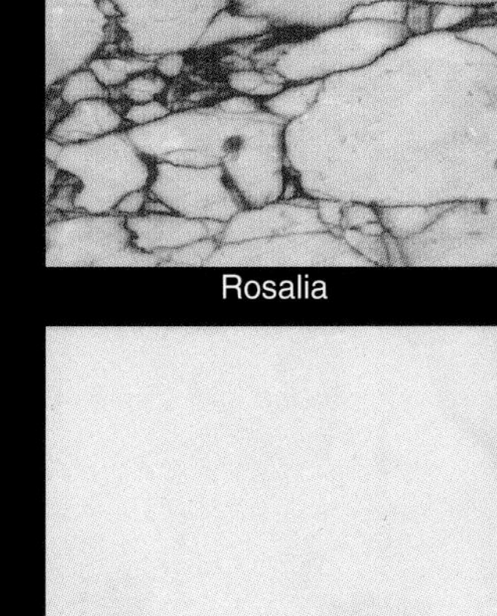

Rosalia

Rosa West

Rosa Norvegia

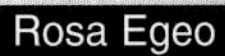

Rosa Egeo

Rosa Aurora

Rosa Portogallo

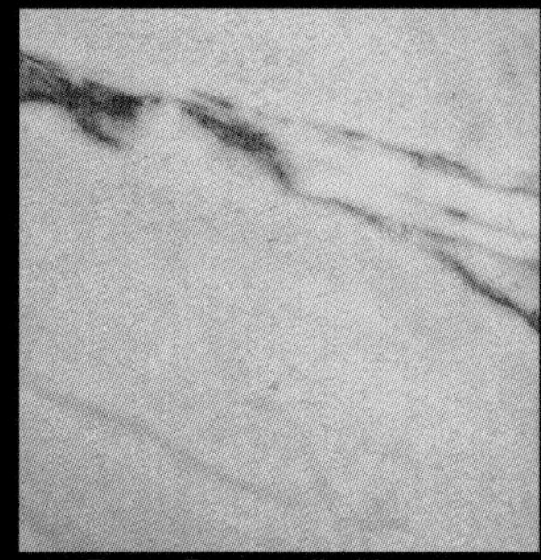

Rosa Portogallo Venato

Quarrying location: Italy
Availability: Medium
Compressive strength: 1334/kg cm²
After freezing: 1214/kg cm²
Ultimate tensile strength: 239/kg cm²
Coef. thermal expansion: 0,0064mm/m°C
Water absorption: 0,12%
Impact test / min. fall height: 48,8 cm
Frictional wear test: 5,79 mm
Bulk density: 2702 kg/m³

CD file number: 0113

Quarrying location: Italy
Availability: Scarse
Compressive strength: 1280/kg cm²
After freezing: 1243/kg cm²
Ultimate tensile strength: 125/kg cm²
Coef. thermal expansion: 0,0039mm/m°C
Water absorption: 0,215%
Impact test / min. fall height: 36 cm
Frictional wear test: 0,58 mm
Bulk density: 2313 kg/m³

CD file number: 0114

Quarrying location: Italy
Availability: Scarse
Compressive strength: 1359/kg cm²
After freezing: 1290/kg cm²
Ultimate tensile strength: 239/kg cm²
Coef. thermal expansion: 0,0061mm/m°C
Water absorption: 0,14%
Impact test / min. fall height: 42,5 cm
Frictional wear test: 3,79 mm
Bulk density: 2708 kg/m³

CD file number: 0115

Quarrying location: Ital
Availability: Mediun
Compressive strength: 1334/kg cm
After freezing: 1214/kg cm
Ultimate tensile strength: 239/kg cm
Coef. thermal expansion: 0,0064mm/m°C
Water absorption: 0,12%
Impact test / min. fall height: 48,8 cm
Frictional wear test: 5,79 mm
Bulk density: 2702 kg/m

CD file number: 0116

Breccia Capraia

Quarrying location: France
Availability: Limited
Compressive strength: 1611/kg cm²
After freezing: 1602/kg cm²
Ultimate tensile strength: 126/kg cm²
Coef. thermal expansion: 0,0052mm/m°C
Water absorption: 0,13%
Impact test / min. fall height: 37 cm
Frictional wear test: –
Bulk density: 2702 kg/m³

CD file number: 0117

Breccia Vagli Rosata

Quarrying location: Italy
Availability: Scarse
Compressive strength: 1611/kg cm²
After freezing: 1602/kg cm²
Ultimate tensile strength: 126/kg cm²
Coef. thermal expansion: 0,0052mm/m°C
Water absorption: 0,13%
Impact test / min. fall height: 37 cm
Frictional wear test: –
Bulk density: 2702 kg/m³

CD file number: 0118

Breccia Stazzema

Quarrying location: France
Availability: Limited
Compressive strength: 1611/kg cm²
After freezing: 1602/kg cm²
Ultimate tensile strength: 126/kg cm²
Coef. thermal expansion: 0,0052mm/m°C
Water absorption: 0,13%
Impact test / min. fall height: 37 cm
Frictional wear test: –
Bulk density: 2702 kg/m³

CD file number: 0119

Breccia Paonazza

Quarrying location: Franc
Availability: Limitec
Compressive strength: 1611/kg cm
After freezing: 1602/kg cm
Ultimate tensile strength: 126/kg cm
Coef. thermal expansion: 0,0052mm/m°C
Water absorption: 0,13%
Impact test / min. fall height: 37 cn
Frictional wear test: -
Bulk density: 2702 kg/m

CD file number: 0120

Breche de Vendome

Quarrying location: France
Availability: Medium
Compressive strength: 1580/kg cm²
After freezing: 1584/kg cm²
Ultimate tensile strength: 210/kg cm²
Coef. thermal expansion: –
Water absorption: 0,40%
Impact test / min. fall height: 35 cm
Frictional wear test: 1,90 mm
Bulk density: 2702 kg/m³

CD file number: 0121

Breccia Multicolore

Quarrying location: Italy
Availability: Scarse
Compressive strength: 1611/kg cm²
After freezing: 1602/kg cm²
Ultimate tensile strength: 126/kg cm²
Coef. thermal expansion: 0,0052mm/m°C
Water absorption: 0,13%
Impact test / min. fall height: 37 cm
Frictional wear test: –
Bulk density: 2702 kg/m³

CD file number: 0122

Sarrancolin

Quarrying location: Italy
Availability: Scarse
Compressive strength: 1611/kg cm²
After freezing: 1602/kg cm²
Ultimate tensile strength: 126/kg cm²
Coef. thermal expansion: 0,0052mm/m°C
Water absorption: 0,13%
Impact test / min. fall height: 37 cm
Frictional wear test: –
Bulk density: 2702 kg/m³

CD file number: 0123

Opera Fantastico

Quarrying location: Franc
Availability: Mediun
Compressive strength: 1611/kg cm
After freezing: 1602/kg cm
Ultimate tensile strength: 126/kg cm
Coef. thermal expansion: 0,0052mm/m°C
Water absorption: 0,13%
Impact test / min. fall height: 37 cn
Frictional wear test: -
Bulk density: 2702 kg/m

CD file number: 0124

Breccia Novella

Quarrying location: France
Availability: Medium
Compressive strength: 1580/kg cm²
After freezing: 1584/kg cm²
Ultimate tensile strength: 210/kg cm²
Coef. thermal expansion: –
Water absorption: 0,40%
Impact test / min. fall height: 35 cm
Frictional wear test: 1,90 mm
Bulk density: 2702 kg/m³

CD file number: 0125

Breccia di Montepulciano

Quarrying location: Italy
Availability: Scarse
Compressive strength: 1611/kg cm²
After freezing: 1602/kg cm²
Ultimate tensile strength: 126/kg cm²
Coef. thermal expansion: 0,0052mm/m°C
Water absorption: 0,13%
Impact test / min. fall height: 37 cm
Frictional wear test: –
Bulk density: 2702 kg/m³

CD file number: 0126

Broccatello

Quarrying location: Portugal
Availability: Medium
Compressive strength: 1580/kg cm²
After freezing: 1584/kg cm²
Ultimate tensile strength: 210/kg cm²
Coef. thermal expansion: –
Water absorption: 0,40%
Impact test / min. fall height: 35 cm
Frictional wear test: 1,90 mm
Bulk density: 2702 kg/m³

CD file number: 0127

Noisette Fleury

Quarrying location: Portuga
Availability: Limitec
Compressive strength: 1580/kg cm
After freezing: 1584/kg cm
Ultimate tensile strength: 210/kg cm
Coef. thermal expansion: -
Water absorption: 0,40%
Impact test / min. fall height: 35 cn
Frictional wear test: 1,90 mn
Bulk density: 2702 kg/m

CD file number: 0128

Breche de Honefleure

Breccia Colorata

Breccia Tavira

Breccia Estrella

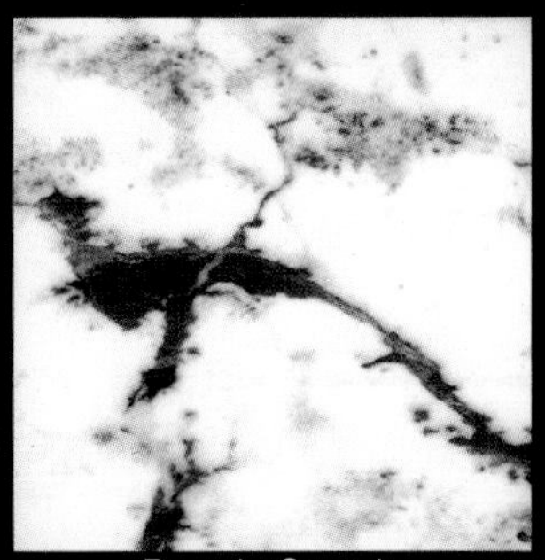
Breccia Capraia

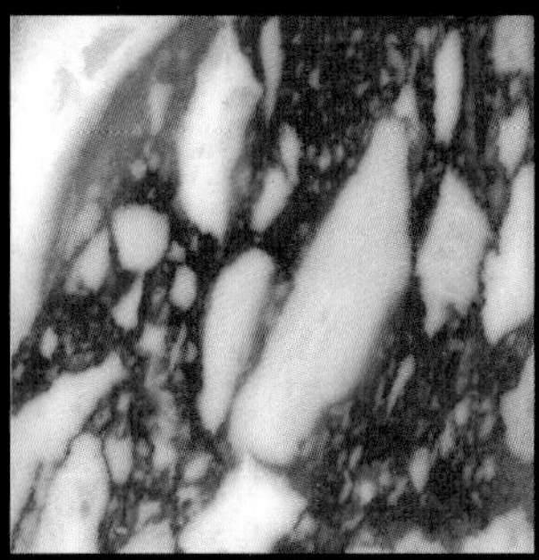
Breccia Vagli Rosata

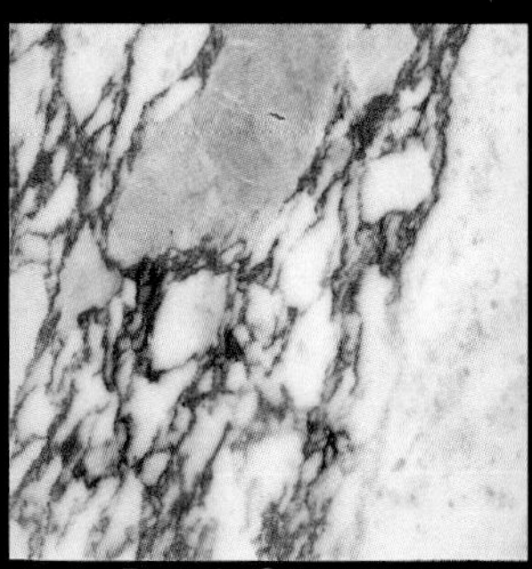
Breccia Stazzema

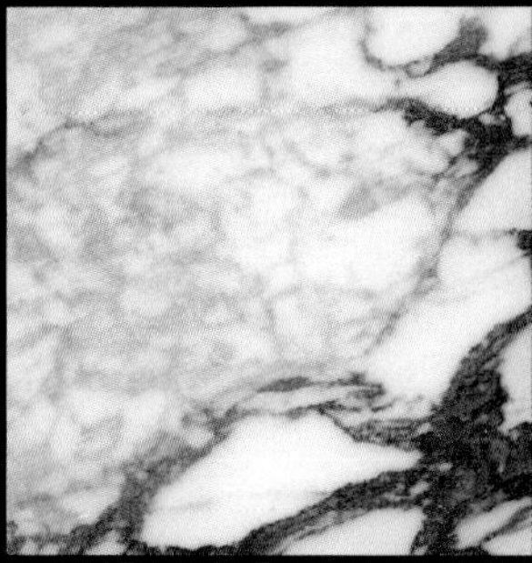
Breccia Paonazza

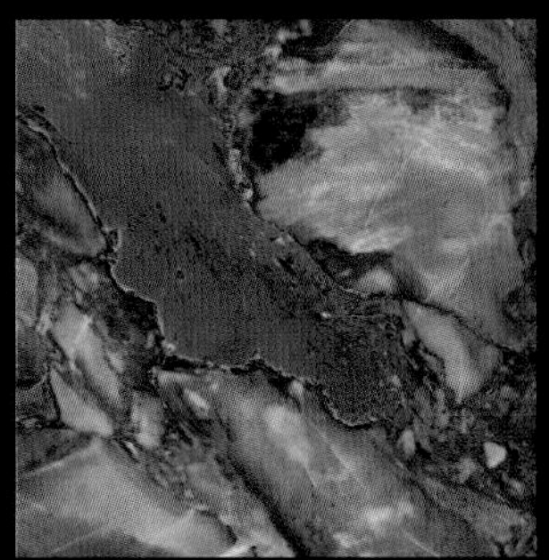
Breche de Vendome

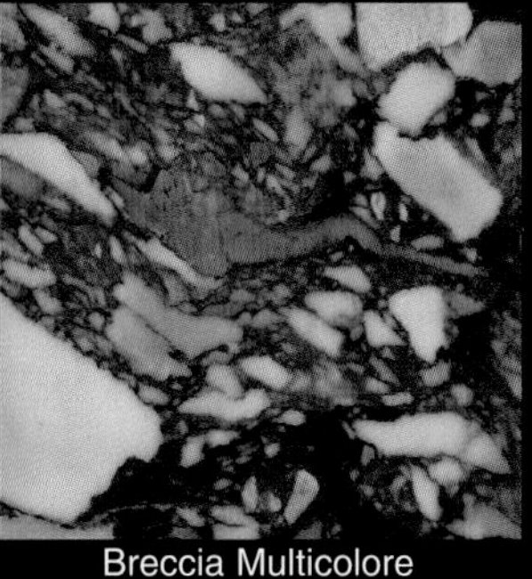
Breccia Multicolore

Sarrancolin

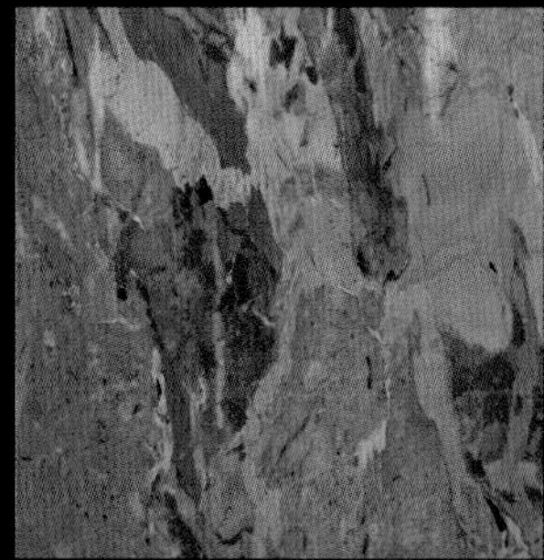
Opera Fantastico

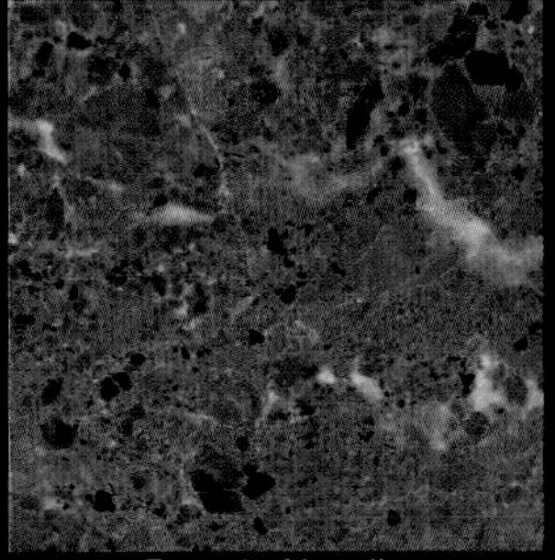
Breccia Novella

Breccia di Montepulciano

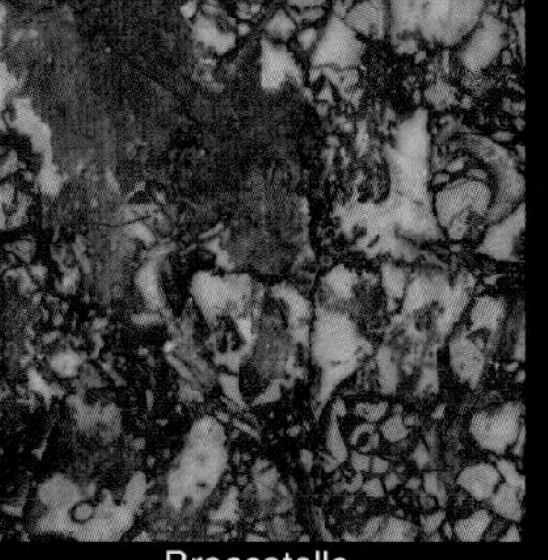
Broccatello

Noisette Fleury

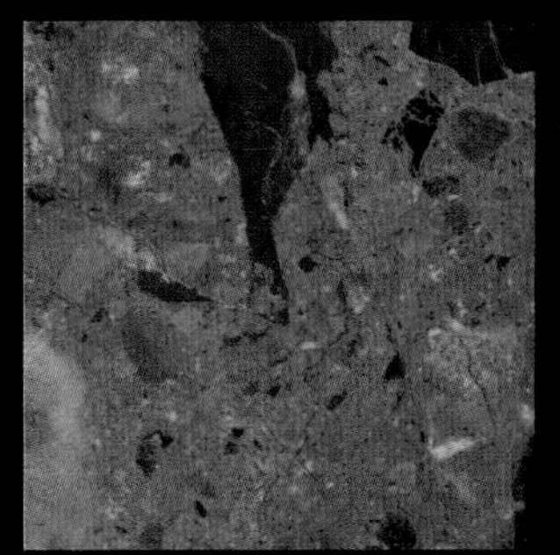
Breche de Honefleure

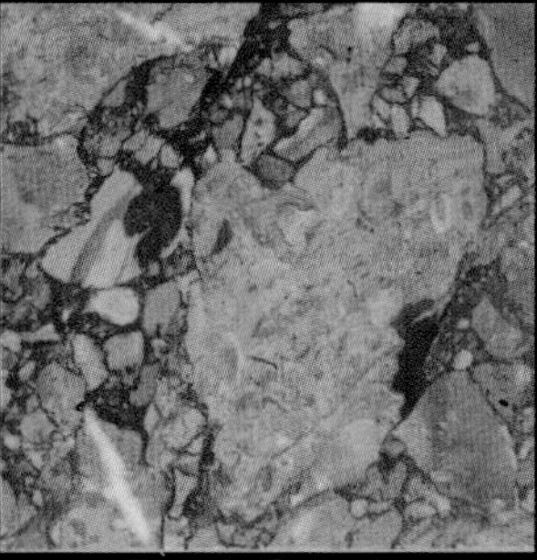
Breccia Colorata

Breccia Tavira

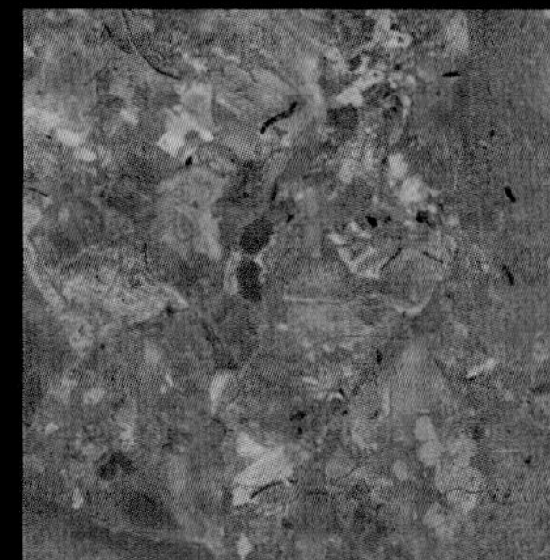
Breccia Estrella

Quarrying location:	Italy
Availability:	Limited
Compressive strength:	1611/kg cm^2
After freezing:	1602/kg cm^2
Ultimate tensile strength:	126/kg cm^2
Coef. thermal expansion:	0,0052 mm/m°C
Water absorption:	0,13%
Impact test / min. fall height:	37 cm
Frictional wear test:	–
Bulk density:	2702 kg/m^3

CD file number: 0129

Quarrying location:	Italy
Availability:	Limited
Compressive strength:	1611/kg cm^2
After freezing:	1602/kg cm^2
Ultimate tensile strength:	126/kg cm^2
Coef. thermal expansion:	0,0052 mm/m°C
Water absorption:	0,13%
Impact test / min. fall height:	37 cm
Frictional wear test:	–
Bulk density:	2702 kg/m^3

CD file number: 0130

Quarrying location:	Italy
Availability:	Limited
Compressive strength:	1611/kg cm^2
After freezing:	1602/kg cm^2
Ultimate tensile strength:	126/kg cm^2
Coef. thermal expansion:	0,0052 mm/m°C
Water absorption:	0,13%
Impact test / min. fall height:	37 cm
Frictional wear test:	–
Bulk density:	2702 kg/m^3

CD file number: 0131

Quarrying location:	Italy
Availability:	Limited
Compressive strength:	1562/kg cm^2
After freezing:	1261/kg cm^2
Ultimate tensile strength:	139/kg cm^2
Coef. thermal expansion:	–
Water absorption:	0,13%
Impact test / min. fall height:	32 cm
Frictional wear test:	–
Bulk density:	2688 kg/m^3

CD file number: 0132

Arabescato Orobico Rosso

Quarrying location:	Spain
Availability:	Medium
Compressive strength:	1562/kg cm^2
After freezing:	1261/kg cm^2
Ultimate tensile strength:	139/kg cm^2
Coef. thermal expansion:	–
Water absorption:	0,13%
Impact test / min. fall height:	32 cm
Frictional wear test:	–
Bulk density:	2688 kg/m^3

CD file number: 0133

Breccia Pernice

Quarrying location:	Spain
Availability:	Medium
Compressive strength:	1562/kg cm^2
After freezing:	1261/kg cm^2
Ultimate tensile strength:	139/kg cm^2
Coef. thermal expansion:	–
Water absorption:	0,13%
Impact test / min. fall height:	32 cm
Frictional wear test:	–
Bulk density:	2688 kg/m^3

CD file number: 0134

Breccia Pernice Chiara

Quarrying location:	Spain
Availability:	Medium
Compressive strength:	1562/kg cm^2
After freezing:	1261/kg cm^2
Ultimate tensile strength:	139/kg cm^2
Coef. thermal expansion:	–
Water absorption:	0,13%
Impact test / min. fall height:	32 cm
Frictional wear test:	–
Bulk density:	2688 kg/m^3

CD file number: 0135

Diaspro Sicilia

Quarrying location:	Albania
Availability:	Medium
Compressive strength:	1611/kg cm^2
After freezing:	1602/kg cm^2
Ultimate tensile strength:	126/kg cm^2
Coef. thermal expansion:	0,0052 mm/m°C
Water absorption:	0,13%
Impact test / min. fall height:	37 cm
Frictional wear test:	–
Bulk density:	2702 kg/m^3

CD file number: 0136

Rojo Alicante

Quarrying location:	France
Availability:	Medium
Compressive strength:	1562/kg cm^2
After freezing:	1261/kg cm^2
Ultimate tensile strength:	139/kg cm^2
Coef. thermal expansion:	–
Water absorption:	0,13%
Impact test / min. fall height:	32 cm
Frictional wear test:	–
Bulk density:	2688 kg/m^3

CD file number: 0137

Rojo Daniel

Quarrying location:	France
Availability:	Medium
Compressive strength:	1562/kg cm^2
After freezing:	1261/kg cm^2
Ultimate tensile strength:	139/kg cm^2
Coef. thermal expansion:	–
Water absorption:	0,13%
Impact test / min. fall height:	32 cm
Frictional wear test:	–
Bulk density:	2688 kg/m^3

CD file number: 0138

Rosso Bilbao

Quarrying location:	France
Availability:	Medium
Compressive strength:	1562/kg cm^2
After freezing:	1261/kg cm^2
Ultimate tensile strength:	139/kg cm^2
Coef. thermal expansion:	–
Water absorption:	0,13%
Impact test / min. fall height:	32 cm
Frictional wear test:	–
Bulk density:	2688 kg/m^3

CD file number: 0139

Rosso Carpazi

Quarrying location:	Turkey
Availability:	Limited
Compressive strength:	1630/kg cm^2
After freezing:	1159/kg cm^2
Ultimate tensile strength:	130/kg cm^2
Coef. thermal expansion:	–
Water absorption:	0,20%
Impact test / min. fall height:	33 cm
Frictional wear test:	–
Bulk density:	2695 kg/m^3

CD file number: 0140

Rouge France Incarnat

Quarrying location:	Italy
Availability:	Limited
Compressive strength:	1377/kg cm^2
After freezing:	1208/kg cm^2
Ultimate tensile strength:	98/kg cm^2
Coef. thermal expansion:	0,0053 mm/m°C
Water absorption:	0,57%
Impact test / min. fall height:	31 cm
Frictional wear test:	–
Bulk density:	2629 kg/m^3

CD file number: 0141

Rouge France Languedoc

Quarrying location:	France
Availability:	Limited
Compressive strength:	1377/kg cm^2
After freezing:	1208/kg cm^2
Ultimate tensile strength:	98/kg cm^2
Coef. thermal expansion:	0,0071mm/m°C
Water absorption:	0,13%
Impact test / min. fall height:	37 cm
Frictional wear test:	–
Bulk density:	2692 kg/m^3

CD file number: 0142

Rouge France Isabelle

Quarrying location:	France
Availability:	Limited
Compressive strength:	1562/kg cm^2
After freezing:	1261/kg cm^2
Ultimate tensile strength:	139/kg cm^2
Coef. thermal expansion:	–
Water absorption:	0,13%
Impact test / min. fall height:	32 cm
Frictional wear test:	–
Bulk density:	2688 kg/m^3

CD file number: 0143

Rosso Laguna

Quarrying location:	Italy
Availability:	Limited
Compressive strength:	1562/kg cm^2
After freezing:	1261/kg cm^2
Ultimate tensile strength:	139/kg cm^2
Coef. thermal expansion:	–
Water absorption:	0,13%
Impact test / min. fall height:	32 cm
Frictional wear test:	–
Bulk density:	2688 kg/m^3

CD file number: 0144

Rosso Levanto

Rouge Griotte

Rouge Antique

Rosso Collemandina

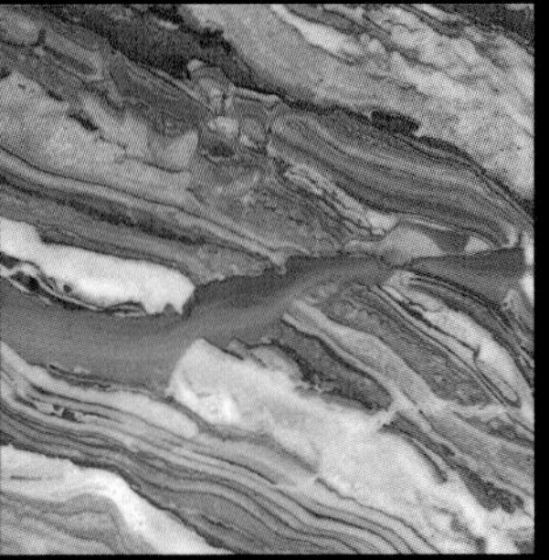
Arabescato Orobico Rosso

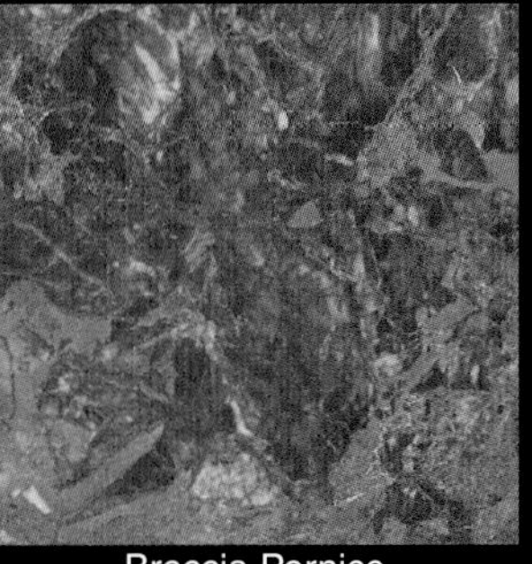
Breccia Pernice

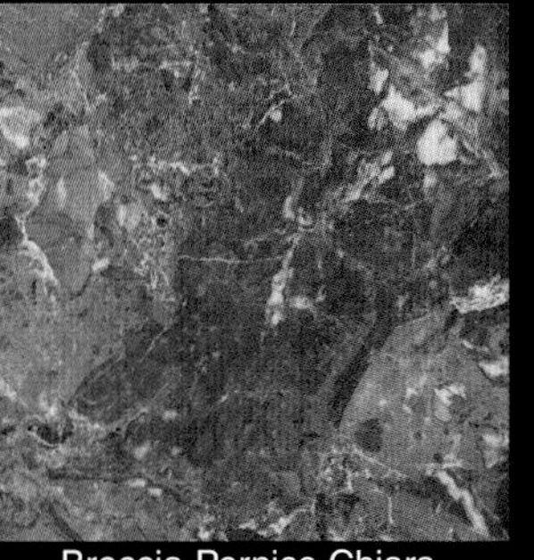
Breccia Pernice Chiara

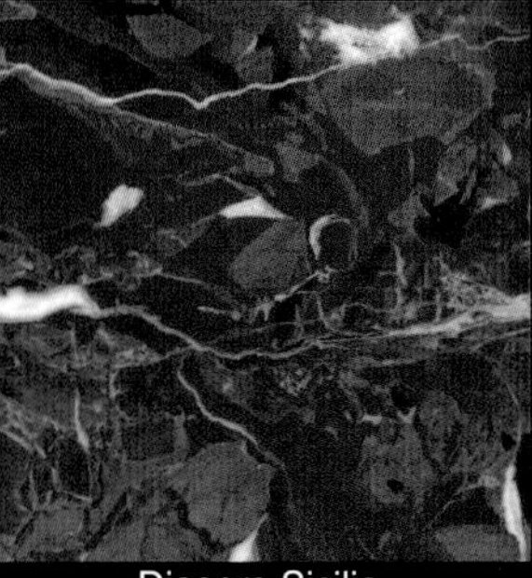
Diaspro Sicilia

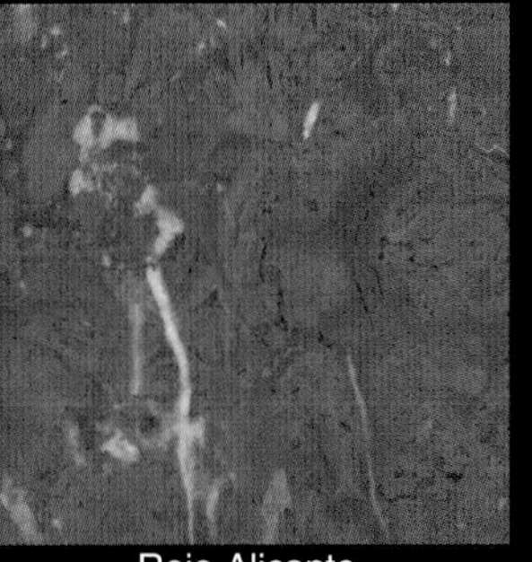
Rojo Alicante

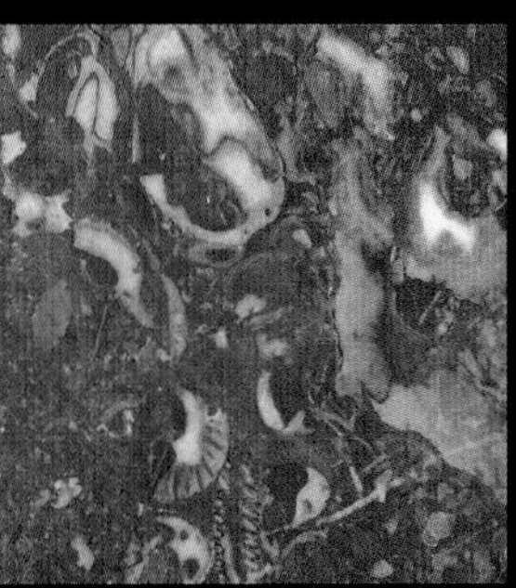
Rojo Daniel

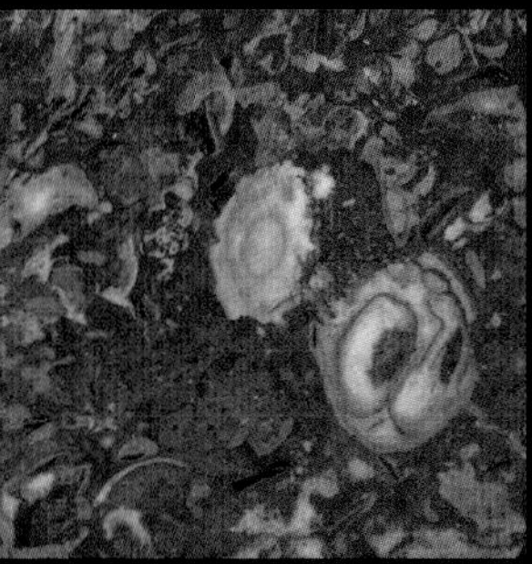
Rosso Bilbao

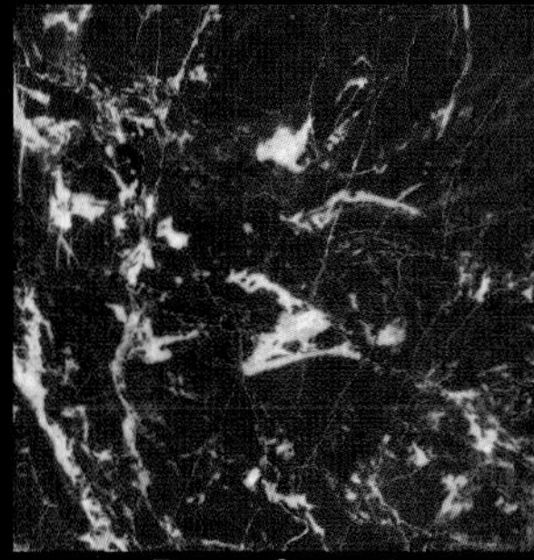
Rosso Carpazi

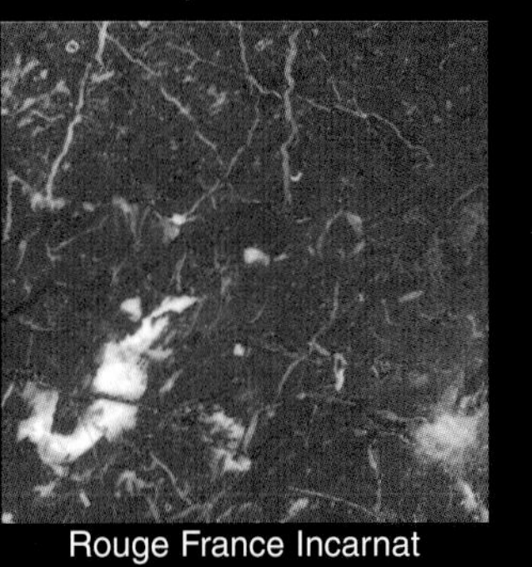
Rouge France Incarnat

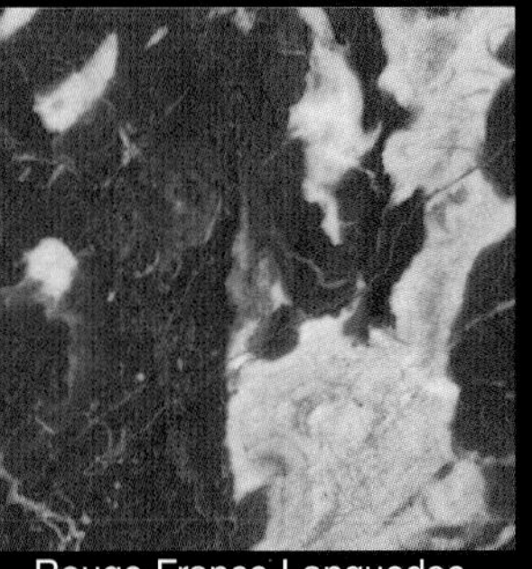
Rouge France Languedoc

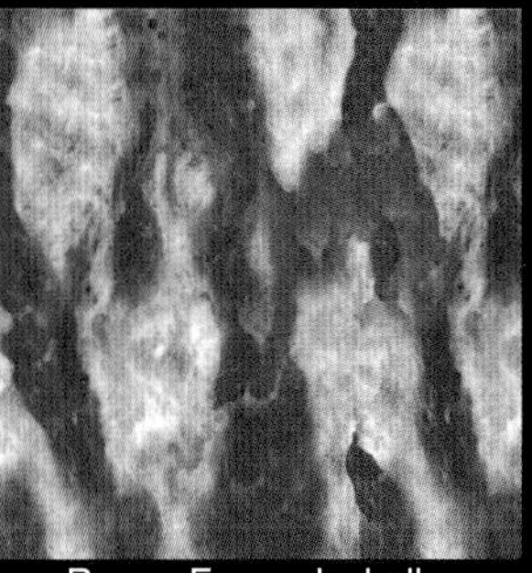
Rouge France Isabelle

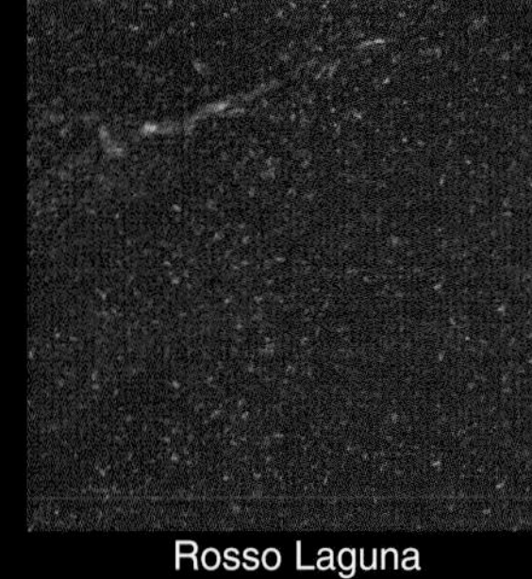
Rosso Laguna

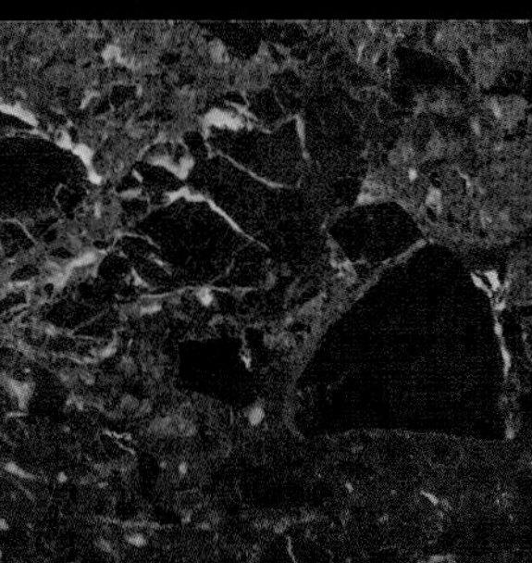
Rosso Levanto

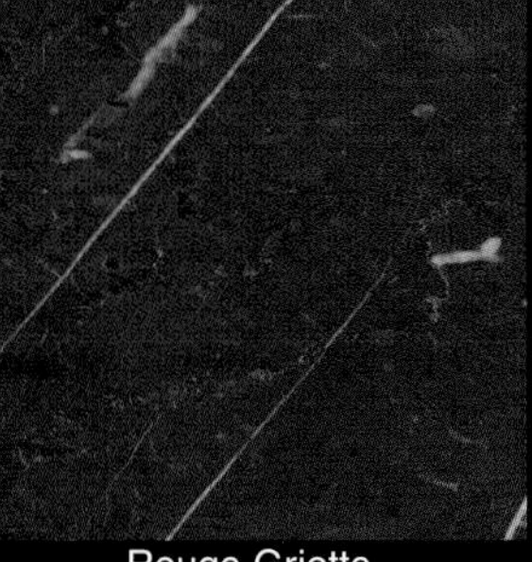
Rouge Griotte

Rouge Antique

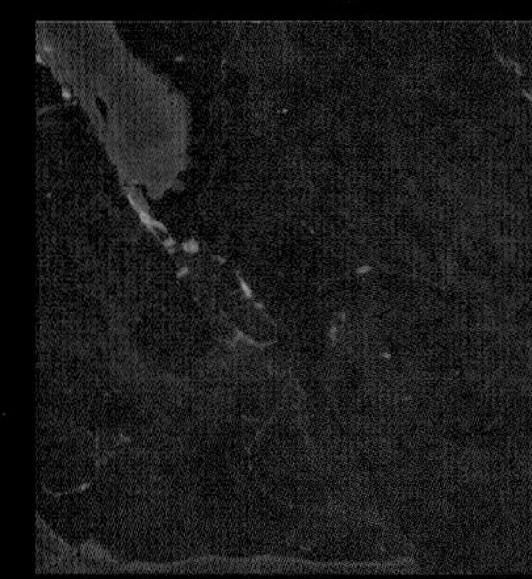
Rosso Collemandina

Quarrying location:	Turkey
Availability:	Limited
Compressive strength:	1377/kg cm^2
After freezing:	1208/kg cm^2
Ultimate tensile strength:	98/kg cm^2
Coef. thermal expansion:	0,0053 mm/m°C
Water absorption:	0,57%
Impact test / min. fall height:	31 cm
Frictional wear test:	–
Bulk density:	2629 kg/m^3

CD file number: 0145

Quarrying location:	Italy
Availability:	Limited
Compressive strength:	1377/kg cm^2
After freezing:	1208/kg cm^2
Ultimate tensile strength:	98/kg cm^2
Coef. thermal expansion:	0,0053 mm/m°C
Water absorption:	0,57%
Impact test / min. fall height:	31 cm
Frictional wear test:	–
Bulk density:	2629 kg/m^3

CD file number: 0146

Quarrying location:	Italy
Availability:	Medium
Compressive strength:	1377/kg cm^2
After freezing:	1208/kg cm^2
Ultimate tensile strength:	98/kg cm^2
Coef. thermal expansion:	0,0071mm/m°C
Water absorption:	0,13%
Impact test / min. fall height:	37 cm
Frictional wear test:	–
Bulk density:	2692 kg/m^3

CD file number: 0147

Quarrying location:	Italy
Availability:	Medium
Compressive strength:	1377/kg cm^2
After freezing:	1208/kg cm^2
Ultimate tensile strength:	98/kg cm^2
Coef. thermal expansion:	0,0071mm/m°C
Water absorption:	0,13%
Impact test / min. fall height:	37 cm
Frictional wear test:	–
Bulk density:	2692 kg/m^3

CD file number: 0148

Rosso Lepanto

Quarrying location:	Marocco
Availability:	Medium
Compressive strength:	1562/kg cm^2
After freezing:	1261/kg cm^2
Ultimate tensile strength:	139/kg cm^2
Coef. thermal expansion:	–
Water absorption:	0,13%
Impact test / min. fall height:	32 cm
Frictional wear test:	–
Bulk density:	2688 kg/m^3

CD file number: 0149

Rosso Antico d'Italia

Quarrying location:	Italy
Availability:	Limited
Compressive strength:	1562/kg cm^2
After freezing:	1261/kg cm^2
Ultimate tensile strength:	139/kg cm^2
Coef. thermal expansion:	–
Water absorption:	0,13%
Impact test / min. fall height:	32 cm
Frictional wear test:	–
Bulk density:	2688 kg/m^3

CD file number: 0150

Rosso Asiago

Quarrying location:	Italy
Availability:	Limited
Compressive strength:	1562/kg cm^2
After freezing:	1261/kg cm^2
Ultimate tensile strength:	139/kg cm^2
Coef. thermal expansion:	–
Water absorption:	0,13%
Impact test / min. fall height:	32 cm
Frictional wear test:	–
Bulk density:	2688 kg/m^3

CD file number: 0151

Rosso Verona

Quarrying location:	Spain
Availability:	Good
Compressive strength:	1805kg cm^2
After freezing:	1727/kg cm^2
Ultimate tensile strength:	139/kg cm^2
Coef. thermal expansion:	0,0045mm/m°C
Water absorption:	0,12%
Impact test / min. fall height:	29 cm
Frictional wear test:	–
Bulk density:	2686 kg/m^3

CD file number: 0152

Rosso Agadir

Quarrying location:	Spain
Availability:	Medium
Compressive strength:	1562/kg cm^2
After freezing:	1261/kg cm^2
Ultimate tensile strength:	139/kg cm^2
Coef. thermal expansion:	–
Water absorption:	0,13%
Impact test / min. fall height:	32 cm
Frictional wear test:	–
Bulk density:	2688 kg/m^3

CD file number: 0153

Rosso Rubino

Quarrying location:	Spain
Availability:	Medium
Compressive strength:	1562/kg cm^2
After freezing:	1261/kg cm^2
Ultimate tensile strength:	139/kg cm^2
Coef. thermal expansion:	–
Water absorption:	0,13%
Impact test / min. fall height:	32 cm
Frictional wear test:	–
Bulk density:	2688 kg/m^3

CD file number: 0154

Fior di Pesco Apuano

Quarrying location:	Italy
Availability:	Limited
Compressive strength:	1377/kg cm^2
After freezing:	1208/kg cm^2
Ultimate tensile strength:	98/kg cm^2
Coef. thermal expansion:	0,0071mm/m°C
Water absorption:	0,13%
Impact test / min. fall height:	37 cm
Frictional wear test:	–
Bulk density:	2692 kg/m^3

CD file number: 0155

Rosa Zarci

Quarrying location:	Turkey
Availability:	Medium
Compressive strength:	1377/kg cm^2
After freezing:	1208/kg cm^2
Ultimate tensile strength:	98/kg cm^2
Coef. thermal expansion:	0,0071mm/m°C
Water absorption:	0,13%
Impact test / min. fall height:	37 cm
Frictional wear test:	–
Bulk density:	2692 kg/m^3

CD file number: 0156

Rosa Doucquesa

Quarrying location:	Italy
Availability:	Limited
Compressive strength:	1377/kg cm^2
After freezing:	1208/kg cm^2
Ultimate tensile strength:	98/kg cm^2
Coef. thermal expansion:	0,0071mm/m°C
Water absorption:	0,13%
Impact test / min. fall height:	37 cm
Frictional wear test:	–
Bulk density:	2692 kg/m^3

CD file number: 0157

Rosa Doucquesa Scura

Quarrying location:	Italy
Availability:	Medium
Compressive strength:	1377/kg cm^2
After freezing:	1208/kg cm^2
Ultimate tensile strength:	98/kg cm^2
Coef. thermal expansion:	0,0071mm/m°C
Water absorption:	0,13%
Impact test / min. fall height:	37 cm
Frictional wear test:	–
Bulk density:	2692 kg/m^3

CD file number: 0158

Porfirico Ramello

Quarrying location:	Italy
Availability:	Limited
Compressive strength:	1562/kg cm^2
After freezing:	1261/kg cm^2
Ultimate tensile strength:	139/kg cm^2
Coef. thermal expansion:	–
Water absorption:	0,13%
Impact test / min. fall height:	32 cm
Frictional wear test:	–
Bulk density:	2688 kg/m^3

CD file number: 0159

Rosso Bellini

Quarrying location:	Italy
Availability:	Limited
Compressive strength:	1562/kg cm^2
After freezing:	1261/kg cm^2
Ultimate tensile strength:	139/kg cm^2
Coef. thermal expansion:	–
Water absorption:	0,13%
Impact test / min. fall height:	32 cm
Frictional wear test:	–
Bulk density:	2688 kg/m^3

CD file number: 0160

Rosso Lepanto

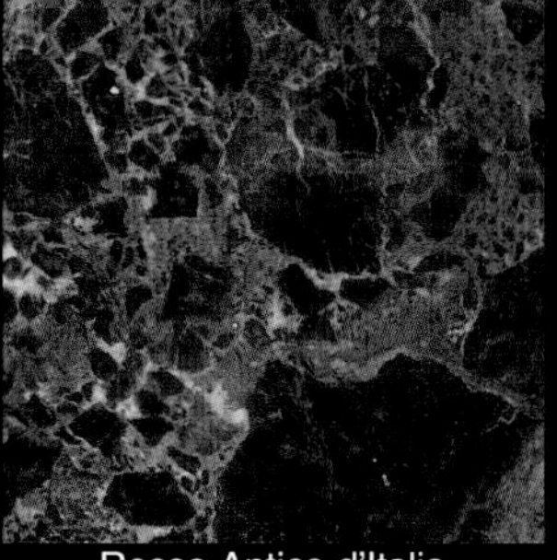

Rosso Antico d’Italia

Rosso Asiago

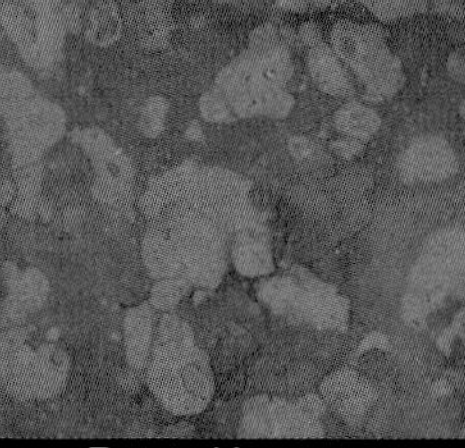

Rosso Verona

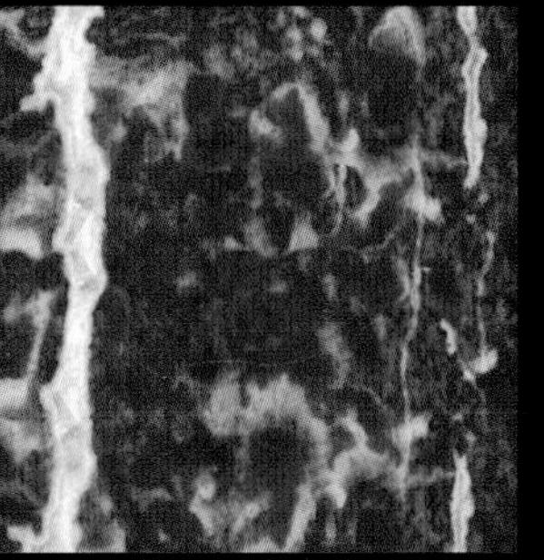

Rosso Agadir

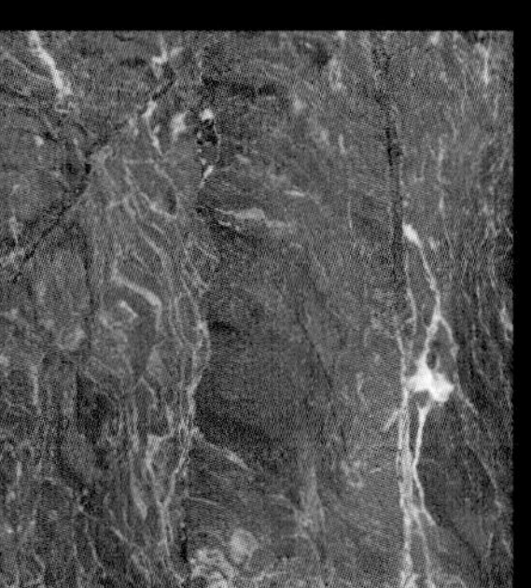

Rosso Rubino

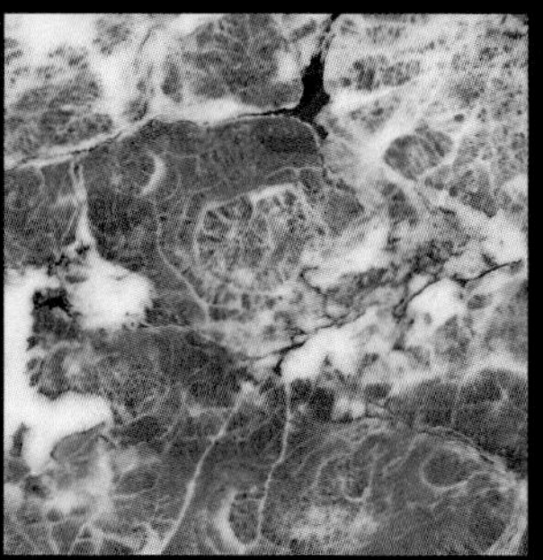

Fior di Pesco Apuano

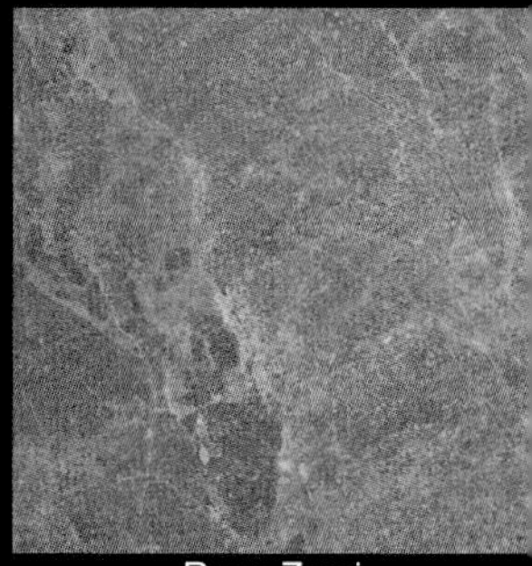

Rosa Zarci

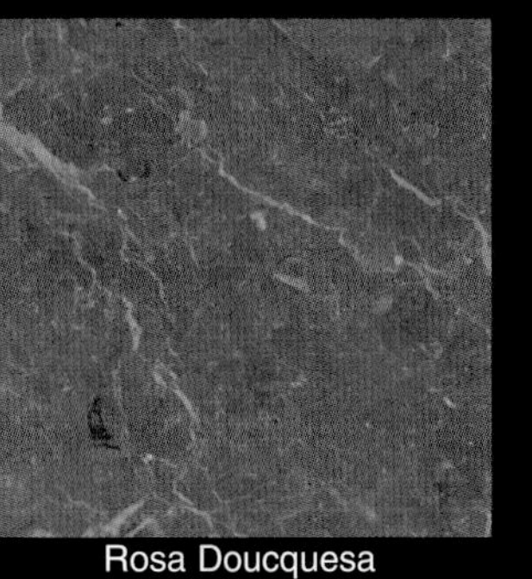

Rosa Doucquesa

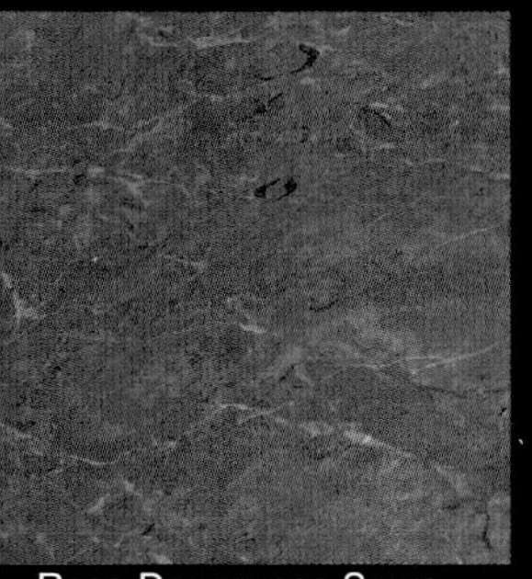

Rosa Doucquesa Scura

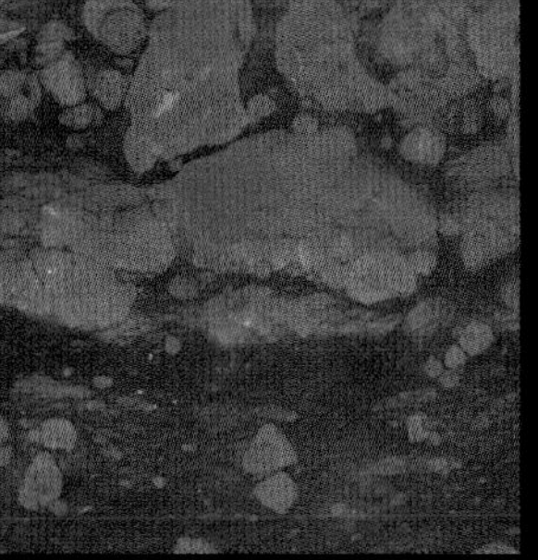

Porfirico Ramello

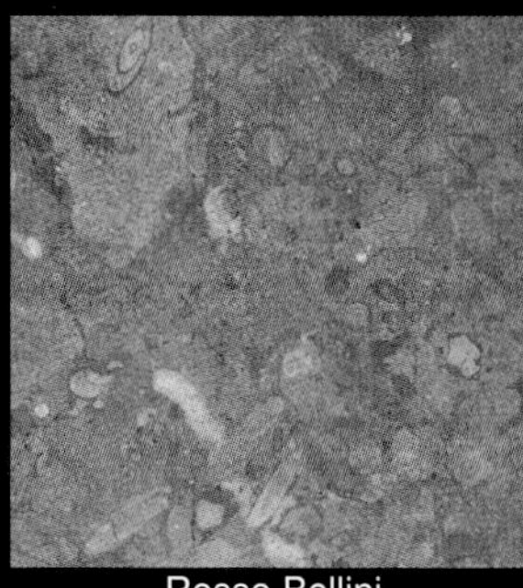

Rosso Bellini

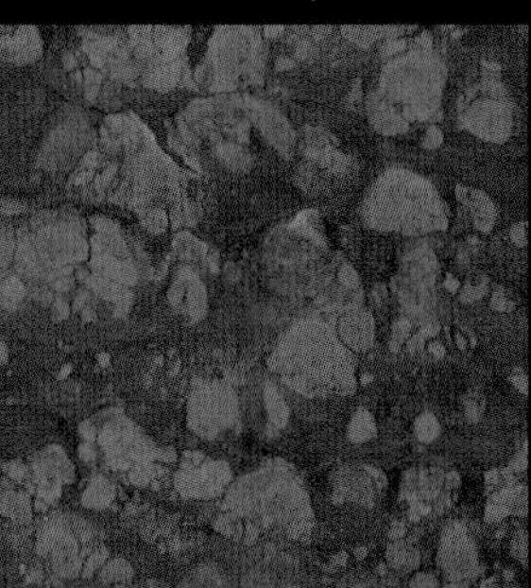

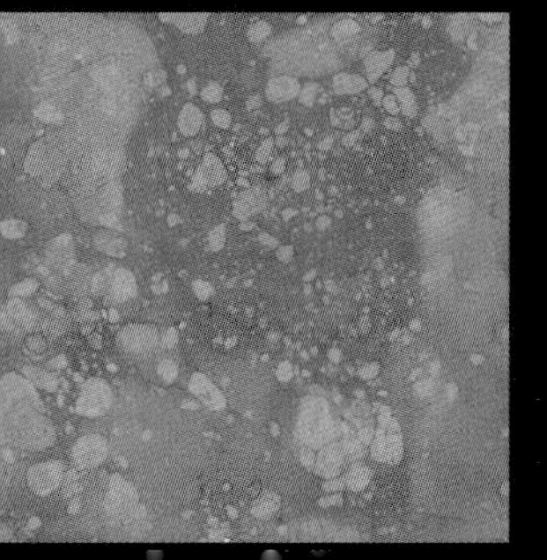

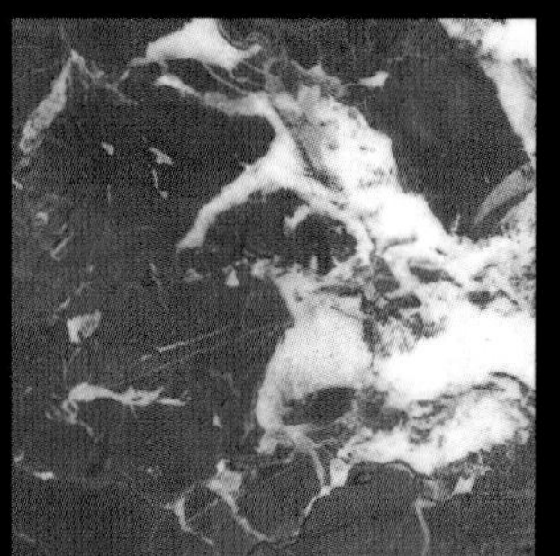

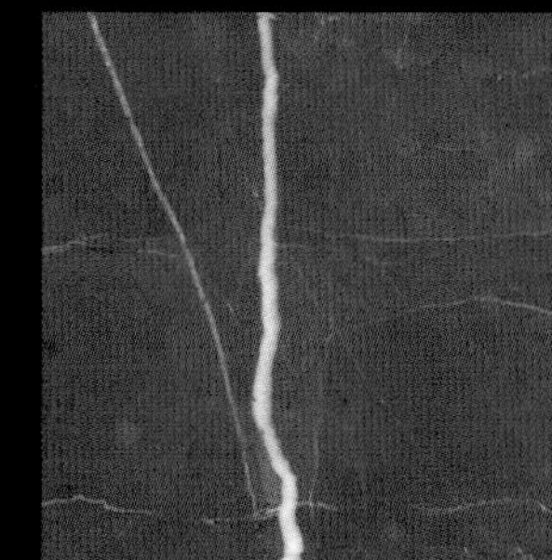

Quarrying location: Portugal
Availability: Medium
Compressive strength: 729/kg cm^2
After freezing: –
Ultimate tensile strength: 129/kg cm^2
Coef. thermal expansion: –
Water absorption: –
Impact test / min. fall height: –
Frictional wear test: –
Bulk density: 2710 kg/m^3

CD file number: 0161

Quarrying location: Marocco
Availability: Medium
Compressive strength: 729/kg cm^2
After freezing: –
Ultimate tensile strength: 129/kg cm^2
Coef. thermal expansion: –
Water absorption: –
Impact test / min. fall height: –
Frictional wear test: –
Bulk density: 2710 kg/m^3

CD file number: 0162

Quarrying location: Italy
Availability: Limited
Compressive strength: 1803/kg cm^2
After freezing: 1738/kg cm^2
Ultimate tensile strength: 180/kg cm^2
Coef. thermal expansion: 0,0071mm/m°C
Water absorption: 0,35%
Impact test / min. fall height: 29 cm
Frictional wear test: –
Bulk density: 2800 kg/m^3

CD file number: 0163

Quarrying location: Italy
Availability: Limited
Compressive strength: 1803/kg cm^2
After freezing: 1738/kg cm^2
Ultimate tensile strength: 180/kg cm^2
Coef. thermal expansion: 0,0071mm/m°C
Water absorption: 0,35%
Impact test / min. fall height: 29 cm
Frictional wear test: –
Bulk density: 2800 kg/m^3

CD file number: 0164

Amarello Negrais

Quarrying location: Italy
Availability: Medium
Compressive strength: 1975/kg cm^2
After freezing: 1876/kg cm^2
Ultimate tensile strength: 120/kg cm^2
Coef. thermal expansion: 0,0071mm/m°C
Water absorption: 0,30%
Impact test / min. fall height: 30 cm
Frictional wear test: –
Bulk density: 2675 kg/m^3

CD file number: 0165

Giallo Atlantide

Quarrying location: Italy
Availability: Medium
Compressive strength: 1975/kg cm^2
After freezing: 1876/kg cm^2
Ultimate tensile strength: 120/kg cm^2
Coef. thermal expansion: 0,0071mm/m°C
Water absorption: 0,30%
Impact test / min. fall height: 30 cm
Frictional wear test: –
Bulk density: 2675 kg/m^3

CD file number: 0166

Giallo Siena

Quarrying location: Australia
Availability: Medium
Compressive strength: 1975/kg cm^2
After freezing: 1876/kg cm^2
Ultimate tensile strength: 120/kg cm^2
Coef. thermal expansion: 0,0071mm/m°C
Water absorption: 0,30%
Impact test / min. fall height: 30 cm
Frictional wear test: –
Bulk density: 2675 kg/m^3

CD file number: 0167

Calacatta Siena

Quarrying location: Spain
Availability: Medium
Compressive strength: 1563/kg cm^2
After freezing: 1286/kg cm^2
Ultimate tensile strength: 601/kg cm^2
Coef. thermal expansion: –
Water absorption: 0,06%
Impact test / min. fall height: 35 cm
Frictional wear test: –
Bulk density: 2667 kg/m^3

CD file number: 0168

Giallo Reale

Quarrying location: Israel
Availability: Medium
Compressive strength: 1975/kg cm^2
After freezing: 1876/kg cm^2
Ultimate tensile strength: 120/kg cm^2
Coef. thermal expansion: 0,0071mm/m°C
Water absorption: 0,30%
Impact test / min. fall height: 30 cm
Frictional wear test: –
Bulk density: 2675 kg/m^3

CD file number: 0169

Giallo Reale Scuro

Quarrying location: Spain
Availability: Medium
Compressive strength: 729/kg cm^2
After freezing: –
Ultimate tensile strength: 129/kg cm^2
Coef. thermal expansion: –
Water absorption: –
Impact test / min. fall height: –
Frictional wear test: –
Bulk density: 2710 kg/m^3

CD file number: 0170

Giallo Dune

Quarrying location: Brazil
Availability: Limited
Compressive strength: 2440/kg cm^2
After freezing: 2300/kg cm^2
Ultimate tensile strength: 120/kg cm^2
Coef. thermal expansion: 0,0050mm/m°C
Water absorption: 0,30%
Impact test / min. fall height: 35 cm
Frictional wear test: –
Bulk density: 2760 kg/m^3

CD file number: 0171

Amarello Macael

Quarrying location: Spain
Availability: Limited
Compressive strength: 1580/kg cm^2
After freezing: 1584/kg cm^2
Ultimate tensile strength: 210/kg cm^2
Coef. thermal expansion: –
Water absorption: 0,40%
Impact test / min. fall height: 35 cm
Frictional wear test: 1,90 mm
Bulk density: 2702 kg/m^3

CD file number: 0172

Giallo Tafouk

Quarrying location: Spain
Availability: Limited
Compressive strength: 1580/kg cm^2
After freezing: 1584/kg cm^2
Ultimate tensile strength: 210/kg cm^2
Coef. thermal expansion: –
Water absorption: 0,40%
Impact test / min. fall height: 35 cm
Frictional wear test: 1,90 mm
Bulk density: 2702 kg/m^3

CD file number: 0173

Crema Valencia

Quarrying location: Spain
Availability: Limited
Compressive strength: 1580/kg cm^2
After freezing: 1584/kg cm^2
Ultimate tensile strength: 210/kg cm^2
Coef. thermal expansion: –
Water absorption: 0,40%
Impact test / min. fall height: 35 cm
Frictional wear test: 1,90 mm
Bulk density: 2702 kg/m^3

CD file number: 0174

Chocolate

Quarrying location: Italy
Availability: Limited
Compressive strength: 1580/kg cm^2
After freezing: 1584/kg cm^2
Ultimate tensile strength: 210/kg cm^2
Coef. thermal expansion: –
Water absorption: 0,40%
Impact test / min. fall height: 35 cm
Frictional wear test: 1,90 mm
Bulk density: 2702 kg/m^3

CD file number: 0175

Emperador Light

Quarrying location: Marocco
Availability: Limited
Compressive strength: 1580/kg cm^2
After freezing: 1584/kg cm^2
Ultimate tensile strength: 210/kg cm^2
Coef. thermal expansion: –
Water absorption: 0,40%
Impact test / min. fall height: 35 cm
Frictional wear test: 1,90 mm
Bulk density: 2702 kg/m^3

CD file number: 0176

Dark Emperador

Marron Emperador

Breccia Paradiso

Fossil Brown

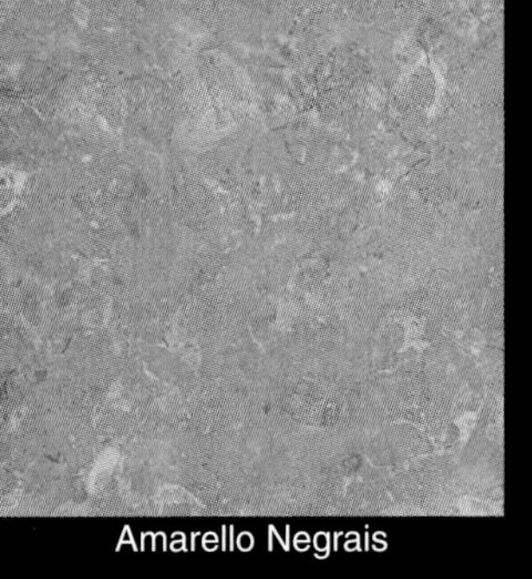
Amarello Negrais

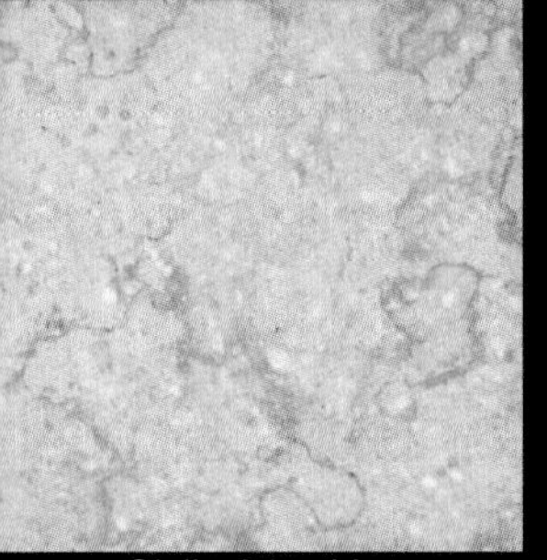
Giallo Atlantide

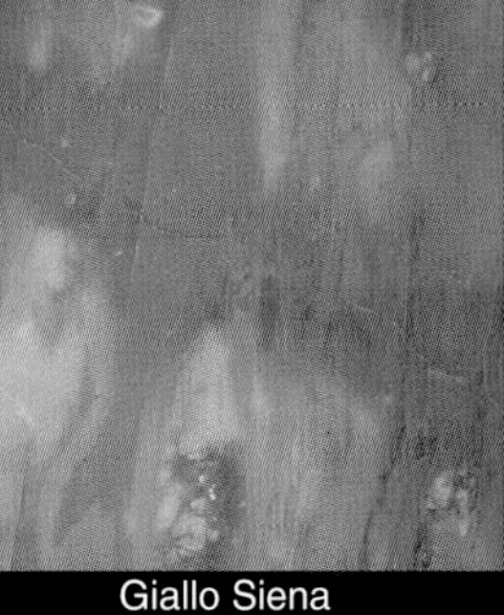
Giallo Siena

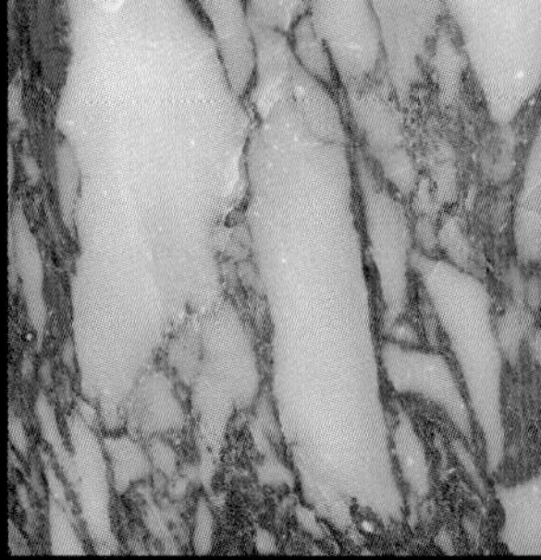
Calacatta Siena

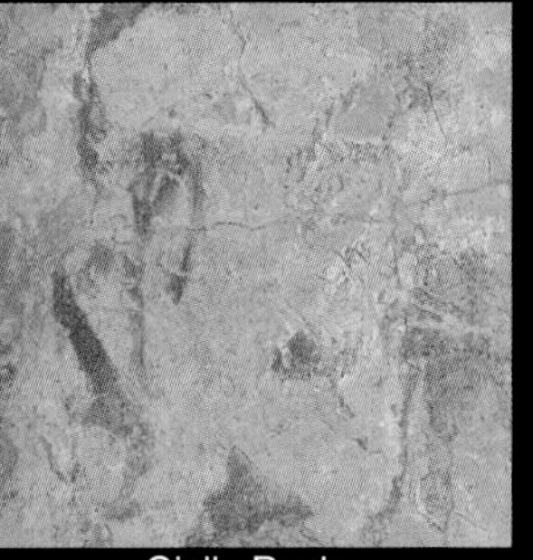
Giallo Reale

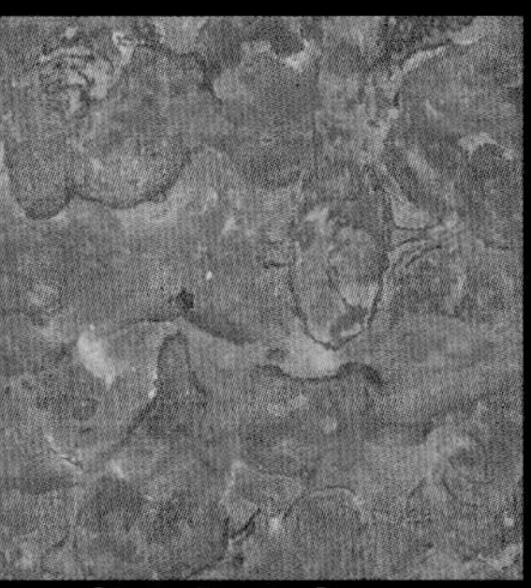
Giallo Reale Scuro

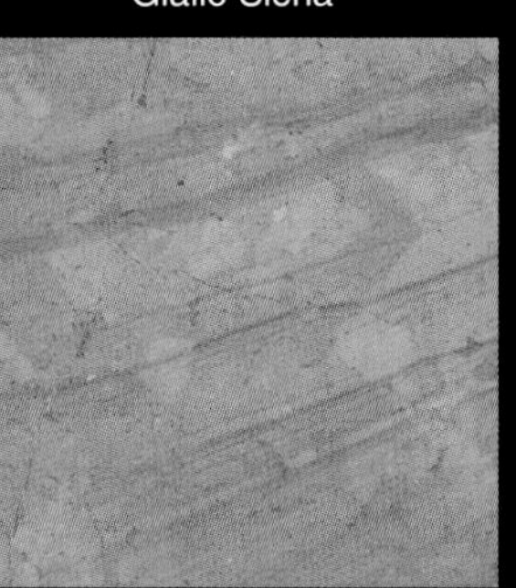
Giallo Dune

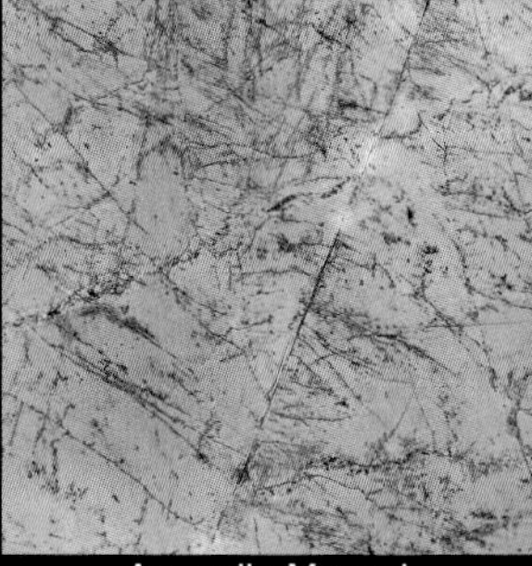
Amarello Macael

Giallo Tafouk

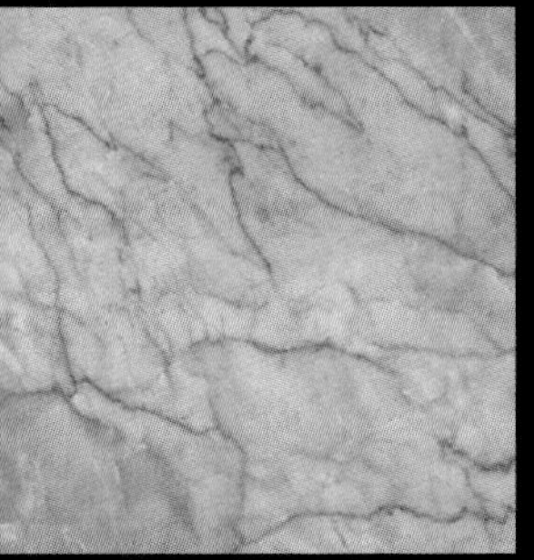
Crema Valencia

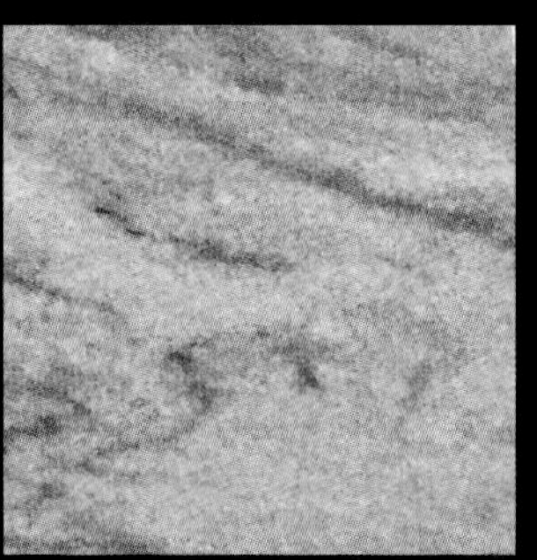
Chocolate

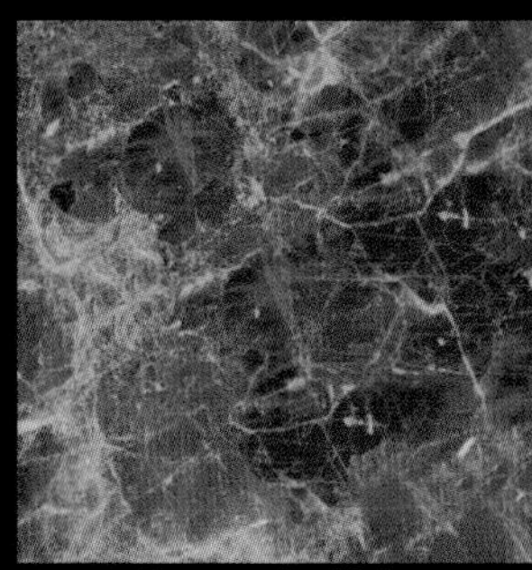
Emperador Light

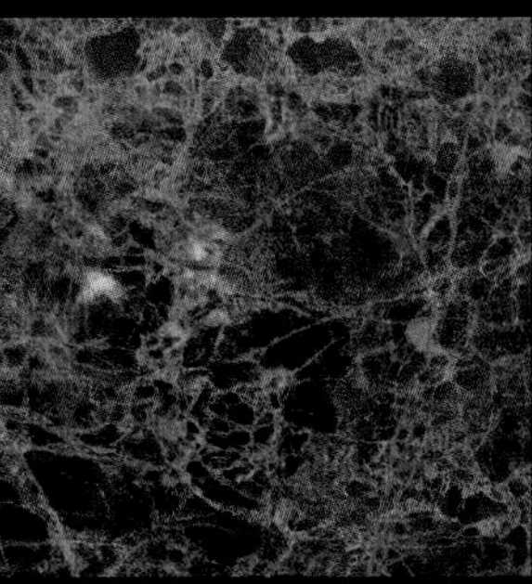
Dark Emperador

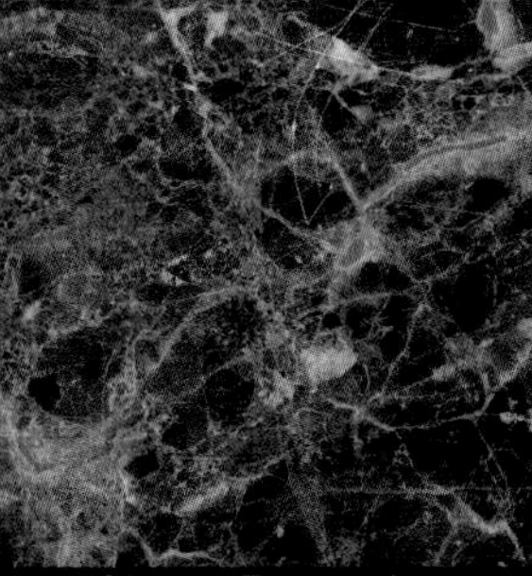
Marron Emperador

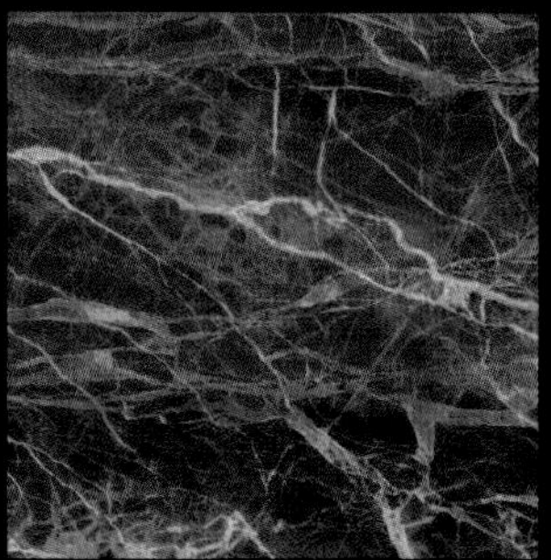
Breccia Paradiso

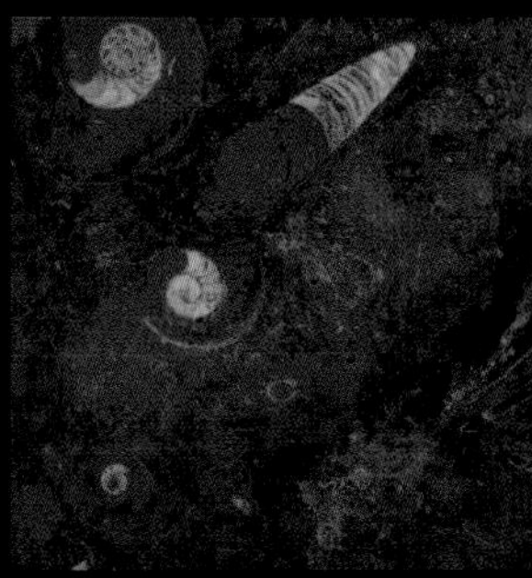
Fossil Brown

- Quarrying location: Italy
- Availability: Limited
- Compressive strength: 1260/kg cm^2
- After freezing: 1150/kg cm^2
- Ultimate tensile strength: 89/kg cm^2
- Coef. thermal expansion: 0,0080mm/m°C
- Water absorption: 0,30%
- Impact test / min. fall height: 38 cm
- Frictional wear test: –
- Bulk density: 2740 kg/m^3

CD file number: 0177

- Quarrying location: Italy
- Availability: Limited
- Compressive strength: 1260/kg cm^2
- After freezing: 1150/kg cm^2
- Ultimate tensile strength: 89/kg cm^2
- Coef. thermal expansion: 0,0080mm/m°C
- Water absorption: 0,30%
- Impact test / min. fall height: 38 cm
- Frictional wear test: –
- Bulk density: 2740 kg/m^3

CD file number: 0178

- Quarrying location: Italy
- Availability: Limited
- Compressive strength: 1260/kg cm^2
- After freezing: 1150/kg cm^2
- Ultimate tensile strength: 89/kg cm^2
- Coef. thermal expansion: 0,0080mm/m°C
- Water absorption: 0,30%
- Impact test / min. fall height: 38 cm
- Frictional wear test: –
- Bulk density: 2740 kg/m^3

CD file number: 0179

- Quarrying location: Italy
- Availability: Limited
- Compressive strength: 1260/kg cm^2
- After freezing: 1150/kg cm^2
- Ultimate tensile strength: 89/kg cm^2
- Coef. thermal expansion: 0,0080mm/m°C
- Water absorption: 0,30%
- Impact test / min. fall height: 38 cm
- Frictional wear test: –
- Bulk density: 2740 kg/m^3

CD file number: 0180

Cipollino al Contro

- Quarrying location: Iran
- Availability: Medium
- Compressive strength: 1427/kg cm^2
- After freezing: 1215/kg cm^2
- Ultimate tensile strength: 141/kg cm^2
- Coef. thermal expansion: 0,0058mm/m°C
- Water absorption: 0,44%
- Impact test / min. fall height: 49 cm
- Frictional wear test: –
- Bulk density: 2680 kg/m^3

CD file number: 0181

Cipollino al Verso

- Quarrying location: France
- Availability: Limited
- Compressive strength: 1260/kg cm^2
- After freezing: 1150/kg cm^2
- Ultimate tensile strength: 89/kg cm^2
- Coef. thermal expansion: 0,0080mm/m°C
- Water absorption: 0,30%
- Impact test / min. fall height: 38 cm
- Frictional wear test: –
- Bulk density: 2740 kg/m^3

CD file number: 0182

Cremo Tirreno

- Quarrying location: China
- Availability: Good
- Compressive strength: 1260/kg cm^2
- After freezing: 1150/kg cm^2
- Ultimate tensile strength: 89/kg cm^2
- Coef. thermal expansion: 0,0080mm/m°C
- Water absorption: 0,30%
- Impact test / min. fall height: 38 cm
- Frictional wear test: –
- Bulk density: 2740 kg/m^3

CD file number: 0183

Venato Fantastico

- Quarrying location: data not available
- Availability: –
- Compressive strength: –
- After freezing: –
- Ultimate tensile strength: –
- Coef. thermal expansion: –
- Water absorption: –
- Impact test / min. fall height: –
- Frictional wear test: –
- Bulk density: –

CD file number: 0184

Verde Antigua

- Quarrying location: France
- Availability: Limited
- Compressive strength: 2470/kg cm^2
- After freezing: 1270/kg cm^2
- Ultimate tensile strength: 625/kg cm^2
- Coef. thermal expansion: 0,0070mm/m°C
- Water absorption: 0,03%
- Impact test / min. fall height: 50 cm
- Frictional wear test: –
- Bulk density: 2800 kg/m^3

CD file number: 0185

Verde Chassagne

- Quarrying location: China
- Availability: Good
- Compressive strength: 1427/kg cm^2
- After freezing: 1215/kg cm^2
- Ultimate tensile strength: 141/kg cm^2
- Coef. thermal expansion: 0,0058mm/m°C
- Water absorption: 0,44%
- Impact test / min. fall height: 49 cm
- Frictional wear test: –
- Bulk density: 2680 kg/m^3

CD file number: 0186

Verde Cina

- Quarrying location: China
- Availability: Good
- Compressive strength: 1427/kg cm^2
- After freezing: 1215/kg cm^2
- Ultimate tensile strength: 141/kg cm^2
- Coef. thermal expansion: 0,0058mm/m°C
- Water absorption: 0,44%
- Impact test / min. fall height: 49 cm
- Frictional wear test: –
- Bulk density: 2680 kg/m^3

CD file number: 0187

Azzurro d'Oriente

- Quarrying location: Italy
- Availability: Medium
- Compressive strength: 1427/kg cm^2
- After freezing: 1215/kg cm^2
- Ultimate tensile strength: 141/kg cm^2
- Coef. thermal expansion: 0,0058mm/m°C
- Water absorption: 0,44%
- Impact test / min. fall height: 49 cm
- Frictional wear test: –
- Bulk density: 2680 kg/m^3

CD file number: 0188

Irish Connemarble

- Quarrying location: India
- Availability: Medium
- Compressive strength: 1427/kg cm^2
- After freezing: 1215/kg cm^2
- Ultimate tensile strength: 141/kg cm^2
- Coef. thermal expansion: 0,0058mm/m°C
- Water absorption: 0,44%
- Impact test / min. fall height: 49 cm
- Frictional wear test: –
- Bulk density: 2680 kg/m^3

CD file number: 0189

Ming Green

- Quarrying location: Italy
- Availability: Limited
- Compressive strength: 1427/kg cm^2
- After freezing: 1215/kg cm^2
- Ultimate tensile strength: 141/kg cm^2
- Coef. thermal expansion: 0,0058mm/m°C
- Water absorption: 0,44%
- Impact test / min. fall height: 49 cm
- Frictional wear test: –
- Bulk density: 2680 kg/m^3

CD file number: 0190

Verde Apollo

- Quarrying location: Italy
- Availability: Limited
- Compressive strength: 1427/kg cm^2
- After freezing: 1215/kg cm^2
- Ultimate tensile strength: 141/kg cm^2
- Coef. thermal expansion: 0,0058mm/m°C
- Water absorption: 0,44%
- Impact test / min. fall height: 49 cm
- Frictional wear test: –
- Bulk density: 2680 kg/m^3

CD file number: 0191

Verde S. Denise

- Quarrying location: Italy
- Availability: Limited
- Compressive strength: 1427/kg cm^2
- After freezing: 1215/kg cm^2
- Ultimate tensile strength: 141/kg cm^2
- Coef. thermal expansion: 0,0058mm/m°C
- Water absorption: 0,44%
- Impact test / min. fall height: 49 cm
- Frictional wear test: –
- Bulk density: 2680 kg/m^3

CD file number: 0192

Rajastan Green

Verde Issoire

Verde Patricia Scuro

Verde Patricia

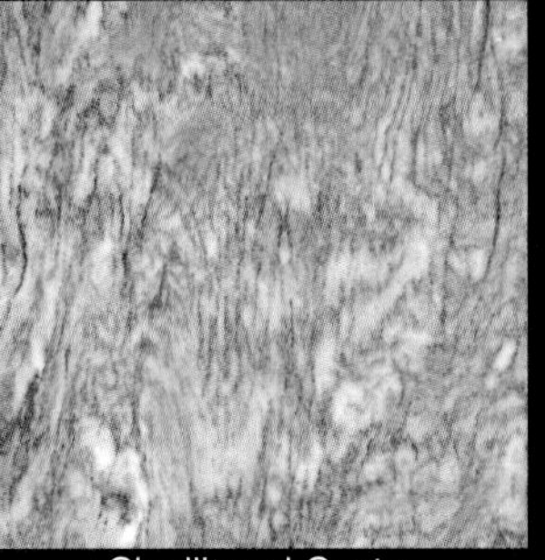
Cipollino al Contro

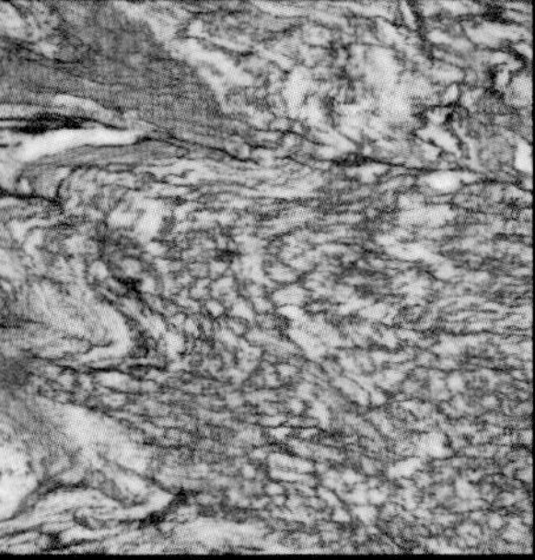
Cipollino al Verso

Cremo Tirreno

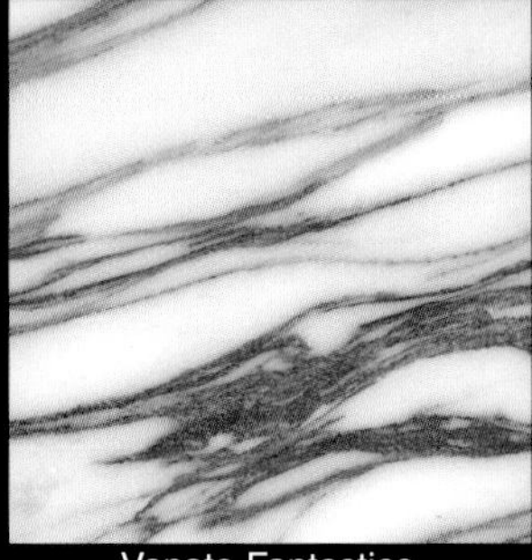
Venato Fantastico

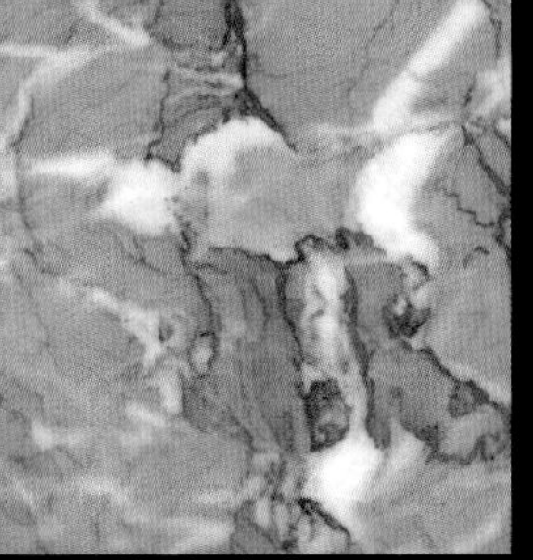
Verde Antigua

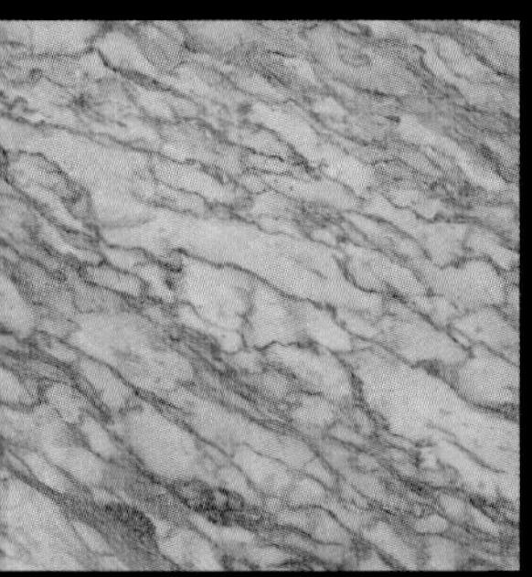
Verde Chassagne

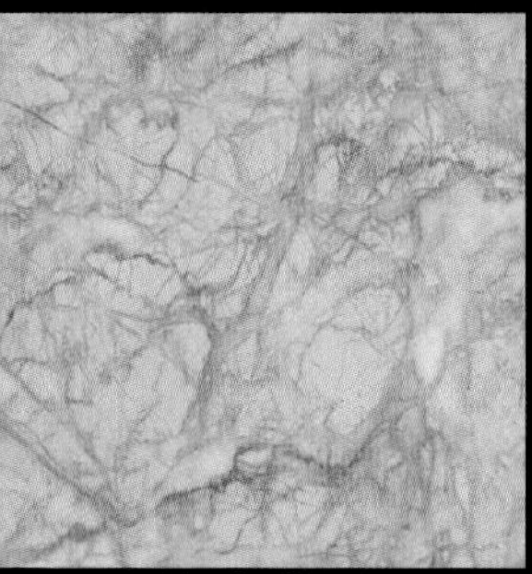
Verde Cina

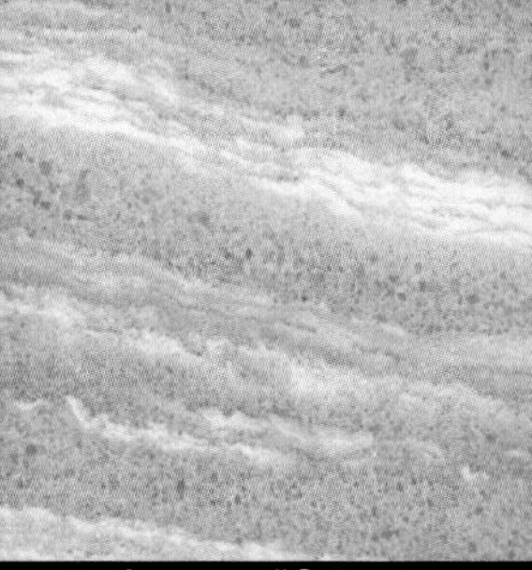
Azzurro d'Oriente

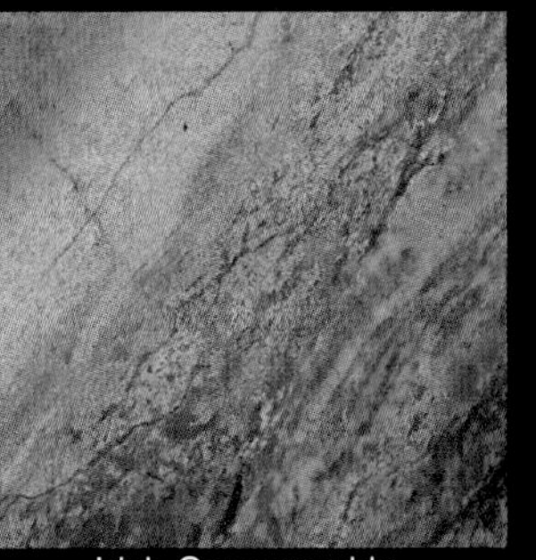
Irish Connemarble

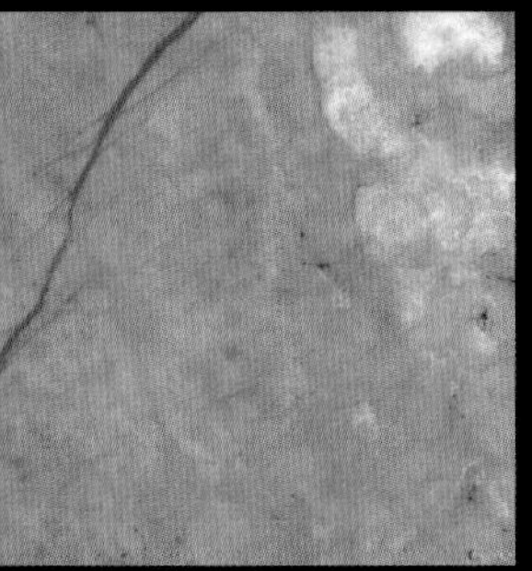
Ming Green

Verde Apollo

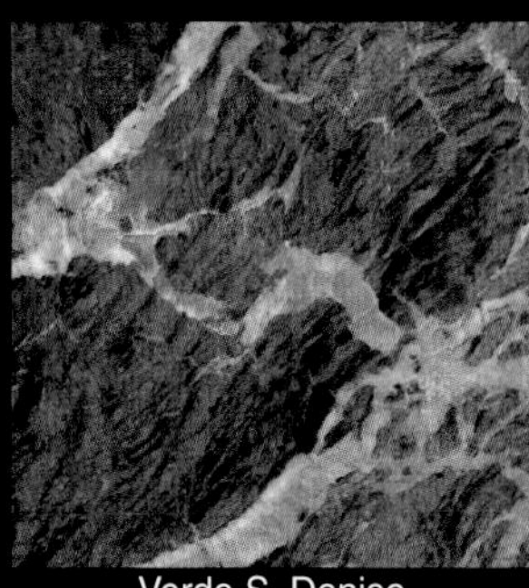
Verde S. Denise

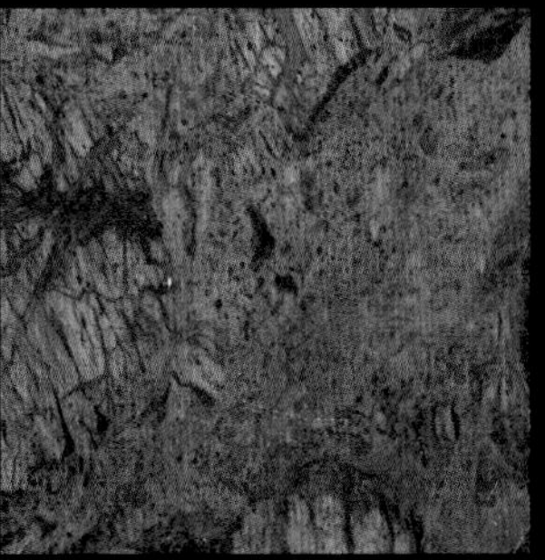
Rajastan Green

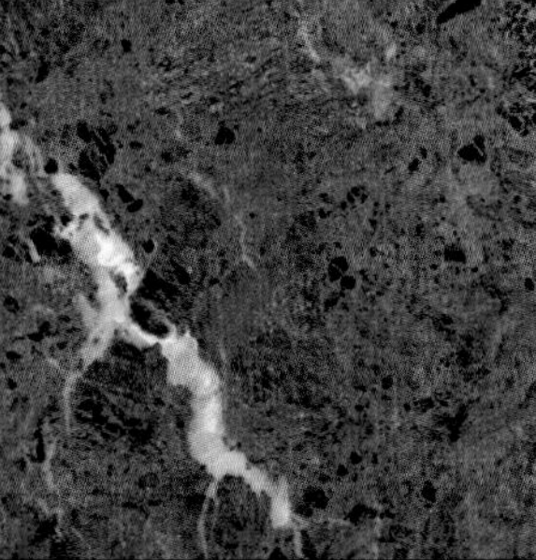
Verde Issoire

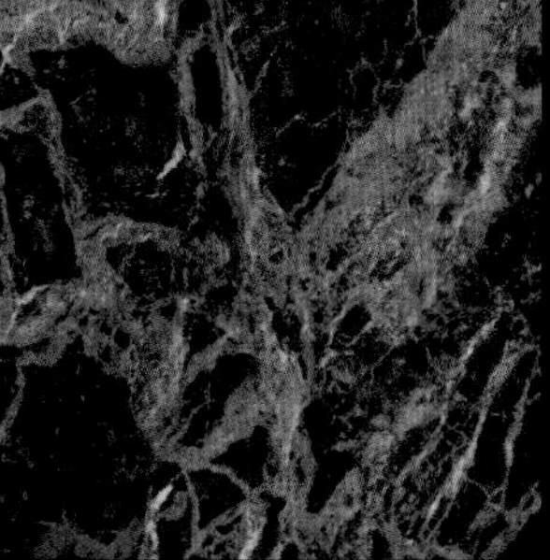
Verde Patricia Scuro

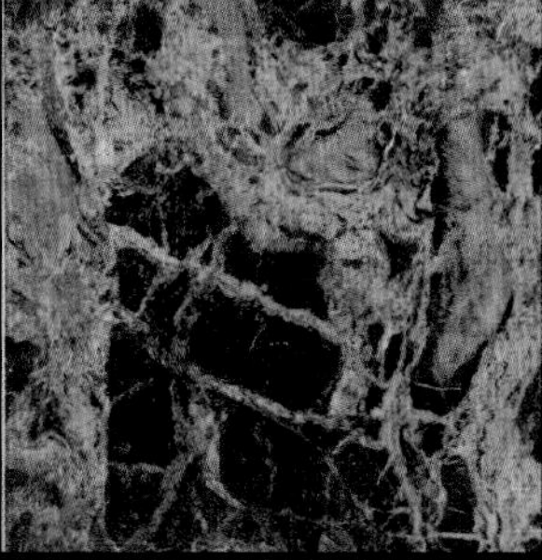
Verde Patricia

Quarrying location:	China
Availability:	Medium
Compressive strength:	1427/kg cm^2
After freezing:	1215/kg cm^2
Ultimate tensile strength:	141/kg cm^2
Coef. thermal expansion:	0,0058mm/m°C
Water absorption:	0,44%
Impact test / min. fall height:	49 cm
Frictional wear test:	–
Bulk density:	2680 kg/m^3

CD file number: 0193

Empress Green

Quarrying location:	USA
Availability:	Medium
Compressive strength:	1427/kg cm^2
After freezing:	1215/kg cm^2
Ultimate tensile strength:	141/kg cm^2
Coef. thermal expansion:	0,0058mm/m°C
Water absorption:	0,44%
Impact test / min. fall height:	49 cm
Frictional wear test:	–
Bulk density:	2680 kg/m^3

CD file number: 0194

Verde Vermont

Quarrying location:	Italy
Availability:	Medium
Compressive strength:	1427/kg cm^2
After freezing:	1215/kg cm^2
Ultimate tensile strength:	141/kg cm^2
Coef. thermal expansion:	0,0058mm/m°C
Water absorption:	0,44%
Impact test / min. fall height:	49 cm
Frictional wear test:	–
Bulk density:	2680 kg/m^3

CD file number: 0195

Verde Rameggiato

Quarrying location:	Greece
Availability:	Medium
Compressive strength:	1427/kg cm^2
After freezing:	1215/kg cm^2
Ultimate tensile strength:	141/kg cm^2
Coef. thermal expansion:	0,0058mm/m°C
Water absorption:	0,44%
Impact test / min. fall height:	49 cm
Frictional wear test:	–
Bulk density:	2680 kg/m^3

CD file number: 0196

Verde Tinos

Quarrying location:	Taiwan
Availability:	Medium
Compressive strength:	1427/kg cm^2
After freezing:	1215/kg cm^2
Ultimate tensile strength:	141/kg cm^2
Coef. thermal expansion:	0,0058mm/m°C
Water absorption:	0,44%
Impact test / min. fall height:	49 cm
Frictional wear test:	–
Bulk density:	2680 kg/m^3

CD file number: 0197

Taiwan Green

Quarrying location:	Italy
Availability:	Medium
Compressive strength:	1427/kg cm^2
After freezing:	1215/kg cm^2
Ultimate tensile strength:	141/kg cm^2
Coef. thermal expansion:	0,0058mm/m°C
Water absorption:	0,44%
Impact test / min. fall height:	49 cm
Frictional wear test:	–
Bulk density:	2680 kg/m^3

CD file number: 0198

Verde Alpi

Quarrying location:	Italy
Availability:	Limited
Compressive strength:	1427/kg cm^2
After freezing:	1215/kg cm^2
Ultimate tensile strength:	141/kg cm^2
Coef. thermal expansion:	0,0058mm/m°C
Water absorption:	0,44%
Impact test / min. fall height:	49 cm
Frictional wear test:	–
Bulk density:	2680 kg/m^3

CD file number: 0199

Verde Gressoney

Quarrying location:	Italy
Availability:	Medium
Compressive strength:	1427/kg cm^2
After freezing:	1215/kg cm^2
Ultimate tensile strength:	141/kg cm^2
Coef. thermal expansion:	0,0058mm/m°C
Water absorption:	0,44%
Impact test / min. fall height:	49 cm
Frictional wear test:	–
Bulk density:	2680 kg/m^3

CD file number: 0200

Verde Acceglio

Quarrying location:	Guatemala
Availability:	Limited
Compressive strength:	1427/kg cm^2
After freezing:	1215/kg cm^2
Ultimate tensile strength:	141/kg cm^2
Coef. thermal expansion:	0,0058mm/m°C
Water absorption:	0,44%
Impact test / min. fall height:	49 cm
Frictional wear test:	–
Bulk density:	2680 kg/m^3

CD file number: 0201

Verde Guatemala

Quarrying location:	data not available
Availability:	–
Compressive strength:	–
After freezing:	–
Ultimate tensile strength:	–
Coef. thermal expansion:	–
Water absorption:	–
Impact test / min. fall height:	–
Frictional wear test:	–
Bulk density:	–

CD file number: 0202

Verde Antico d'Oriente

Quarrying location:	Italy
Availability:	Medium
Compressive strength:	2470/kg cm^2
After freezing:	2270/kg cm^2
Ultimate tensile strength:	625/kg cm^2
Coef. thermal expansion:	0,0070mm/m°C
Water absorption:	0,03%
Impact test / min. fall height:	50 cm
Frictional wear test:	–
Bulk density:	2800 kg/m^3

CD file number: 0203

Serpentino

Quarrying location:	marocco
Availability:	Medium
Compressive strength:	2470/kg cm^2
After freezing:	2270/kg cm^2
Ultimate tensile strength:	625/kg cm^2
Coef. thermal expansion:	0,0070mm/m°C
Water absorption:	0,03%
Impact test / min. fall height:	50 cm
Frictional wear test:	–
Bulk density:	2800 kg/m^3

CD file number: 0204

Verde Chaine

Quarrying location:	Egypt
Availability:	Limited
Compressive strength:	1427/kg cm^2
After freezing:	1215/kg cm^2
Ultimate tensile strength:	141/kg cm^2
Coef. thermal expansion:	0,0058mm/m°C
Water absorption:	0,44%
Impact test / min. fall height:	49 cm
Frictional wear test:	–
Bulk density:	2680 kg/m^3

CD file number: 0205

Breccia Fawakir

Quarrying location:	Italy
Availability:	Limited
Compressive strength:	1427/kg cm^2
After freezing:	1215/kg cm^2
Ultimate tensile strength:	141/kg cm^2
Coef. thermal expansion:	0,0058mm/m°C
Water absorption:	0,44%
Impact test / min. fall height:	49 cm
Frictional wear test:	–
Bulk density:	2680 kg/m^3

CD file number: 0206

Verde Aver

Quarrying location:	Italy
Availability:	Limited
Compressive strength:	1427/kg cm^2
After freezing:	1215/kg cm^2
Ultimate tensile strength:	141/kg cm^2
Coef. thermal expansion:	0,0058mm/m°C
Water absorption:	0,44%
Impact test / min. fall height:	49 cm
Frictional wear test:	–
Bulk density:	2680 kg/m^3

CD file number: 0207

Verde Giada

Quarrying location:	Italy
Availability:	Medium
Compressive strength:	1427/kg cm^2
After freezing:	1215/kg cm^2
Ultimate tensile strength:	141/kg cm^2
Coef. thermal expansion:	0,0058mm/m°C
Water absorption:	0,44%
Impact test / min. fall height:	49 cm
Frictional wear test:	–
Bulk density:	2680 kg/m^3

CD file number: 0208

Verde Issogne

Empress Green

Verde Vermont

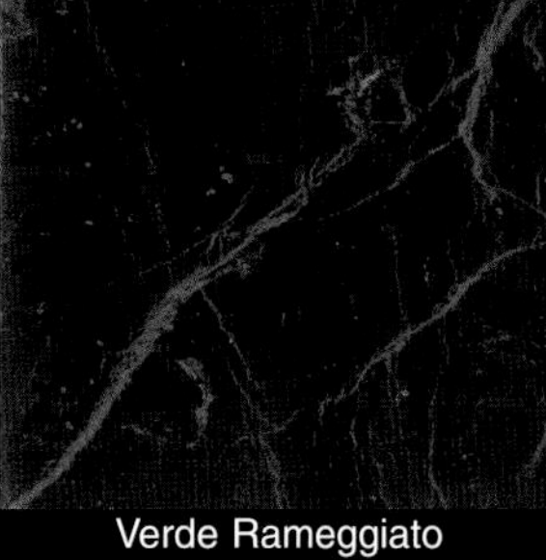
Verde Rameggiato

Verde Tinos

Taiwan Green

Verde Alpi

Verde Gressoney

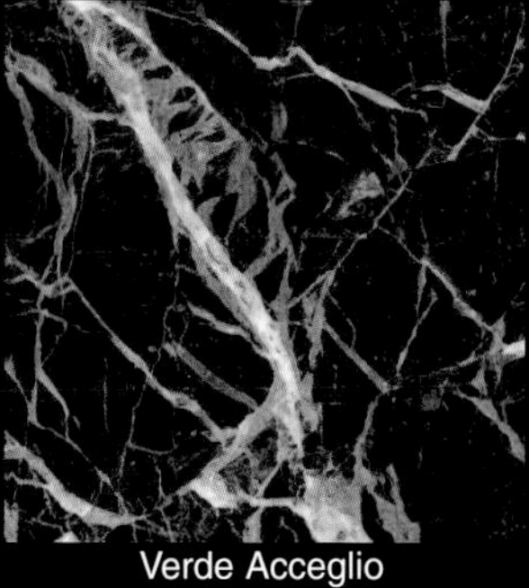
Verde Acceglio

Verde Guatemala

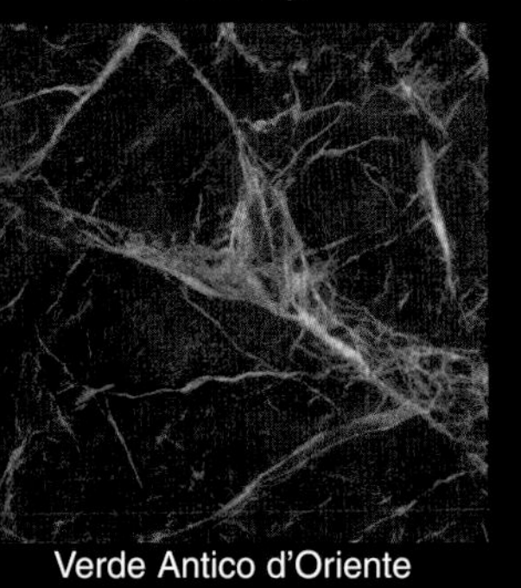
Verde Antico d’Oriente

Serpentino

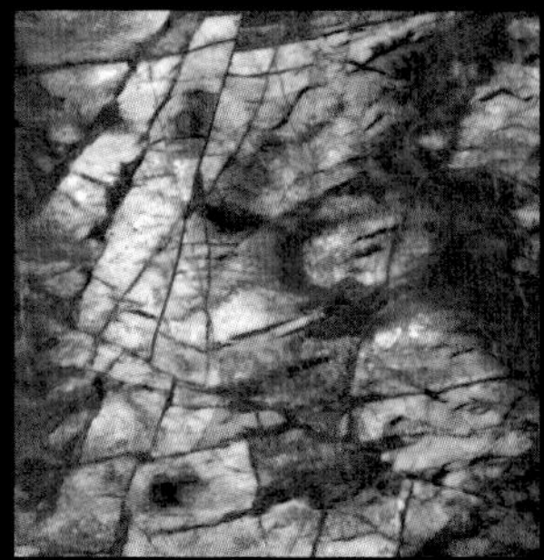
Verde Chaine

Breccia Fawakir

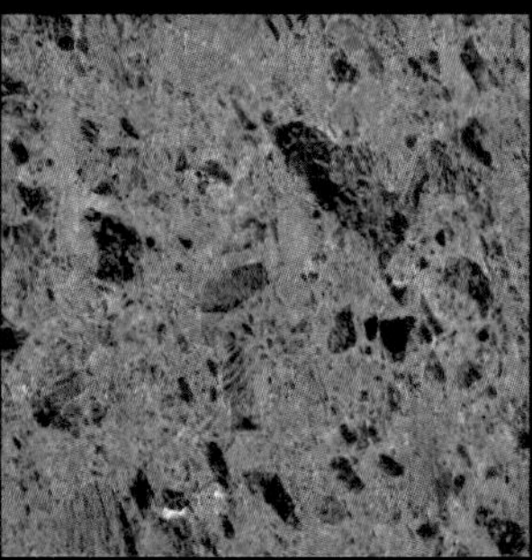
Verde Aver

Verde Giada

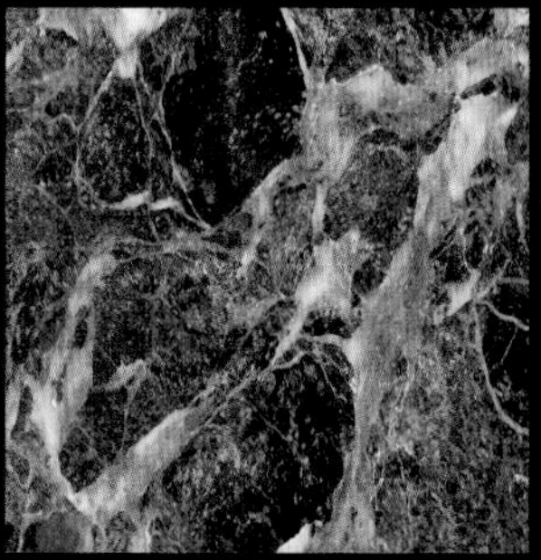
Verde Issogne

Quarrying location: Italy
Availability: Medium
Compressive strength: 1439/kg cm^2
After freezing: 1322/kg cm^2
Ultimate tensile strength: 163/kg cm^2
Coef. thermal expansion: 0,0048mm/m°C
Water absorption: 0,21%
Impact test / min. fall height: 57 cm
Frictional wear test: –
Bulk density: 2682 kg/m^3

CD file number: 0209

Bardiglio Carrara

Quarrying location: Italy
Availability: Limited
Compressive strength: 1439/kg cm^2
After freezing: 1322/kg cm^2
Ultimate tensile strength: 163/kg cm^2
Coef. thermal expansion: 0,0048mm/m°C
Water absorption: 0,21%
Impact test / min. fall height: 57 cm
Frictional wear test: –
Bulk density: 2682 kg/m^3

CD file number: 0210

Bardiglio Imperiale

Quarrying location: Italy
Availability: Limited
Compressive strength: 1439/kg cm^2
After freezing: 1322/kg cm^2
Ultimate tensile strength: 163/kg cm^2
Coef. thermal expansion: 0,0048mm/m°C
Water absorption: 0,21%
Impact test / min. fall height: 57 cm
Frictional wear test: –
Bulk density: 2682 kg/m^3

CD file number: 0211

Bardiglio Cappella

Quarrying location: Italy
Availability: Medium
Compressive strength: 1439/kg cm^2
After freezing: 1322/kg cm^2
Ultimate tensile strength: 163/kg cm^2
Coef. thermal expansion: 0,0048mm/m°C
Water absorption: 0,21%
Impact test / min. fall height: 57 cm
Frictional wear test: –
Bulk density: 2682 kg/m^3

CD file number: 0212

Bardiglio Fumo di Londra

Quarrying location: Italy
Availability: Limited
Compressive strength: 1439/kg cm^2
After freezing: 1322/kg cm^2
Ultimate tensile strength: 163/kg cm^2
Coef. thermal expansion: 0,0048mm/m°C
Water absorption: 0,21%
Impact test / min. fall height: 57 cm
Frictional wear test: –
Bulk density: 2682 kg/m^3

CD file number: 0213

Bardiglio Costa

Quarrying location: Turkey
Availability: Good
Compressive strength: 1315/kg cm^2
After freezing: 1215/kg cm^2
Ultimate tensile strength: 141/kg cm^2
Coef. thermal expansion: 0,0049mm/m°C
Water absorption: 0,09%
Impact test / min. fall height: 43 cm
Frictional wear test: –
Bulk density: 2687 kg/m^3

CD file number: 0214

Dove

Quarrying location: TItaly
Availability: Good
Compressive strength: 1315/kg cm^2
After freezing: 1215/kg cm^2
Ultimate tensile strength: 141/kg cm^2
Coef. thermal expansion: 0,0049mm/m°C
Water absorption: 0,09%
Impact test / min. fall height: 43 cm
Frictional wear test: –
Bulk density: 2687 kg/m^3

CD file number: 0215

Fior di Pesco Carnico

Quarrying location: Italy
Availability: Limited
Compressive strength: 1562/kg cm^2
After freezing: 1261/kg cm^2
Ultimate tensile strength: 139/kg cm^2
Coef. thermal expansion: –
Water absorption: 0,13%
Impact test / min. fall height: 32 cm
Frictional wear test: –
Bulk density: 2688 kg/m^3

CD file number: 0216

Fior di Bosco

Quarrying location: Italy
Availability: Medium
Compressive strength: 1562/kg cm^2
After freezing: 1261/kg cm^2
Ultimate tensile strength: 139/kg cm^2
Coef. thermal expansion: –
Water absorption: 0,13%
Impact test / min. fall height: 32 cm
Frictional wear test: –
Bulk density: 2688 kg/m^3

CD file number: 0217

Grigio Carnico

Quarrying location: Italy
Availability: Limited
Compressive strength: 1439/kg cm^2
After freezing: 1322/kg cm^2
Ultimate tensile strength: 163/kg cm^2
Coef. thermal expansion: 0,0048mm/m°C
Water absorption: 0,21%
Impact test / min. fall height: 57 cm
Frictional wear test: –
Bulk density: 2682 kg/m^3

CD file number: 0218

Grigio Orobico

Quarrying location: Italy
Availability: Limited
Compressive strength: 1562/kg cm^2
After freezing: 1261/kg cm^2
Ultimate tensile strength: 139/kg cm^2
Coef. thermal expansion: –
Water absorption: 0,13%
Impact test / min. fall height: 32 cm
Frictional wear test: –
Bulk density: 2688 kg/m^3

CD file number: 0219

Gris Bowere

Quarrying location: Greece
Availability: Medium
Compressive strength: 1562/kg cm^2
After freezing: 1261/kg cm^2
Ultimate tensile strength: 139/kg cm^2
Coef. thermal expansion: –
Water absorption: 0,13%
Impact test / min. fall height: 32 cm
Frictional wear test: –
Bulk density: 2688 kg/m^3

CD file number: 0220

Grigio Creta

Quarrying location: France
Availability: Limited
Compressive strength: 1439/kg cm^2
After freezing: 1322/kg cm^2
Ultimate tensile strength: 163/kg cm^2
Coef. thermal expansion: 0,0048mm/m°C
Water absorption: 0,21%
Impact test / min. fall height: 57 cm
Frictional wear test: –
Bulk density: 2682 kg/m^3

CD file number: 0221

Gris Antique

Quarrying location: Italy
Availability: Limited
Compressive strength: 1439/kg cm^2
After freezing: 1322/kg cm^2
Ultimate tensile strength: 163/kg cm^2
Coef. thermal expansion: 0,0048mm/m°C
Water absorption: 0,21%
Impact test / min. fall height: 57 cm
Frictional wear test: –
Bulk density: 2682 kg/m^3

CD file number: 0222

Blu Venato d'Italia

Quarrying location: Turkey
Availability: Good
Compressive strength: 1315/kg cm^2
After freezing: 1215/kg cm^2
Ultimate tensile strength: 141/kg cm^2
Coef. thermal expansion: 0,0049mm/m°C
Water absorption: 0,09%
Impact test / min. fall height: 43 cm
Frictional wear test: –
Bulk density: 2687 kg/m^3

CD file number: 0223

Supren

Quarrying location: Turkey
Availability: Good
Compressive strength: 1315/kg cm^2
After freezing: 1215/kg cm^2
Ultimate tensile strength: 141/kg cm^2
Coef. thermal expansion: 0,0049mm/m°C
Water absorption: 0,09%
Impact test / min. fall height: 43 cm
Frictional wear test: –
Bulk density: 2687 kg/m^3

CD file number: 0224

Salomé

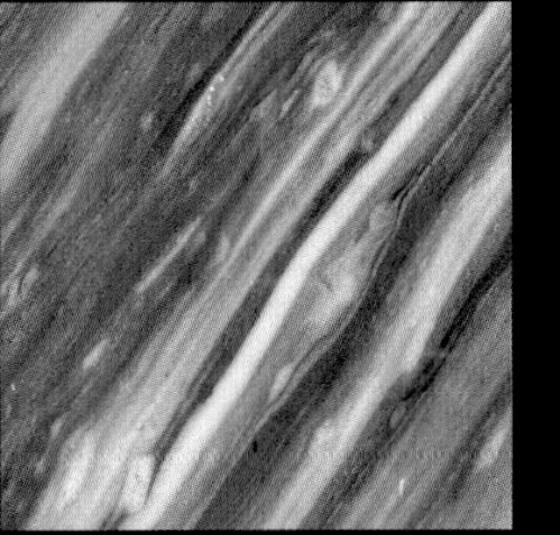
Bardiglio Carrara

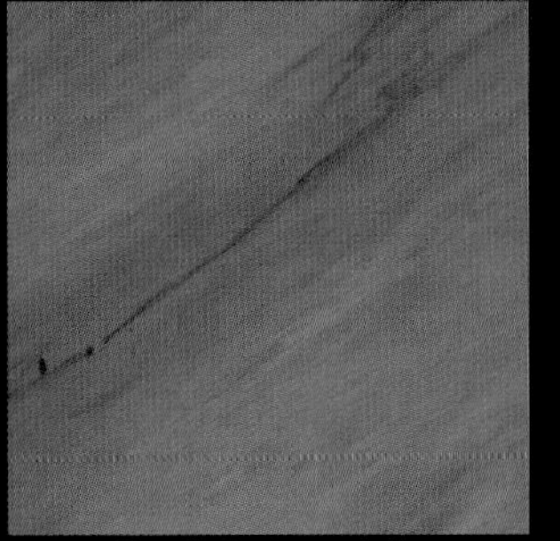
Bardiglio Imperiale

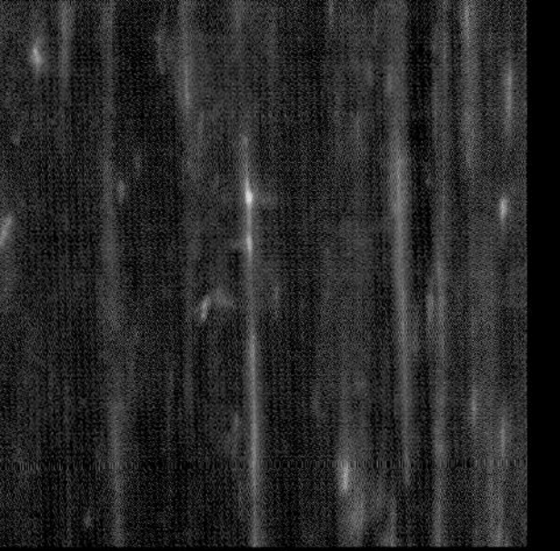
Bardiglio Cappella

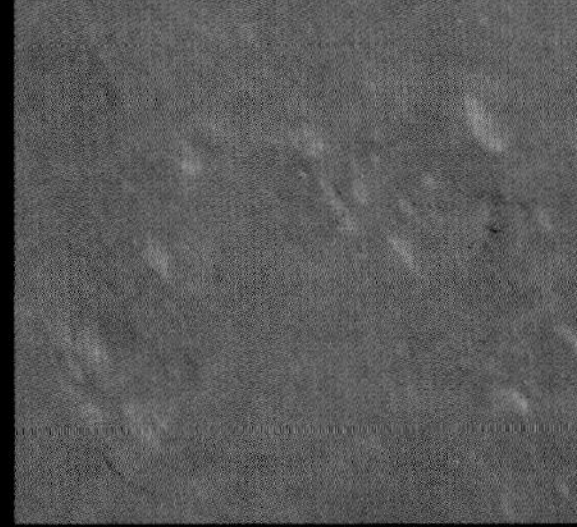
Bardiglio Fumo di Londra

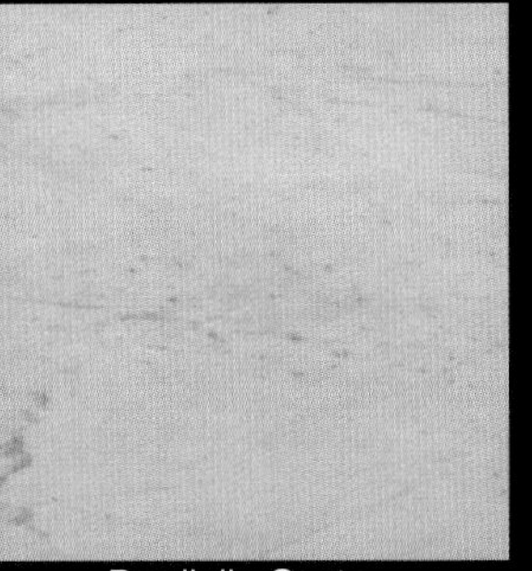
Bardiglio Costa

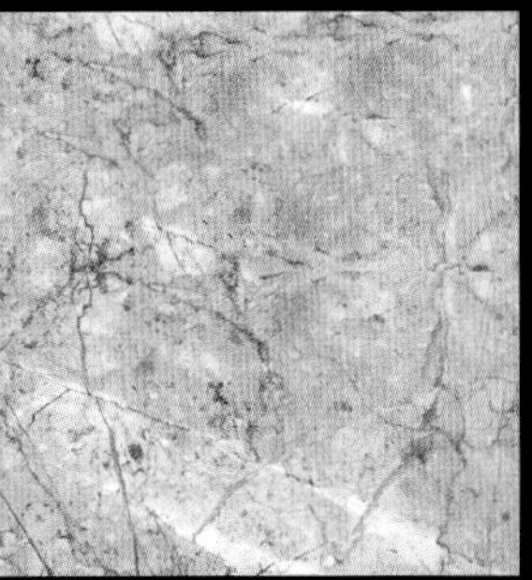
Dove

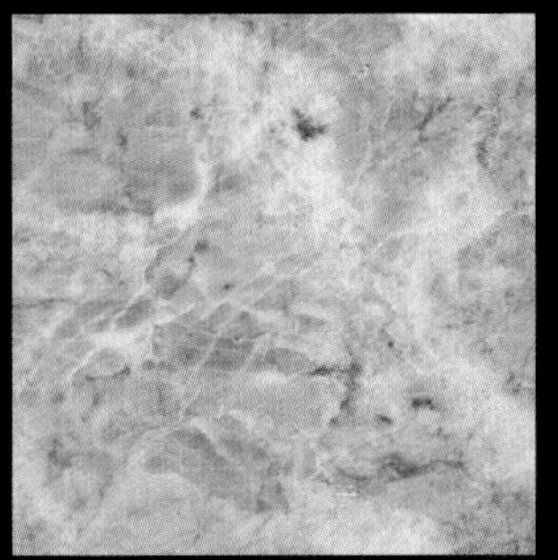
Fior di Pesco Carnico

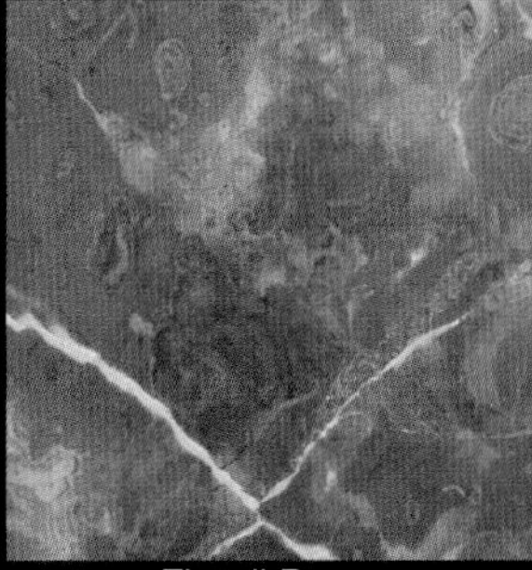
Fior di Bosco

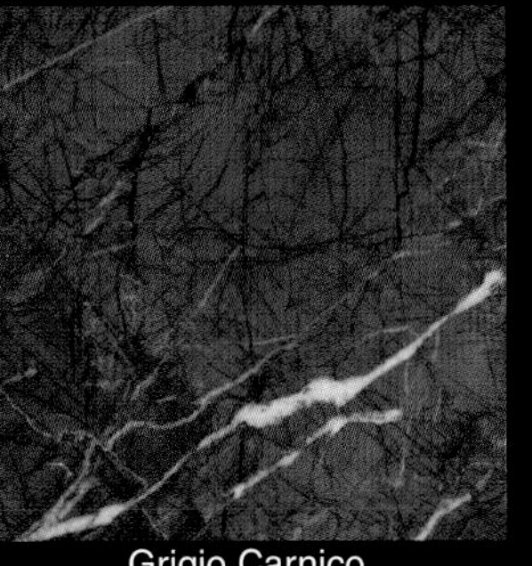
Grigio Carnico

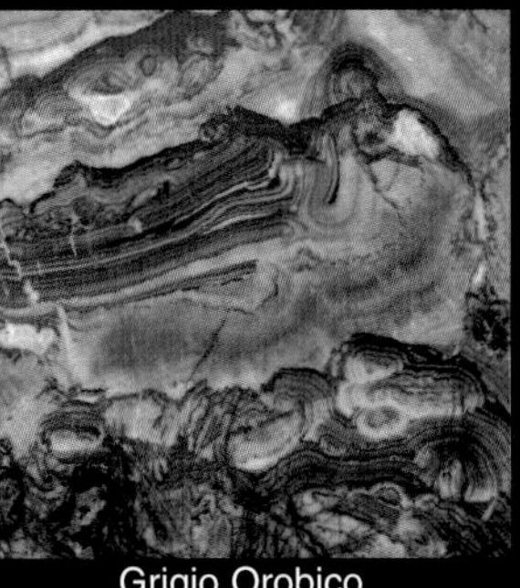
Grigio Orobico

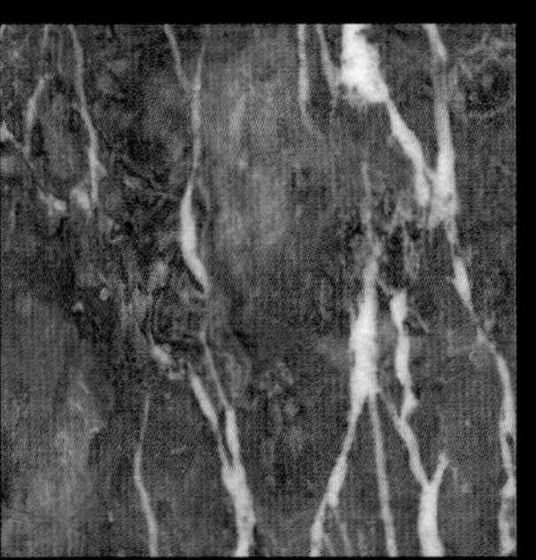
Gris Bowere

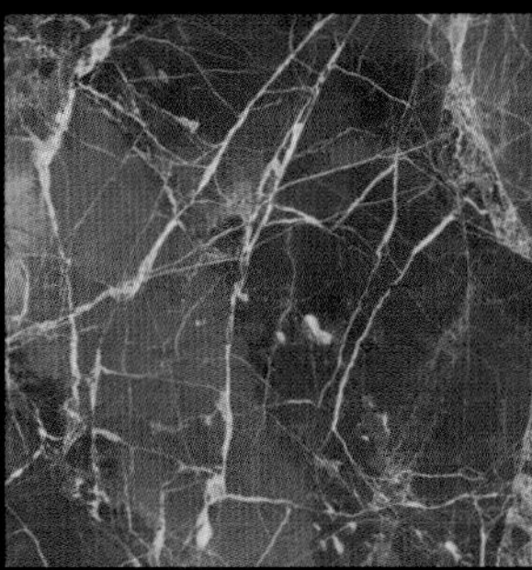
Grigio Creta

Gris Antique

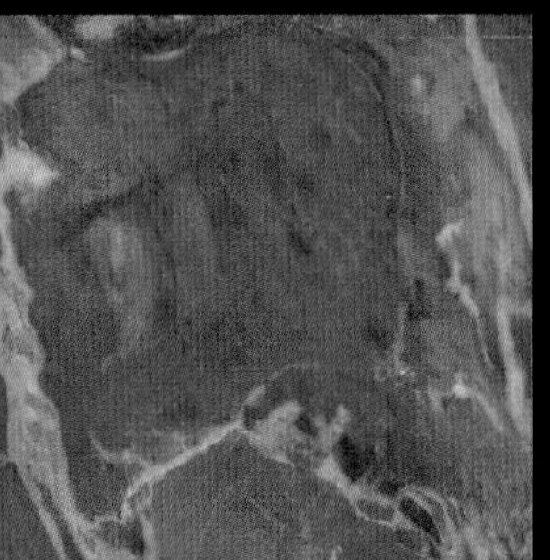
Blu Venato d'Italia

Supren

Salomé

Quarrying location: Italy
Availability: Limited
Compressive strength: 1563/kg cm^2
After freezing: 1478/kg cm^2
Ultimate tensile strength: 181/kg cm^2
Coef. thermal expansion: 0,0045mm/m°C
Water absorption: 0,23%
Impact test / min. fall height: 48 cm
Frictional wear test: –
Bulk density: 2667 kg/m^3

CD file number: 0225

Palissandro Bluette

Quarrying location: Argentina
Availability: Medium
Compressive strength: –
After freezing: –
Ultimate tensile strength: –
Coef. thermal expansion: –
Water absorption: –
Impact test / min. fall height: –
Frictional wear test: –
Bulk density: –

CD file number: 0226

Azul Cielo

Quarrying location: Bolivia
Availability: Limited
Compressive strength: –
After freezing: –
Ultimate tensile strength: –
Coef. thermal expansion: –
Water absorption: –
Impact test / min. fall height: –
Frictional wear test: –
Bulk density: –

CD file number: 0227

Sodalite Blu

Quarrying location: Chile
Availability: Limited
Compressive strength: –
After freezing: –
Ultimate tensile strength: –
Coef. thermal expansion: –
Water absorption: –
Impact test / min. fall height: –
Frictional wear test: –
Bulk density: –

CD file number: 0228

Lapislazuli

Quarrying location: Greece
Availability: Medium
Compressive strength: 988/kg cm^2
After freezing: –
Ultimate tensile strength: 122/kg cm^2
Coef. thermal expansion: 0,0041mm/m°C
Water absorption: 0,13%
Impact test / min. fall height: 27 cm
Frictional wear test: –
Bulk density: 2689 kg/m^3

CD file number: 0229

Nero Kawala

Quarrying location: Marocco
Availability: Medium
Compressive strength: 988/kg cm^2
After freezing: –
Ultimate tensile strength: 122/kg cm^2
Coef. thermal expansion: 0,0041mm/m°C
Water absorption: 0,13%
Impact test / min. fall height: 27 cm
Frictional wear test: –
Bulk density: 2689 kg/m^3

CD file number: 0230

Fossil Black

Quarrying location: Spain
Availability: Medium
Compressive strength: 988/kg cm^2
After freezing: –
Ultimate tensile strength: 122/kg cm^2
Coef. thermal expansion: 0,0041mm/m°C
Water absorption: 0,13%
Impact test / min. fall height: 27 cm
Frictional wear test: –
Bulk density: 2689 kg/m^3

CD file number: 0231

Nero Marquina Fiorito

Quarrying location: Spain
Availability: Good
Compressive strength: 988/kg cm^2
After freezing: –
Ultimate tensile strength: 122/kg cm^2
Coef. thermal expansion: 0,0041mm/m°C
Water absorption: 0,13%
Impact test / min. fall height: 27 cm
Frictional wear test: –
Bulk density: 2689 kg/m^3

CD file number: 0232

Nero Marquina

Quarrying location: Mexico
Availability: Medium
Compressive strength: 988/kg cm^2
After freezing: –
Ultimate tensile strength: 122/kg cm^2
Coef. thermal expansion: 0,0041mm/m°C
Water absorption: 0,13%
Impact test / min. fall height: 27 cm
Frictional wear test: –
Bulk density: 2689 kg/m^3

CD file number: 0233

Nero Mexico

Quarrying location: India
Availability: Medium
Compressive strength: 988/kg cm^2
After freezing: –
Ultimate tensile strength: 122/kg cm^2
Coef. thermal expansion: 0,0041mm/m°C
Water absorption: 0,13%
Impact test / min. fall height: 27 cm
Frictional wear test: –
Bulk density: 2689 kg/m^3

CD file number: 0234

Black Pearl

Quarrying location: Italy
Availability: Limited
Compressive strength: 988/kg cm^2
After freezing: –
Ultimate tensile strength: 122/kg cm^2
Coef. thermal expansion: 0,0041mm/m°C
Water absorption: 0,13%
Impact test / min. fall height: 27 cm
Frictional wear test: –
Bulk density: 2689 kg/m^3

CD file number: 0235

Nero di Ormea

Quarrying location: Spain
Availability: Limited
Compressive strength: 988/kg cm^2
After freezing: –
Ultimate tensile strength: 122/kg cm^2
Coef. thermal expansion: 0,0041mm/m°C
Water absorption: 0,13%
Impact test / min. fall height: 27 cm
Frictional wear test: –
Bulk density: 2689 kg/m^3

CD file number: 0236

Noir Saint Laurent

Quarrying location: Iyaly
Availability: Limited
Compressive strength: 988/kg cm^2
After freezing: –
Ultimate tensile strength: 122/kg cm^2
Coef. thermal expansion: 0,0041mm/m°C
Water absorption: 0,13%
Impact test / min. fall height: 27 cm
Frictional wear test: –
Bulk density: 2689 kg/m^3

CD file number: 0237

Portoro Macchia Grossa

Quarrying location: Italy
Availability: Limited
Compressive strength: 988/kg cm^2
After freezing: –
Ultimate tensile strength: 122/kg cm^2
Coef. thermal expansion: 0,0041mm/m°C
Water absorption: 0,13%
Impact test / min. fall height: 27 cm
Frictional wear test: –
Bulk density: 2689 kg/m^3

CD file number: 0238

Portoro Macchia FIne

Quarrying location: Uruguay
Availability: Limited
Compressive strength: 988/kg cm^2
After freezing: –
Ultimate tensile strength: 122/kg cm^2
Coef. thermal expansion: 0,0041mm/m°C
Water absorption: 0,13%
Impact test / min. fall height: 27 cm
Frictional wear test: –
Bulk density: 2689 kg/m^3

CD file number: 0239

Negro Uruguay

Quarrying location: Belgium
Availability: Limited
Compressive strength: 988/kg cm^2
After freezing: –
Ultimate tensile strength: 122/kg cm^2
Coef. thermal expansion: 0,0041mm/m°C
Water absorption: 0,13%
Impact test / min. fall height: 27 cm
Frictional wear test: –
Bulk density: 2689 kg/m^3

CD file number: 0240

Nero Belgio

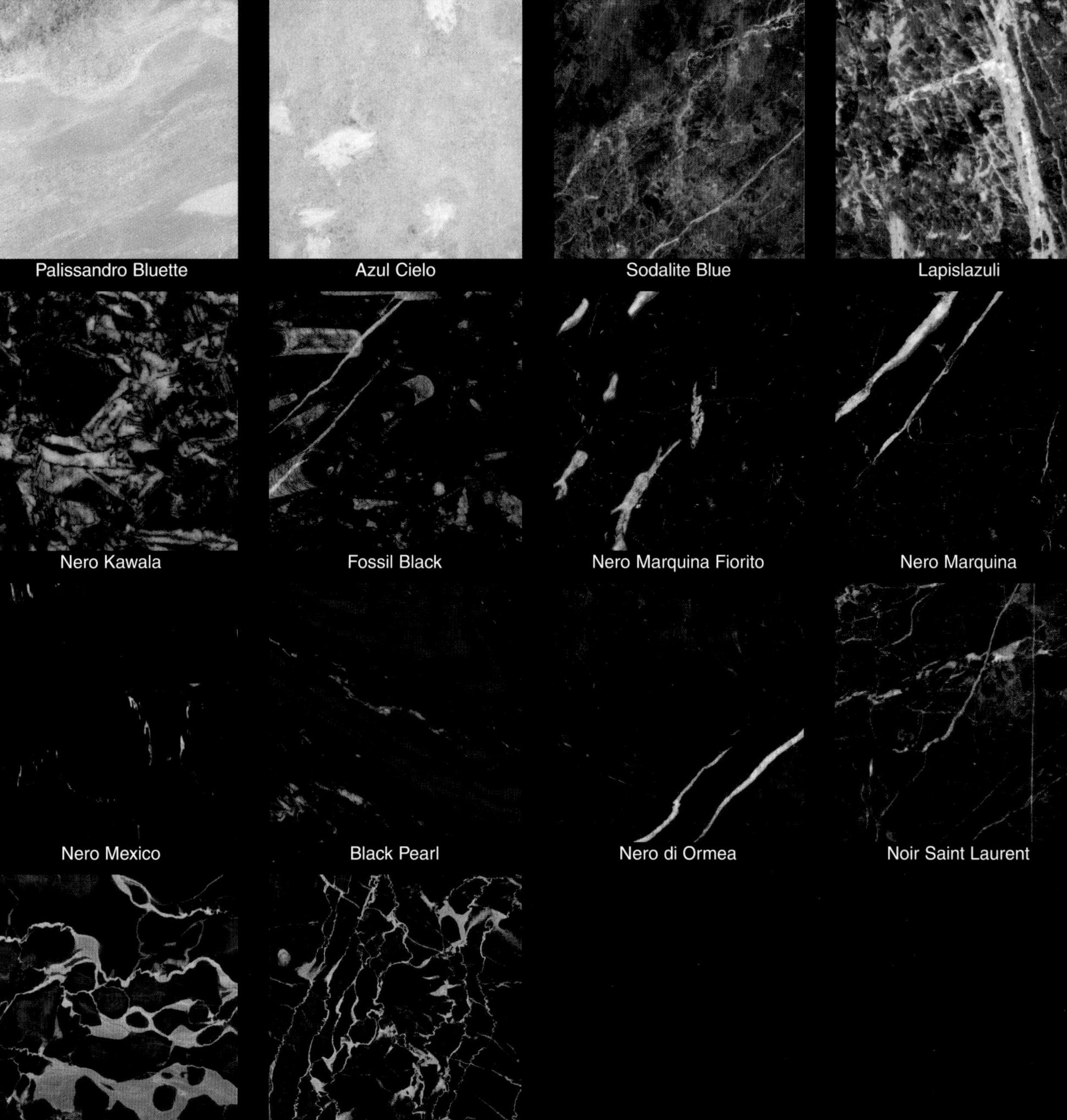
Palissandro Bluette
Azul Cielo
Sodalite Blue
Lapislazuli
Nero Kawala
Fossil Black
Nero Marquina Fiorito
Nero Marquina
Nero Mexico
Black Pearl
Nero di Ormea
Noir Saint Laurent
Portoro Macchia Grossa
Portoro Macchia FIne
Negro Uruguay
Nero Belgio

TRAVERTINE

Quarrying location:	Italy
Availability:	Good
Compressive strength:	957/kg cm^2
After freezing:	880/kg cm^2
Ultimate tensile strength:	127/kg cm^2
Coef. thermal expansion:	0,0045mm/m°C
Water absorption:	1,00%
Impact test / min. fall height:	29 cm
Frictional wear test:	–
Bulk density:	2410 kg/m^3

CD file number: 0241

Quarrying location:	Italy
Availability:	Good
Compressive strength:	957/kg cm^2
After freezing:	880/kg cm^2
Ultimate tensile strength:	127/kg cm^2
Coef. thermal expansion:	0,0045mm/m°C
Water absorption:	1,00%
Impact test / min. fall height:	29 cm
Frictional wear test:	–
Bulk density:	2410 kg/m^3

CD file number: 0242

Quarrying location:	Italy
Availability:	Medium
Compressive strength:	940/kg cm^2
After freezing:	935/kg cm^2
Ultimate tensile strength:	125/kg cm^2
Coef. thermal expansion:	0,0050mm/m°C
Water absorption:	1,30%
Impact test / min. fall height:	30 cm
Frictional wear test:	–
Bulk density:	2430 kg/m^3

CD file number: 0243

Quarrying location:	Italy
Availability:	Good
Compressive strength:	957/kg cm^2
After freezing:	880/kg cm^2
Ultimate tensile strength:	127/kg cm^2
Coef. thermal expansion:	0,0045mm/m°C
Water absorption:	1,00%
Impact test / min. fall height:	29 cm
Frictional wear test:	–
Bulk density:	2410 kg/m^3

CD file number: 0244

Travertino Romano Classico

Quarrying location:	Italy
Availability:	Medium
Compressive strength:	940/kg cm^2
After freezing:	935/kg cm^2
Ultimate tensile strength:	125/kg cm^2
Coef. thermal expansion:	0,0050mm/m°C
Water absorption:	1,30%
Impact test / min. fall height:	30 cm
Frictional wear test:	–
Bulk density:	2430 kg/m^3

CD file number: 0245

Travertino Romano Classico in Falda

Quarrying location:	Spain
Availability:	Medium
Compressive strength:	957/kg cm^2
After freezing:	880/kg cm^2
Ultimate tensile strength:	127/kg cm^2
Coef. thermal expansion:	0,0045mm/m°C
Water absorption:	1,00%
Impact test / min. fall height:	29 cm
Frictional wear test:	–
Bulk density:	2410 kg/m^3

CD file number: 0246

Travertino Bianco

Quarrying location:	Italy
Availability:	Medium
Compressive strength:	1160/kg cm^2
After freezing:	1150/kg cm^2
Ultimate tensile strength:	160/kg cm^2
Coef. thermal expansion:	0,0060mm/m°C
Water absorption:	1,60%
Impact test / min. fall height:	35 cm
Frictional wear test:	–
Bulk density:	2415 kg/m^3

CD file number: 0247

Travertino Navona

Quarrying location:	Italy
Availability:	Medium
Compressive strength:	957/kg cm^2
After freezing:	880/kg cm^2
Ultimate tensile strength:	127/kg cm^2
Coef. thermal expansion:	0,0045mm/m°C
Water absorption:	1,00%
Impact test / min. fall height:	29 cm
Frictional wear test:	–
Bulk density:	2410 kg/m^3

CD file number: 0248

Travertino Silver

Quarrying location:	Turkey
Availability:	Limited
Compressive strength:	1220/kg cm^2
After freezing:	1210/kg cm^2
Ultimate tensile strength:	150/kg cm^2
Coef. thermal expansion:	0,0035mm/m°C
Water absorption:	–
Impact test / min. fall height:	55 cm
Frictional wear test:	–
Bulk density:	2430 kg/m^3

CD file number: 0249

Travertino Iberico

Quarrying location:	Spain
Availability:	Medium
Compressive strength:	957/kg cm^2
After freezing:	880/kg cm^2
Ultimate tensile strength:	127/kg cm^2
Coef. thermal expansion:	0,0045mm/m°C
Water absorption:	1,00%
Impact test / min. fall height:	29 cm
Frictional wear test:	–
Bulk density:	2410 kg/m^3

CD file number: 0250

Travertino Venato

Quarrying location:	Iran
Availability:	Limited
Compressive strength:	1220/kg cm^2
After freezing:	1210/kg cm^2
Ultimate tensile strength:	150/kg cm^2
Coef. thermal expansion:	0,0035mm/m°C
Water absorption:	–
Impact test / min. fall height:	55 cm
Frictional wear test:	–
Bulk density:	2430 kg/m^3

CD file number: 0251

Travertino Striato

Quarrying location:	Iran
Availability:	Limited
Compressive strength:	1220/kg cm^2
After freezing:	1210/kg cm^2
Ultimate tensile strength:	150/kg cm^2
Coef. thermal expansion:	0,0035mm/m°C
Water absorption:	–
Impact test / min. fall height:	55 cm
Frictional wear test:	–
Bulk density:	2430 kg/m^3

CD file number: 0252

Travertino Colorato

Quarrying location:	Italy
Availability:	Good
Compressive strength:	1160/kg cm^2
After freezing:	1150/kg cm^2
Ultimate tensile strength:	160/kg cm^2
Coef. thermal expansion:	0,0060mm/m°C
Water absorption:	1,60%
Impact test / min. fall height:	35 cm
Frictional wear test:	–
Bulk density:	2415 kg/m^3

CD file number: 0253

Travertino Scabas

Quarrying location:	Italy
Availability:	Good
Compressive strength:	1160/kg cm^2
After freezing:	1150/kg cm^2
Ultimate tensile strength:	160/kg cm^2
Coef. thermal expansion:	0,0060mm/m°C
Water absorption:	1,60%
Impact test / min. fall height:	35 cm
Frictional wear test:	–
Bulk density:	2415 kg/m^3

CD file number: 0254

Travertino Rosso

Quarrying location:	Iran
Availability:	Limited
Compressive strength:	–
After freezing:	–
Ultimate tensile strength:	–
Coef. thermal expansion:	–
Water absorption:	–
Impact test / min. fall height:	–
Frictional wear test:	–
Bulk density:	–

CD file number: 0255

Travertino Rosso in Falda

Quarrying location:	Iran
Availability:	Limited
Compressive strength:	–
After freezing:	–
Ultimate tensile strength:	–
Coef. thermal expansion:	–
Water absorption:	–
Impact test / min. fall height:	–
Frictional wear test:	–
Bulk density:	–

CD file number: 0256

Travertino Noce

Travertino Noce in Falda

Travertino Dorato

Travertino Dorato Vein Cut

Travertino Romano Classico

Travertino Romano Classico in Falda

Travertino Bianco

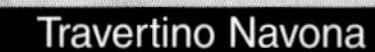

Travertino Navona

Travertino Silver

Travertino Iberico

Travertino Venato

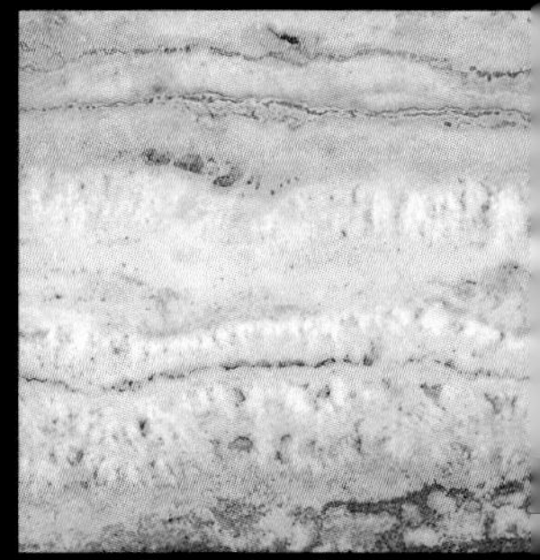

Travertino Striato

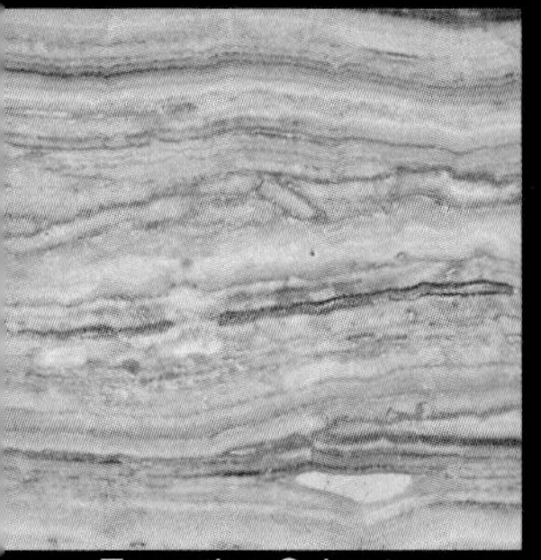

Travertino Colorato

Travertino Scabas

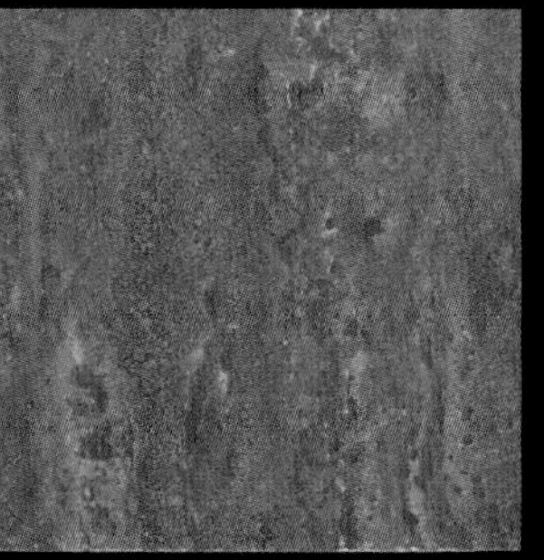

Travertino Rosso

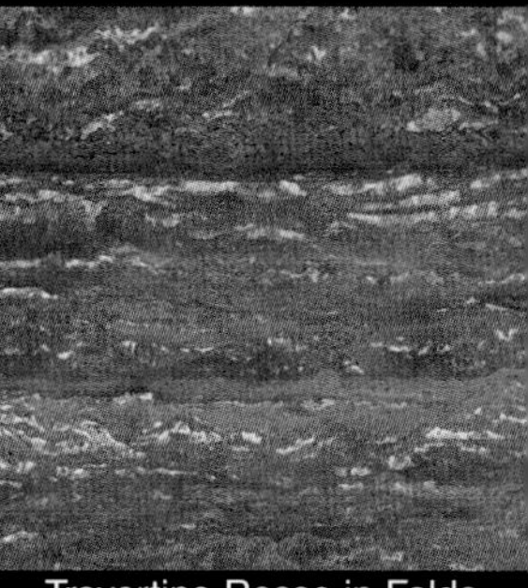

Travertino Rosso in Falda

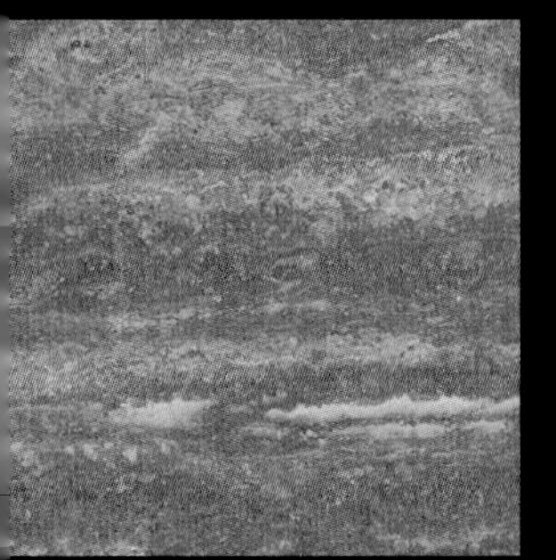

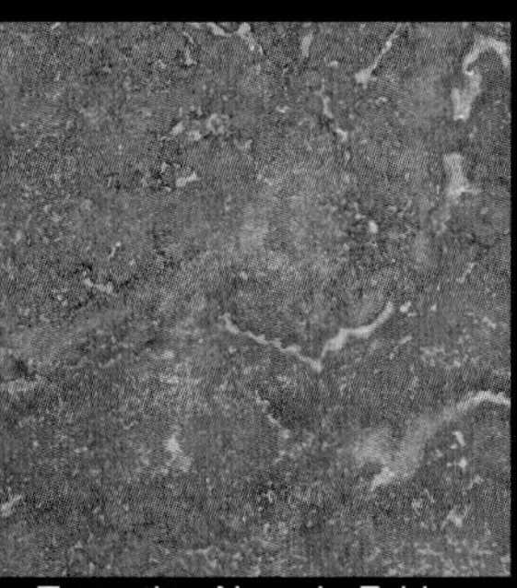

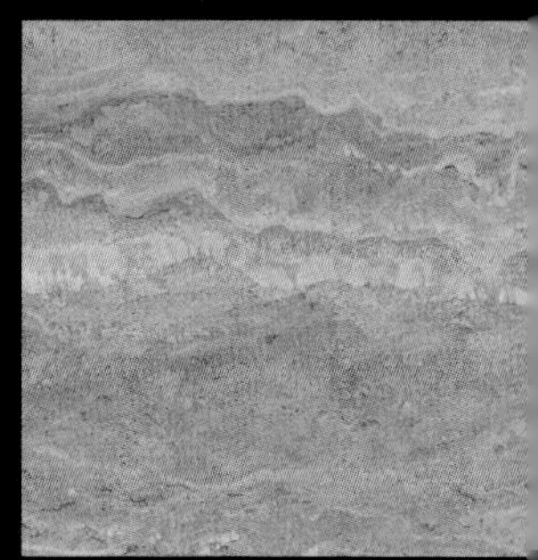

ONYX

Quarrying location: Pakistan
Availability: Limited
Compressive strength: 1760/kg cm^2
After freezing: 1640/kg cm^2
Ultimate tensile strength: –
Coef. thermal expansion: –
Water absorption: 0,15%
Impact test / min. fall height: –
Frictional wear test: –
Bulk density: 2550 kg/m^3

CD file number: 0257

Quarrying location: Pakistan
Availability: Limited
Compressive strength: 1760/kg cm^2
After freezing: 1640/kg cm^2
Ultimate tensile strength: –
Coef. thermal expansion: –
Water absorption: 0,15%
Impact test / min. fall height: –
Frictional wear test: –
Bulk density: 2550 kg/m^3

CD file number: 0258

Quarrying location: Pakistan
Availability: Limited
Compressive strength: 1760/kg cm^2
After freezing: 1640/kg cm^2
Ultimate tensile strength: –
Coef. thermal expansion: –
Water absorption: 0,15%
Impact test / min. fall height: –
Frictional wear test: –
Bulk density: 2550 kg/m^3

CD file number: 0259

Quarrying location: Iran
Availability: Limited
Compressive strength: 1760/kg cm^2
After freezing: 1640/kg cm^2
Ultimate tensile strength: –
Coef. thermal expansion: –
Water absorption: 0,15%
Impact test / min. fall height: –
Frictional wear test: –
Bulk density: 2550 kg/m^3

CD file number: 0260

Onice Bianco

Quarrying location: Egypt
Availability: Limited
Compressive strength: 1760/kg cm^2
After freezing: 1640/kg cm^2
Ultimate tensile strength: –
Coef. thermal expansion: –
Water absorption: 0,15%
Impact test / min. fall height: –
Frictional wear test: –
Bulk density: 2550 kg/m^3

CD file number: 0261

Onice Bianco Venato

Quarrying location: Egypt
Availability: Limited
Compressive strength: 1760/kg cm^2
After freezing: 1640/kg cm^2
Ultimate tensile strength: –
Coef. thermal expansion: –
Water absorption: 0,15%
Impact test / min. fall height: –
Frictional wear test: –
Bulk density: 2550 kg/m^3

CD file number: 0262

Onyx Brown

Quarrying location: Egypt
Availability: Limited
Compressive strength: 1760/kg cm^2
After freezing: 1640/kg cm^2
Ultimate tensile strength: –
Coef. thermal expansion: –
Water absorption: 0,15%
Impact test / min. fall height: –
Frictional wear test: –
Bulk density: 2550 kg/m^3

CD file number: 0263

Onice Giallo

Quarrying location: Iran
Availability: Limited
Compressive strength: 1760/kg cm^2
After freezing: 1640/kg cm^2
Ultimate tensile strength: –
Coef. thermal expansion: –
Water absorption: 0,15%
Impact test / min. fall height: –
Frictional wear test: –
Bulk density: 2550 kg/m^3

CD file number: 0264

Alabastro Egiziano

Quarrying location: Pakistan
Availability: Limited
Compressive strength: 1760/kg cm^2
After freezing: 1640/kg cm^2
Ultimate tensile strength: –
Coef. thermal expansion: –
Water absorption: 0,15%
Impact test / min. fall height: –
Frictional wear test: –
Bulk density: 2550 kg/m^3

CD file number: 0265

Alabastro

Quarrying location: Pakistan
Availability: Limited
Compressive strength: 1760/kg cm^2
After freezing: 1640/kg cm^2
Ultimate tensile strength: –
Coef. thermal expansion: –
Water absorption: 0,15%
Impact test / min. fall height: –
Frictional wear test: –
Bulk density: 2550 kg/m^3

CD file number: 0266

Alabastro Egiziano Cotognino

Quarrying location: Tanzania
Availability: Limited
Compressive strength: 1760/kg cm^2
After freezing: 1640/kg cm^2
Ultimate tensile strength: –
Coef. thermal expansion: –
Water absorption: 0,15%
Impact test / min. fall height: –
Frictional wear test: –
Bulk density: 2550 kg/m^3

CD file number: 0267

Onyx Arcobaleno

Quarrying location: Tanzania
Availability: Limited
Compressive strength: 1760/kg cm^2
After freezing: 1640/kg cm^2
Ultimate tensile strength: –
Coef. thermal expansion: –
Water absorption: 0,15%
Impact test / min. fall height: –
Frictional wear test: –
Bulk density: 2550 kg/m^3

CD file number: 0268

Onyx Verde

Quarrying location: Turkey
Availability: Limited
Compressive strength: 1760/kg cm^2
After freezing: 1640/kg cm^2
Ultimate tensile strength: –
Coef. thermal expansion: –
Water absorption: 0,15%
Impact test / min. fall height: –
Frictional wear test: –
Bulk density: 2550 kg/m^3

CD file number: 0269

Onyx Verde Scuro

Quarrying location: Pakistan
Availability: Limited
Compressive strength: 1760/kg cm^2
After freezing: 1640/kg cm^2
Ultimate tensile strength: –
Coef. thermal expansion: –
Water absorption: 0,15%
Impact test / min. fall height: –
Frictional wear test: –
Bulk density: 2550 kg/m^3

CD file number: 0270

Onice Tanzania Chiaro

Quarrying location: Iran
Availability: Limited
Compressive strength: 1760/kg cm^2
After freezing: 1640/kg cm^2
Ultimate tensile strength: –
Coef. thermal expansion: –
Water absorption: 0,15%
Impact test / min. fall height: –
Frictional wear test: –
Bulk density: 2550 kg/m^3

CD file number: 0271

Onice Tanzania Scuro

Quarrying location: Turkey
Availability: Limited
Compressive strength: 1760/kg cm^2
After freezing: 1640/kg cm^2
Ultimate tensile strength: –
Coef. thermal expansion: –
Water absorption: 0,15%
Impact test / min. fall height: –
Frictional wear test: –
Bulk density: 2550 kg/m^3

CD file number: 0272

Onice Iris Rosso

Onyx Rosso

Onyx Tiger

Onyx Rosso Tartaruga

Onice Bianco

Onice Bianco Venato

Onyx Brown

Onice Giallo

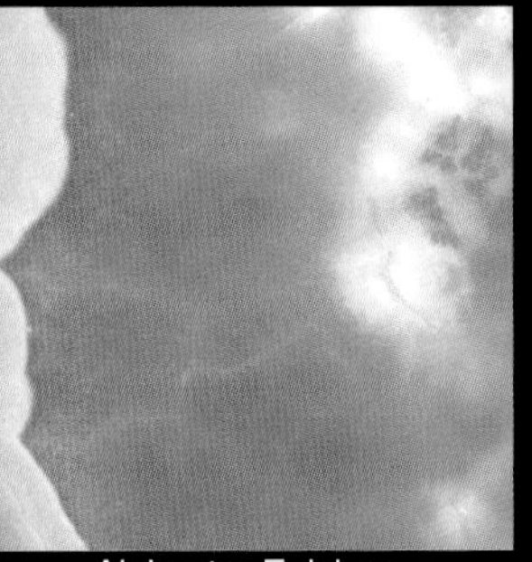

Alabastro Egiziano

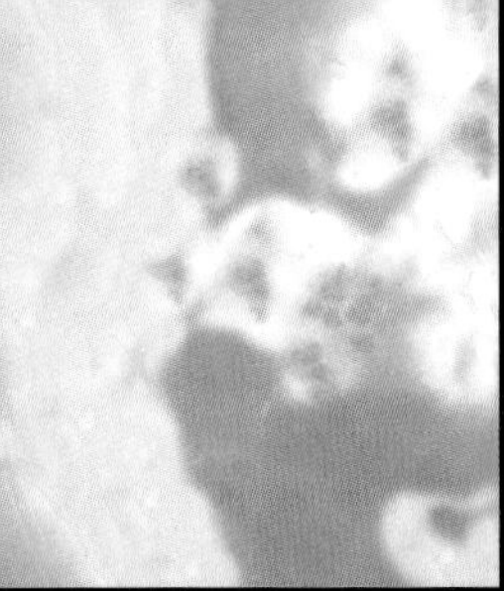

Alabastro

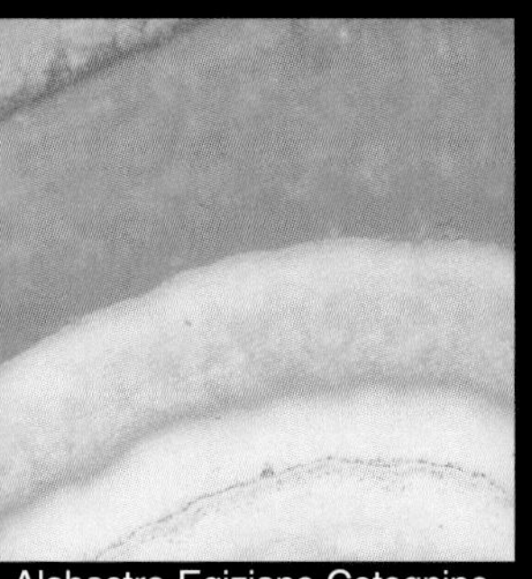

Alabastro Egiziano Cotognino

Onyx Arcobaleno

Onyx Verde

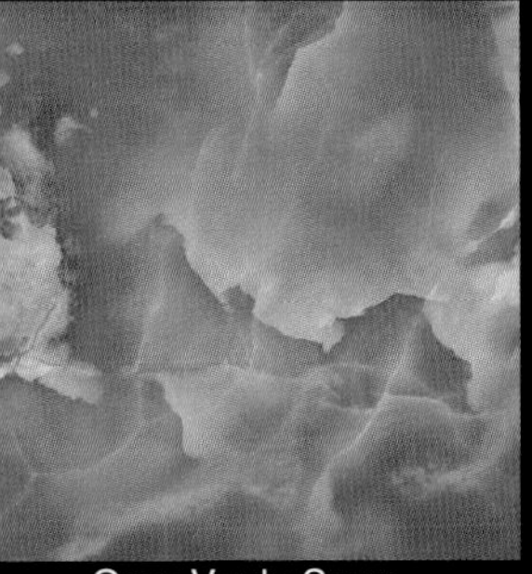

Onyx Verde Scuro

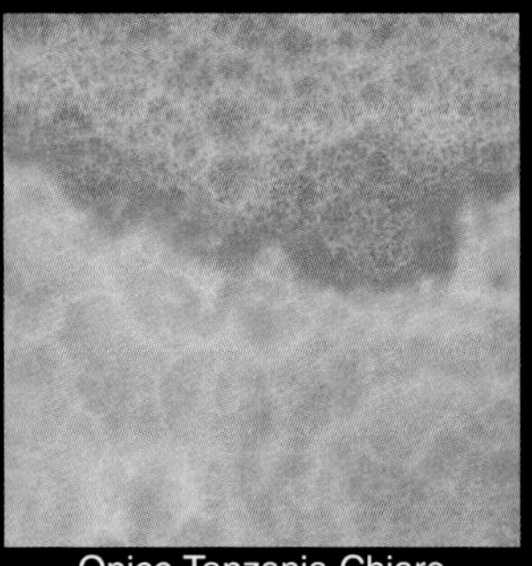

Onice Tanzania Chiaro

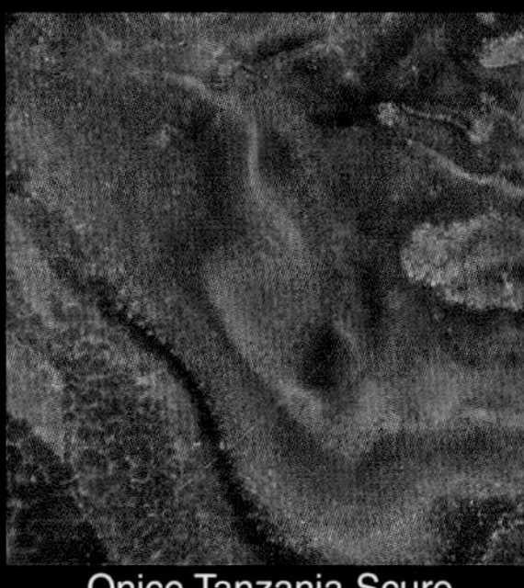

Onice Tanzania Scuro

Onice Iris Rosso

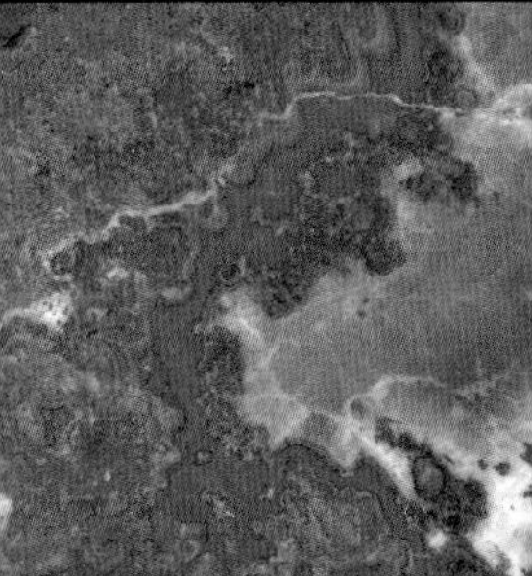

Onyx Rosso

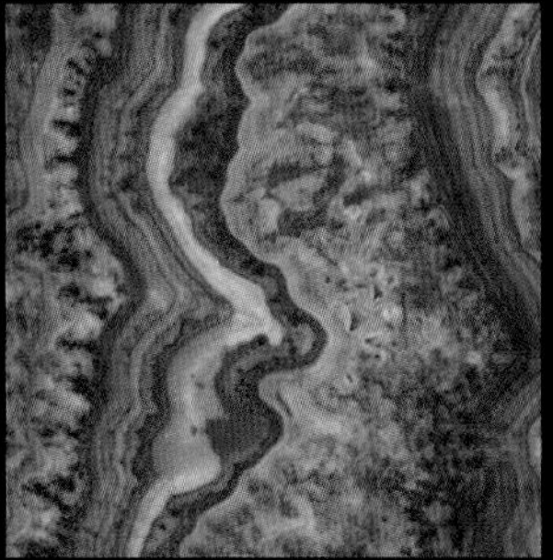

Onyx Tiger

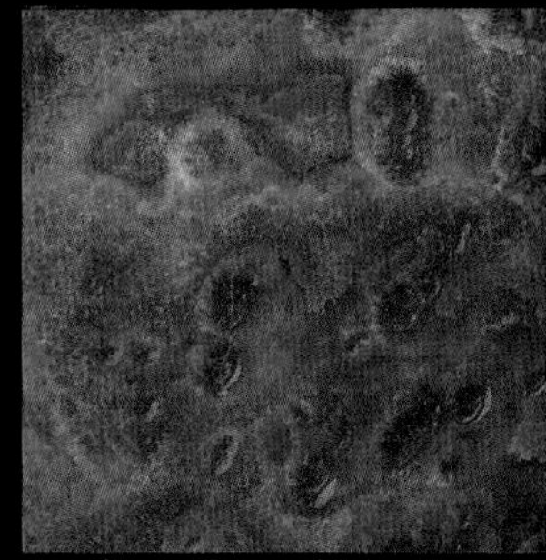

Onyx Rosso Tartaruga

GRANITE

Quarrying location: Spain
Availability: Medium
Compressive strength: 1425/kg cm^2
After freezing: –
Ultimate tensile strength: 139/kg cm^2
Coef. thermal expansion: 0,0069mm/m°C
Water absorption: 0,27%
Impact test / min. fall height: 61 cm
Frictional wear test: 3,5 mm
Bulk density: 2603 kg/m^3

CD file number: 0273

Blanco Berrocal

Quarrying location: Spain
Availability: Good
Compressive strength: 1425/kg cm^2
After freezing: –
Ultimate tensile strength: 139/kg cm^2
Coef. thermal expansion: 0,0069mm/m°C
Water absorption: 0,27%
Impact test / min. fall height: 61 cm
Frictional wear test: 3,5 mm
Bulk density: 2603 kg/m^3

CD file number: 0274

Blanco Cristal

Quarrying location: Spain
Availability: Good
Compressive strength: 1425/kg cm^2
After freezing: –
Ultimate tensile strength: 139/kg cm^2
Coef. thermal expansion: 0,0069mm/m°C
Water absorption: 0,27%
Impact test / min. fall height: 61 cm
Frictional wear test: 3,5 mm
Bulk density: 2603 kg/m^3

CD file number: 0275

Blanco Cristal Extra

Quarrying location: Canada
Availability: Good
Compressive strength: 2051/kg cm^2
After freezing: 1761/kg cm^2
Ultimate tensile strength: 116/kg cm^2
Coef. thermal expansion: 0,0062mm/m°C
Water absorption: 0,35%
Impact test / min. fall height: –
Frictional wear test: –
Bulk density: 2603 kg/m^3

CD file number: 0276

Bethel White

Quarrying location: India
Availability: Medium
Compressive strength: 2051/kg cm^2
After freezing: 1761/kg cm^2
Ultimate tensile strength: 116/kg cm^2
Coef. thermal expansion: 0,0062mm/m°C
Water absorption: 0,35%
Impact test / min. fall height: –
Frictional wear test: –
Bulk density: 2603 kg/m^3

CD file number: 0277

Imperial White

Quarrying location: India
Availability: Medium
Compressive strength: 2051/kg cm^2
After freezing: 1761/kg cm^2
Ultimate tensile strength: 116/kg cm^2
Coef. thermal expansion: 0,0062mm/m°C
Water absorption: 0,35%
Impact test / min. fall height: –
Frictional wear test: –
Bulk density: 2603 kg/m^3

CD file number: 0278

Galaxy White

Quarrying location: India
Availability: Good
Compressive strength: 2080/kg cm^2
After freezing: 1990/kg cm^2
Ultimate tensile strength: 132/kg cm^2
Coef. thermal expansion: 0,0065mm/m°C
Water absorption: 0,40%
Impact test / min. fall height: –
Frictional wear test: –
Bulk density: 2620 kg/m^3

CD file number: 0279

Kashmir White

Quarrying location: Brazil
Availability: Good
Compressive strength: 2080/kg cm^2
After freezing: 1990/kg cm^2
Ultimate tensile strength: 132/kg cm^2
Coef. thermal expansion: 0,0065mm/m°C
Water absorption: 0,40%
Impact test / min. fall height: –
Frictional wear test: –
Bulk density: 2620 kg/m^3

CD file number: 0280

White Andromeda

Quarrying location: Brazil
Availability: Good
Compressive strength: 2080/kg cm^2
After freezing: 1990/kg cm^2
Ultimate tensile strength: 132/kg cm^2
Coef. thermal expansion: 0,0065mm/m°C
Water absorption: 0,40%
Impact test / min. fall height: –
Frictional wear test: –
Bulk density: 2620 kg/m^3

CD file number: 0281

Panama

Quarrying location: Brazil
Availability: Medium
Compressive strength: 2051/kg cm^2
After freezing: 1761/kg cm^2
Ultimate tensile strength: 116/kg cm^2
Coef. thermal expansion: 0,0062mm/m°C
Water absorption: 0,35%
Impact test / min. fall height: –
Frictional wear test: –
Bulk density: 2603 kg/m^3

CD file number: 0282

Panafragola

Quarrying location: Brazil
Availability: Medium
Compressive strength: 2051/kg cm^2
After freezing: 1761/kg cm^2
Ultimate tensile strength: 116/kg cm^2
Coef. thermal expansion: 0,0062mm/m°C
Water absorption: 0,35%
Impact test / min. fall height: –
Frictional wear test: –
Bulk density: 2603 kg/m^3

CD file number: 0283

Rosa Blanca

Quarrying location: Italy
Availability: Limited
Compressive strength: 1425/kg cm^2
After freezing: –
Ultimate tensile strength: 139/kg cm^2
Coef. thermal expansion: 0,0069mm/m°C
Water absorption: 0,27%
Impact test / min. fall height: 61 cm
Frictional wear test: 3,5 mm
Bulk density: 2603 kg/m^3

CD file number: 0284

Bianco Montorfano

Quarrying location: Spain
Availability: Good
Compressive strength: 1425/kg cm^2
After freezing: –
Ultimate tensile strength: 139/kg cm^2
Coef. thermal expansion: 0,0069mm/m°C
Water absorption: 0,27%
Impact test / min. fall height: 61 cm
Frictional wear test: 3,5 mm
Bulk density: 2603 kg/m^3

CD file number: 0285

Bianco Galizia

Quarrying location: Italy
Availability: Good
Compressive strength: 1533/kg cm^2
After freezing: 1556/kg cm^2
Ultimate tensile strength: 150/kg cm^2
Coef. thermal expansion: 0,0080mm/m°C
Water absorption: 0,47%
Impact test / min. fall height: 69 cm
Frictional wear test: –
Bulk density: 2623 kg/m^3

CD file number: 0286

Bianco Sardo

Quarrying location: Italy
Availability: Limited
Compressive strength: 1425/kg cm^2
After freezing: –
Ultimate tensile strength: 139/kg cm^2
Coef. thermal expansion: 0,0069mm/m°C
Water absorption: 0,27%
Impact test / min. fall height: 61 cm
Frictional wear test: 3,5 mm
Bulk density: 2603 kg/m^3

CD file number: 0287

Bianco Sardo Perla

Quarrying location: Spain
Availability: Good
Compressive strength: 1425/kg cm^2
After freezing: –
Ultimate tensile strength: 139/kg cm^2
Coef. thermal expansion: 0,0069mm/m°C
Water absorption: 0,27%
Impact test / min. fall height: 61 cm
Frictional wear test: 3,5 mm
Bulk density: 2603 kg/m^3

CD file number: 0288

Blanco Real

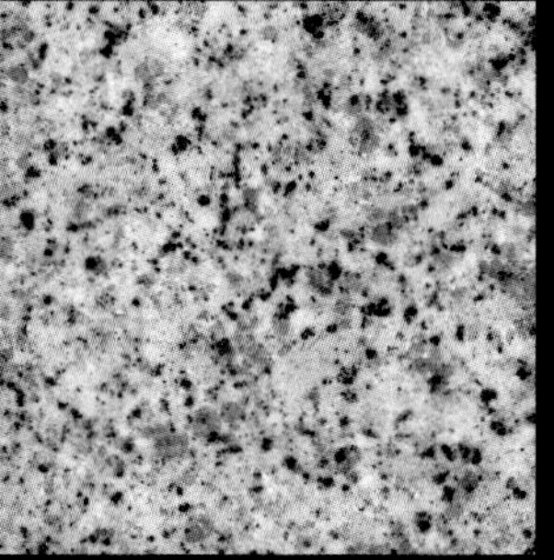

Blanco Berrocal

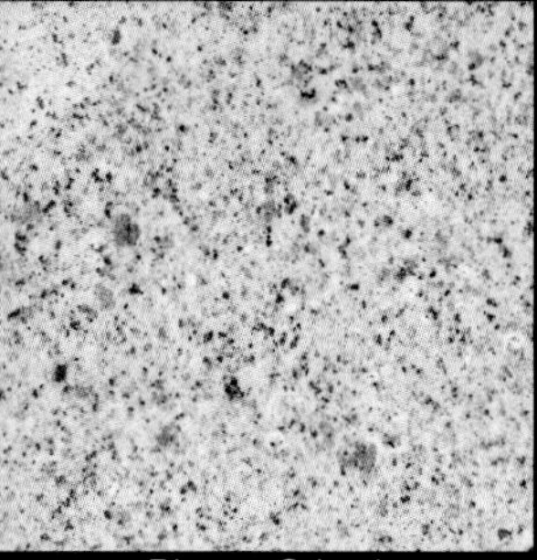

Blanco Cristal

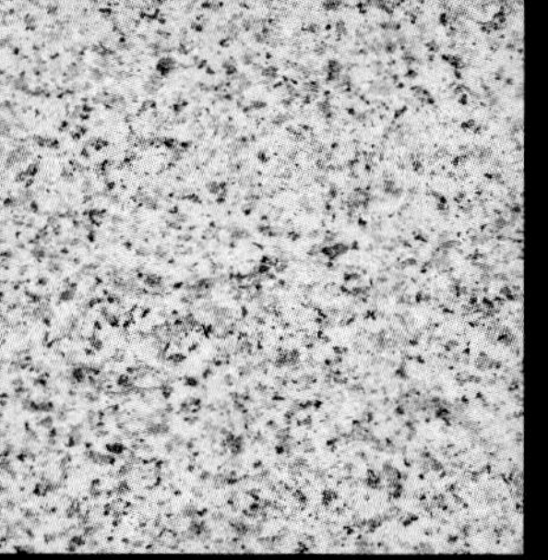

Blanco Cristal Extra

Bethel White

Imperial White

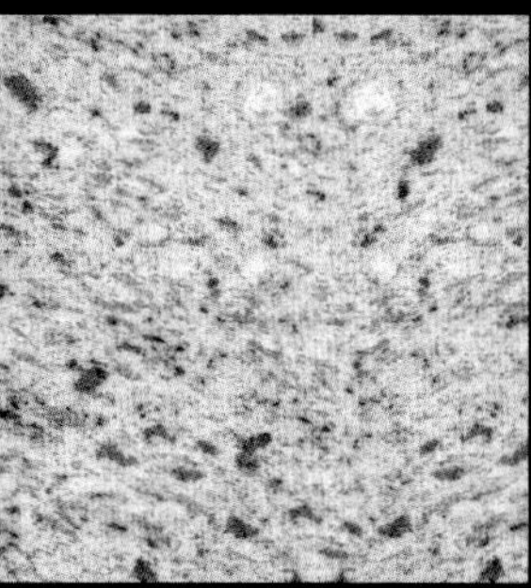

Galaxy White

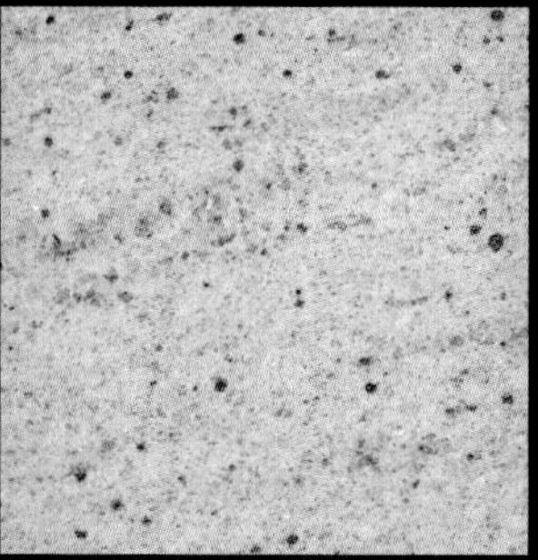

Kashmir White

White Andromeda

Panama

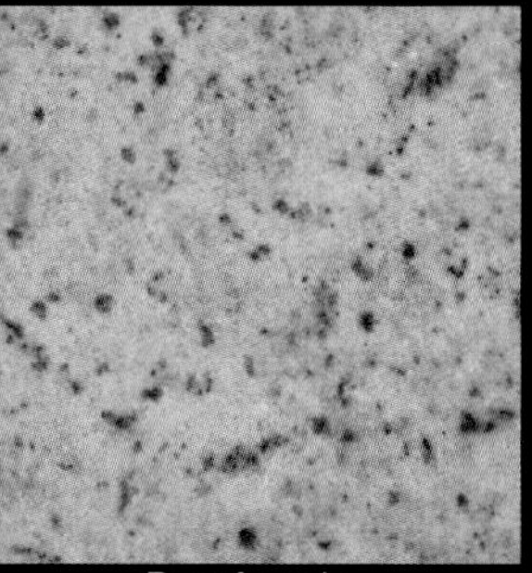

Panafragola

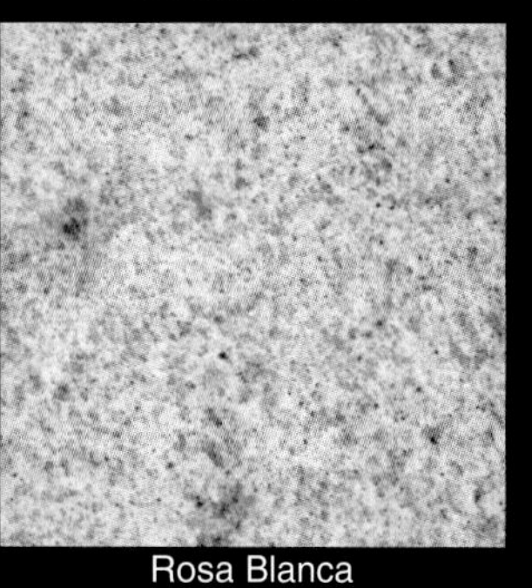

Rosa Blanca

Bianco Montorfano

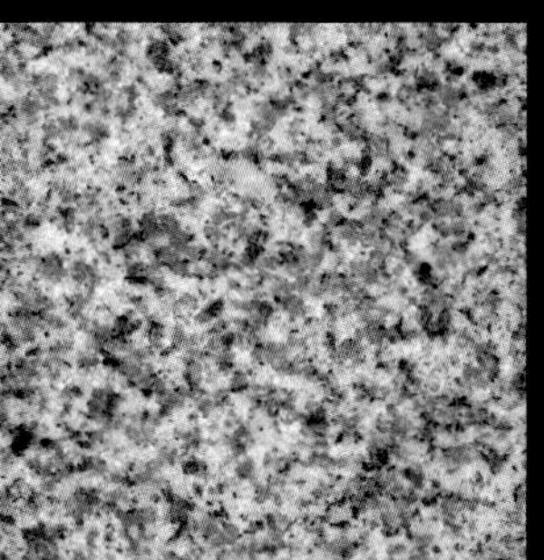

Bianco Galizia

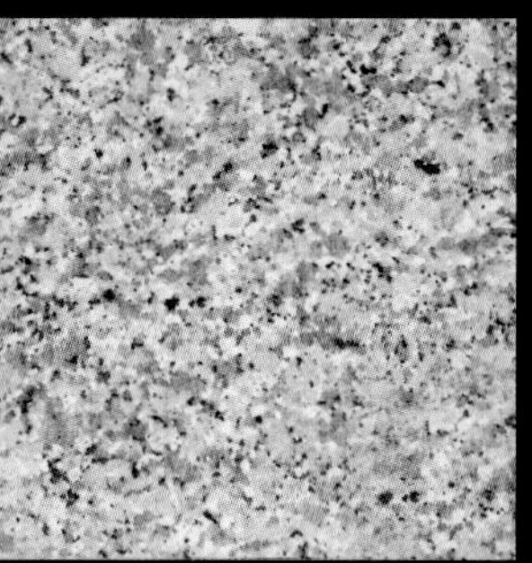

Bianco Sardo

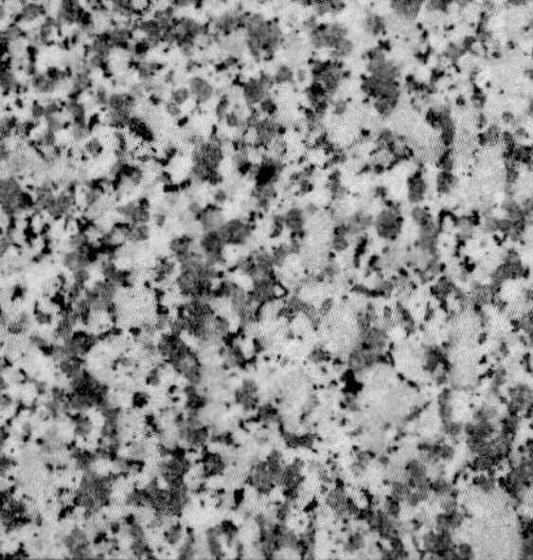

Bianco Sardo Perla

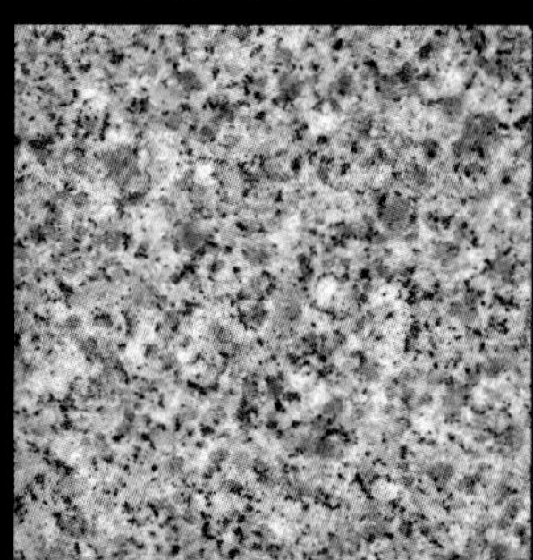

Blanco Real

Quarrying location:	USA
Availability:	Good
Compressive strength:	2051/kg cm^2
After freezing:	1761/kg cm^2
Ultimate tensile strength:	116/kg cm^2
Coef. thermal expansion:	0,0062mm/m°C
Water absorption:	0,35%
Impact test / min. fall height:	–
Frictional wear test:	–
Bulk density:	2603 kg/m^3

CD file number: 0289

Quarrying location:	India
Availability:	Medium
Compressive strength:	2080/kg cm^2
After freezing:	1990/kg cm^2
Ultimate tensile strength:	132/kg cm^2
Coef. thermal expansion:	0,0065mm/m°C
Water absorption:	0,40%
Impact test / min. fall height:	–
Frictional wear test:	–
Bulk density:	2620 kg/m^3

CD file number: 0290

Quarrying location:	USA
Availability:	Good
Compressive strength:	2080/kg cm^2
After freezing:	1990/kg cm^2
Ultimate tensile strength:	132/kg cm^2
Coef. thermal expansion:	0,0065mm/m°C
Water absorption:	0,40%
Impact test / min. fall height:	–
Frictional wear test:	–
Bulk density:	2620 kg/m^3

CD file number: 0291

Quarrying location:	Egypt
Availability:	Medium
Compressive strength:	2051/kg cm^2
After freezing:	1761/kg cm^2
Ultimate tensile strength:	116/kg cm^2
Coef. thermal expansion:	0,0062mm/m°C
Water absorption:	0,35%
Impact test / min. fall height:	–
Frictional wear test:	–
Bulk density:	2603 kg/m^3

CD file number: 0292

Solar White

Quarrying location:	Norway
Availability:	Medium
Compressive strength:	1425/kg cm^2
After freezing:	–
Ultimate tensile strength:	139/kg cm^2
Coef. thermal expansion:	0,0069mm/m°C
Water absorption:	0,27%
Impact test / min. fall height:	61 cm
Frictional wear test:	3,5 mm
Bulk density:	2603 kg/m^3

CD file number: 0293

Viscont White

Quarrying location:	Italy
Availability:	Medium
Compressive strength:	1720/kg cm^2
After freezing:	1664/kg cm^2
Ultimate tensile strength:	139/kg cm^2
Coef. thermal expansion:	0,0050mm/m°C
Water absorption:	0,32%
Impact test / min. fall height:	86 cm
Frictional wear test:	–
Bulk density:	2661 kg/m^3

CD file number: 0294

Silver Cloud

Quarrying location:	Italy
Availability:	Medium
Compressive strength:	1720/kg cm^2
After freezing:	1664/kg cm^2
Ultimate tensile strength:	139/kg cm^2
Coef. thermal expansion:	0,0050mm/m°C
Water absorption:	0,32%
Impact test / min. fall height:	86 cm
Frictional wear test:	–
Bulk density:	2661 kg/m^3

CD file number: 0295

Bianco Halayeb

Quarrying location:	Italy
Availability:	Medium
Compressive strength:	1720/kg cm^2
After freezing:	1664/kg cm^2
Ultimate tensile strength:	139/kg cm^2
Coef. thermal expansion:	0,0050mm/m°C
Water absorption:	0,32%
Impact test / min. fall height:	86 cm
Frictional wear test:	–
Bulk density:	2661 kg/m^3

CD file number: 0296

Tolga White

Quarrying location:	France
Availability:	Medium
Compressive strength:	911/kg cm^2
After freezing:	–
Ultimate tensile strength:	101/kg cm^2
Coef. thermal expansion:	–
Water absorption:	1,00 %
Impact test / min. fall height:	135 cm
Frictional wear test:	–
Bulk density:	2550 kg/m^3

CD file number: 0297

Beola Bianca

Quarrying location:	France
Availability:	Medium
Compressive strength:	911/kg cm^2
After freezing:	–
Ultimate tensile strength:	101/kg cm^2
Coef. thermal expansion:	–
Water absorption:	1,00 %
Impact test / min. fall height:	135 cm
Frictional wear test:	–
Bulk density:	2550 kg/m^3

CD file number: 0298

Beola Ghiandonata

Quarrying location:	Italy
Availability:	Good
Compressive strength:	1533/kg cm^2
After freezing:	1556/kg cm^2
Ultimate tensile strength:	150/kg cm^2
Coef. thermal expansion:	0,0080mm/m°C
Water absorption:	0,47%
Impact test / min. fall height:	69 cm
Frictional wear test:	–
Bulk density:	2623 kg/m^3

CD file number: 0299

Beola Grigia

Quarrying location:	Spain
Availability:	Good
Compressive strength:	1533/kg cm^2
After freezing:	1556/kg cm^2
Ultimate tensile strength:	150/kg cm^2
Coef. thermal expansion:	0,0080mm/m°C
Water absorption:	0,47%
Impact test / min. fall height:	69 cm
Frictional wear test:	–
Bulk density:	2623 kg/m^3

CD file number: 0300

Grigio Tarn Chiaro

Quarrying location:	India
Availability:	Medium
Compressive strength:	911/kg cm^2
After freezing:	–
Ultimate tensile strength:	101/kg cm^2
Coef. thermal expansion:	–
Water absorption:	1,00 %
Impact test / min. fall height:	135 cm
Frictional wear test:	–
Bulk density:	2550 kg/m^3

CD file number: 0301

Grigio Tarn Scuro

Quarrying location:	USA
Availability:	Medium
Compressive strength:	911/kg cm^2
After freezing:	–
Ultimate tensile strength:	101/kg cm^2
Coef. thermal expansion:	–
Water absorption:	1,00 %
Impact test / min. fall height:	135 cm
Frictional wear test:	–
Bulk density:	2550 kg/m^3

CD file number: 0302

Grigio Malaga

Quarrying location:	Spain
Availability:	Good
Compressive strength:	1533/kg cm^2
After freezing:	1556/kg cm^2
Ultimate tensile strength:	150/kg cm^2
Coef. thermal expansion:	0,0080mm/m°C
Water absorption:	0,47%
Impact test / min. fall height:	69 cm
Frictional wear test:	–
Bulk density:	2623 kg/m^3

CD file number: 0303

Gris Perla

Quarrying location:	Spain
Availability:	Good
Compressive strength:	1533/kg cm^2
After freezing:	1556/kg cm^2
Ultimate tensile strength:	150/kg cm^2
Coef. thermal expansion:	0,0080mm/m°C
Water absorption:	0,47%
Impact test / min. fall height:	69 cm
Frictional wear test:	–
Bulk density:	2623 kg/m^3

CD file number: 03041

Tapestry

Duke White

Cinzala

Cinzia Grey

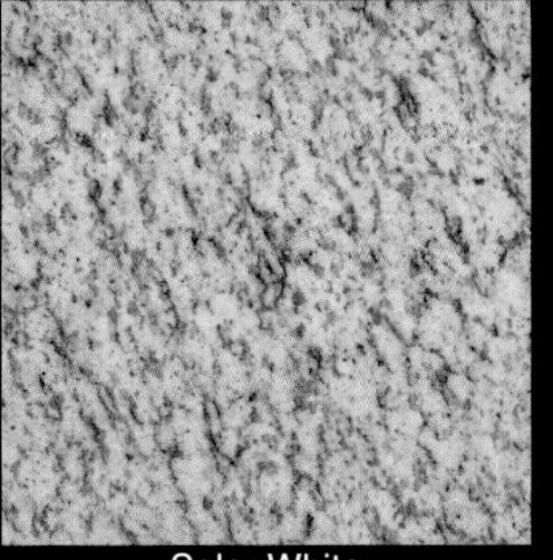
Solar White

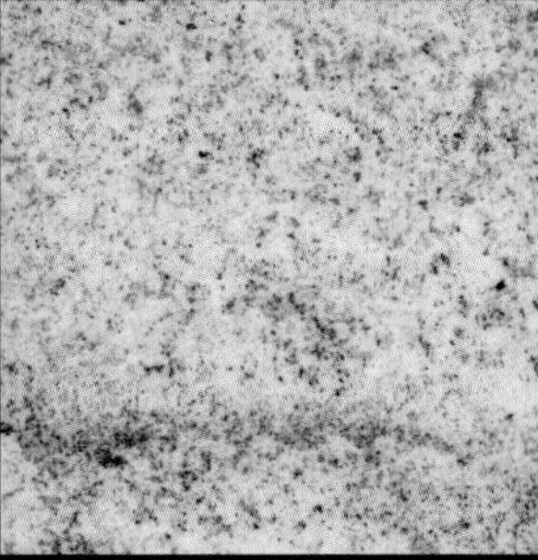
Viscont White

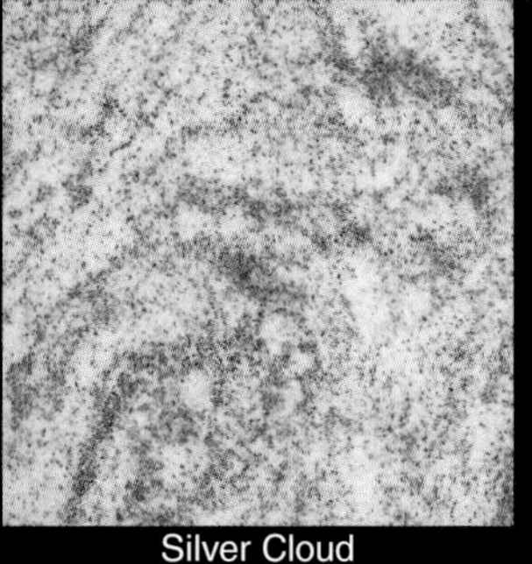
Silver Cloud

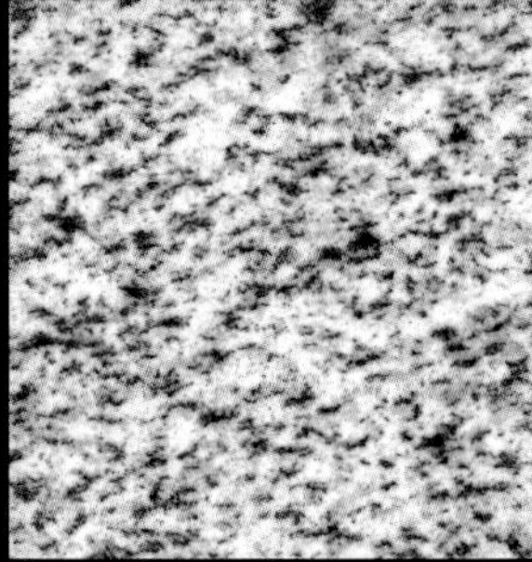
Bianco Halayeb

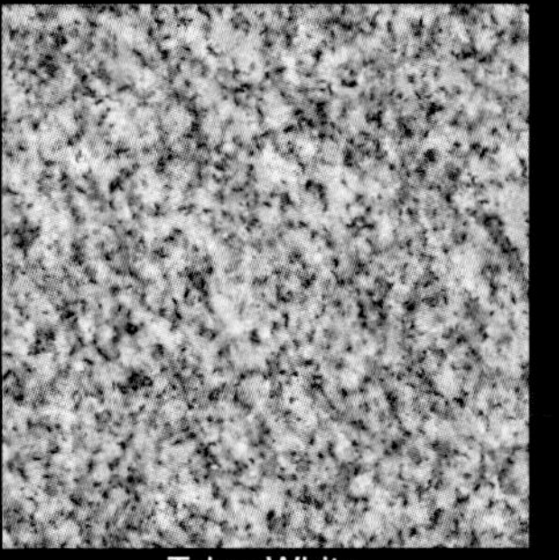
Tolga White

Beola Bianca

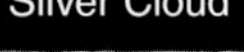
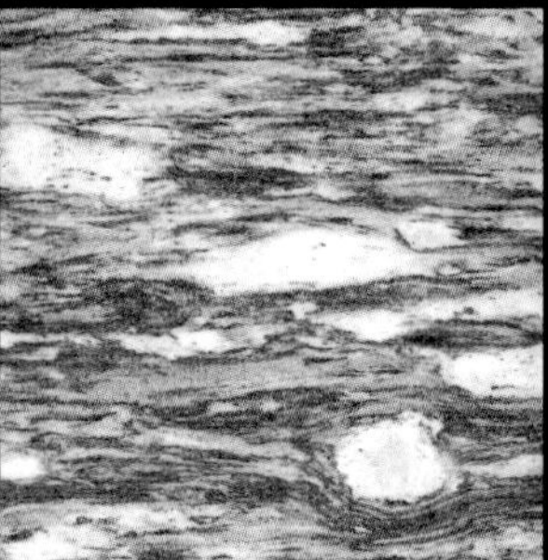
Beola Ghiandonata

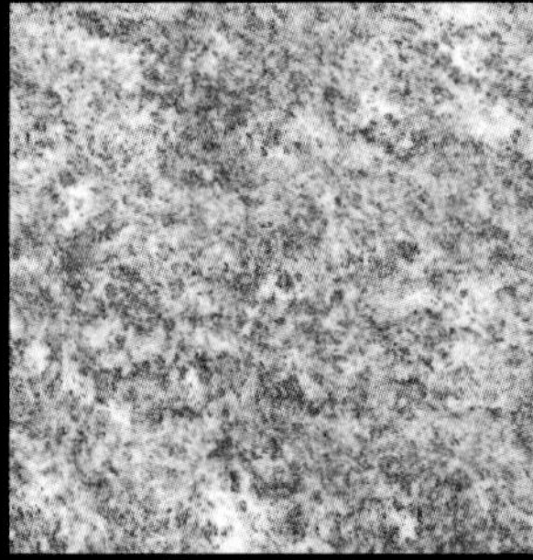
Beola Grigia

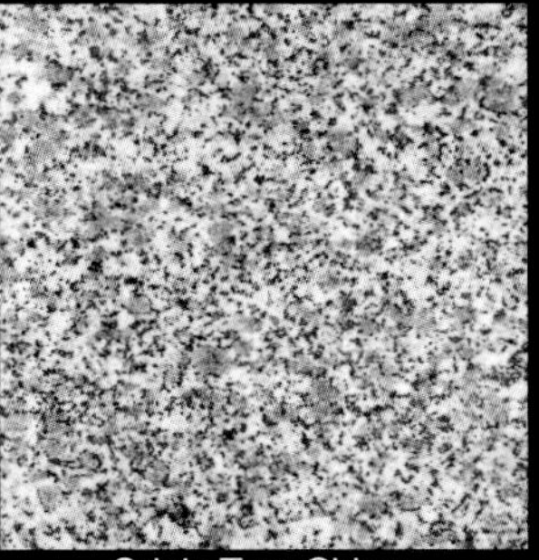
Grigio Tarn Chiaro

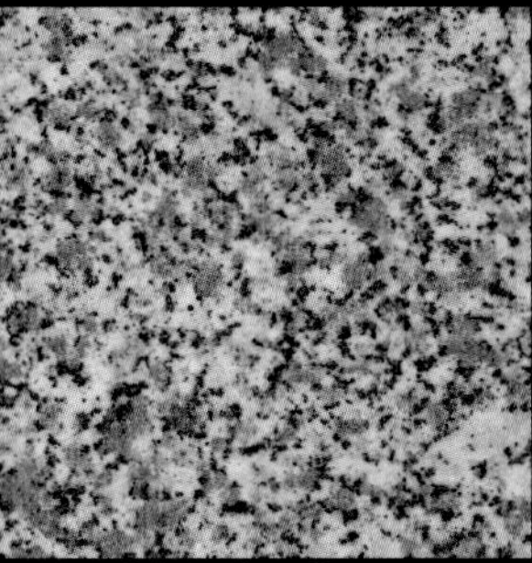
Grigio Tarn Scuro

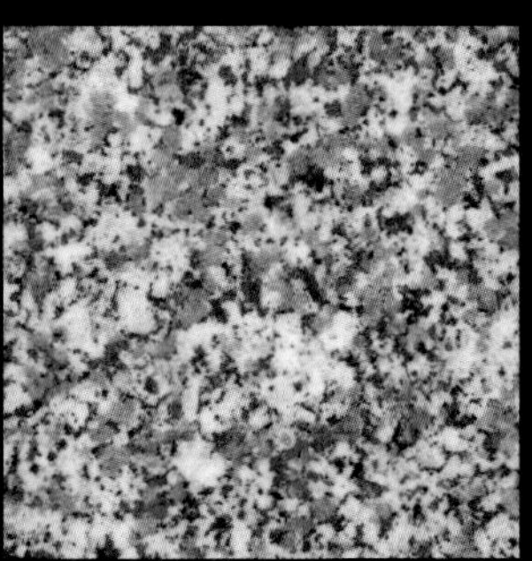
Grigio Malaga

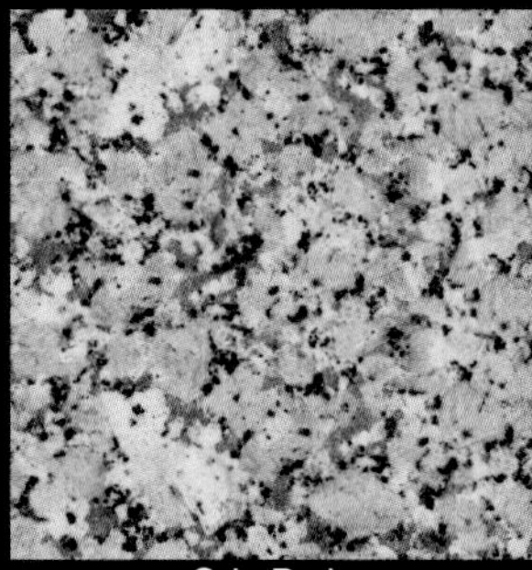
Gris Perla

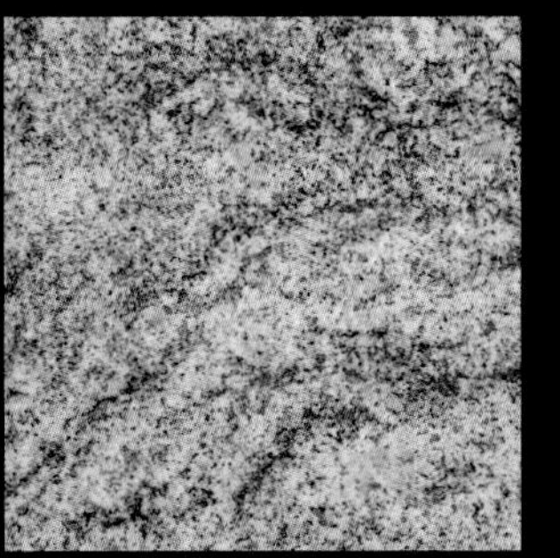
Tapestry

Duke White

Cinzala

Cinzia Grey

Quarrying location: Italy
Availability: Medium
Compressive strength: 1720/kg cm^2
After freezing: 1664/kg cm^2
Ultimate tensile strength: 139/kg cm^2
Coef. thermal expansion: 0,0050mm/m°C
Water absorption: 0,32%
Impact test / min. fall height: 86 cm
Frictional wear test: –
Bulk density: 2661 kg/m^3

CD file number: 0305

Quarrying location: Italy
Availability: Medium
Compressive strength: 1720/kg cm^2
After freezing: 1664/kg cm^2
Ultimate tensile strength: 139/kg cm^2
Coef. thermal expansion: 0,0050mm/m°C
Water absorption: 0,32%
Impact test / min. fall height: 86 cm
Frictional wear test: –
Bulk density: 2661 kg/m^3

CD file number: 0306

Quarrying location: Italy
Availability: Medium
Compressive strength: 1720/kg cm^2
After freezing: 1664/kg cm^2
Ultimate tensile strength: 139/kg cm^2
Coef. thermal expansion: 0,0050mm/m°C
Water absorption: 0,32%
Impact test / min. fall height: 86 cm
Frictional wear test: –
Bulk density: 2661 kg/m^3

CD file number: 0307

Quarrying location: Italy
Availability: Medium
Compressive strength: 1720/kg cm^2
After freezing: 1664/kg cm^2
Ultimate tensile strength: 139/kg cm^2
Coef. thermal expansion: 0,0050mm/m°C
Water absorption: 0,32%
Impact test / min. fall height: 86 cm
Frictional wear test: –
Bulk density: 2661 kg/m^3

CD file number: 0308

Serizzo

Serizzo Formazza

Serizzo Ghiandone

Serizzo Scuro Valmassino

Quarrying location: Spain
Availability: Medium
Compressive strength: 911/kg cm^2
After freezing: –
Ultimate tensile strength: 101/kg cm^2
Coef. thermal expansion: –
Water absorption: 1,00 %
Impact test / min. fall height: 135 cm
Frictional wear test: –
Bulk density: 2550 kg/m^3

CD file number: 0309

Quarrying location: Spain
Availability: Medium
Compressive strength: 911/kg cm^2
After freezing: –
Ultimate tensile strength: 101/kg cm^2
Coef. thermal expansion: –
Water absorption: 1,00 %
Impact test / min. fall height: 135 cm
Frictional wear test: –
Bulk density: 2550 kg/m^3

CD file number: 0310

Quarrying location: South Africa
Availability: Good
Compressive strength: 2080/kg cm^2
After freezing: 1990/kg cm^2
Ultimate tensile strength: 132/kg cm^2
Coef. thermal expansion: 0,0065mm/m°C
Water absorption: 0,40%
Impact test / min. fall height: –
Frictional wear test: –
Bulk density: 2620 kg/m^3

CD file number: 0311

Quarrying location: India
Availability: Medium
Compressive strength: 2080/kg cm^2
After freezing: 1990/kg cm^2
Ultimate tensile strength: 132/kg cm^2
Coef. thermal expansion: 0,0065mm/m°C
Water absorption: 0,40%
Impact test / min. fall height: –
Frictional wear test: –
Bulk density: 2620 kg/m^3

CD file number: 0312

Azul Aran

Azul Platina

Eidelweiss

Kuru Grey

Quarrying location: Brazil
Availability: Medium
Compressive strength: 2051/kg cm^2
After freezing: 1761/kg cm^2
Ultimate tensile strength: 116/kg cm^2
Coef. thermal expansion: 0,0062mm/m°C
Water absorption: 0,35%
Impact test / min. fall height: –
Frictional wear test: –
Bulk density: 2603 kg/m^3

CD file number: 0313

Quarrying location: Brazil
Availability: Medium
Compressive strength: 2080/kg cm^2
After freezing: 1990/kg cm^2
Ultimate tensile strength: 132/kg cm^2
Coef. thermal expansion: 0,0065mm/m°C
Water absorption: 0,40%
Impact test / min. fall height: –
Frictional wear test: –
Bulk density: 2620 kg/m^3

CD file number: 0314

Quarrying location: Spain
Availability: Good
Compressive strength: 1533/kg cm^2
After freezing: 1556/kg cm^2
Ultimate tensile strength: 150/kg cm^2
Coef. thermal expansion: 0,0080mm/m°C
Water absorption: 0,47%
Impact test / min. fall height: 69 cm
Frictional wear test: –
Bulk density: 2623 kg/m^3

CD file number: 0315

Quarrying location: India
Availability: Medium
Compressive strength: 2080/kg cm^2
After freezing: 1990/kg cm^2
Ultimate tensile strength: 132/kg cm^2
Coef. thermal expansion: 0,0065mm/m°C
Water absorption: 0,40%
Impact test / min. fall height: –
Frictional wear test: –
Bulk density: 2620 kg/m^3

CD file number: 0316

Cream Violet

Bianco Piracena

Astir

Diamond White

Quarrying location: Italy
Availability: Medium
Compressive strength: 1720/kg cm^2
After freezing: 1664/kg cm^2
Ultimate tensile strength: 139/kg cm^2
Coef. thermal expansion: 0,0050mm/m°C
Water absorption: 0,32%
Impact test / min. fall height: 86 cm
Frictional wear test: –
Bulk density: 2661 kg/m^3

CD file number: 0317

Quarrying location: China
Availability: Medium
Compressive strength: 1533/kg cm^2
After freezing: 1556/kg cm^2
Ultimate tensile strength: 150/kg cm^2
Coef. thermal expansion: 0,0080mm/m°C
Water absorption: 0,47%
Impact test / min. fall height: 69 cm
Frictional wear test: –
Bulk density: 2623 kg/m^3

CD file number: 0318

Quarrying location: China
Availability: Medium
Compressive strength: 1533/kg cm^2
After freezing: 1556/kg cm^2
Ultimate tensile strength: 150/kg cm^2
Coef. thermal expansion: 0,0080mm/m°C
Water absorption: 0,47%
Impact test / min. fall height: 69 cm
Frictional wear test: –
Bulk density: 2623 kg/m^3

CD file number: 0319

Quarrying location: Spain
Availability: Good
Compressive strength: 1533/kg cm^2
After freezing: 1556/kg cm^2
Ultimate tensile strength: 150/kg cm^2
Coef. thermal expansion: 0,0080mm/m°C
Water absorption: 0,47%
Impact test / min. fall height: 69 cm
Frictional wear test: –
Bulk density: 2623 kg/m^3

CD file number: 0320

Monterosa

Padang TG33

Padang TG34

Gris Perlado

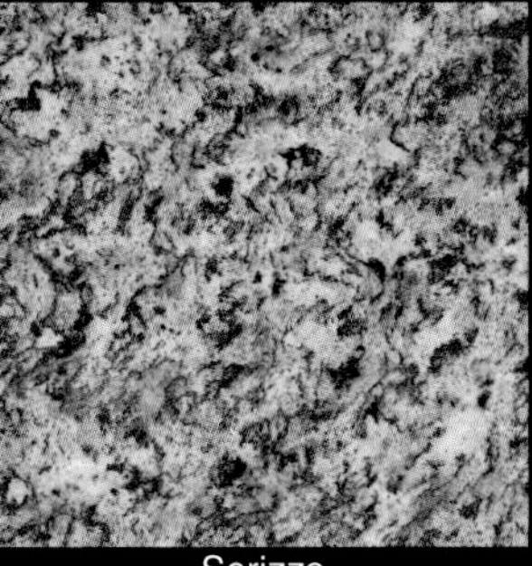
Serizzo

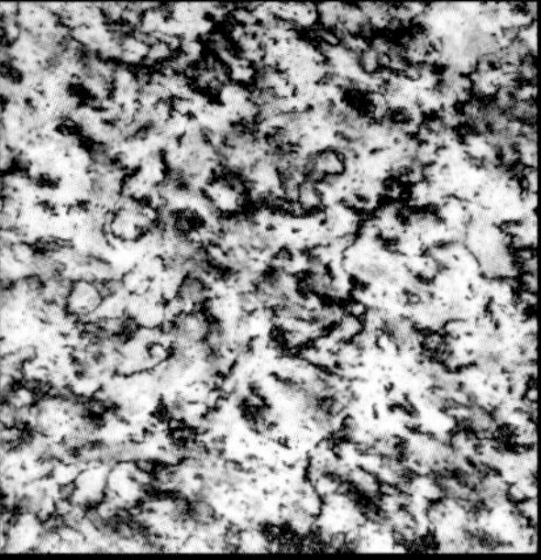
Serizzo Formazza

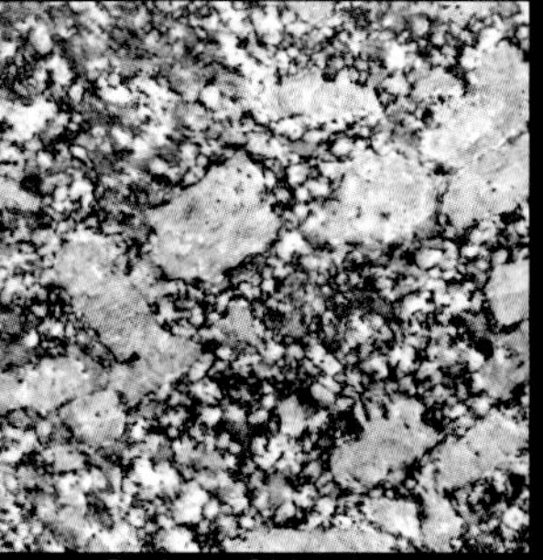
Serizzo Ghiandone

Serizzo Scuro Valmassino

Azul Aran

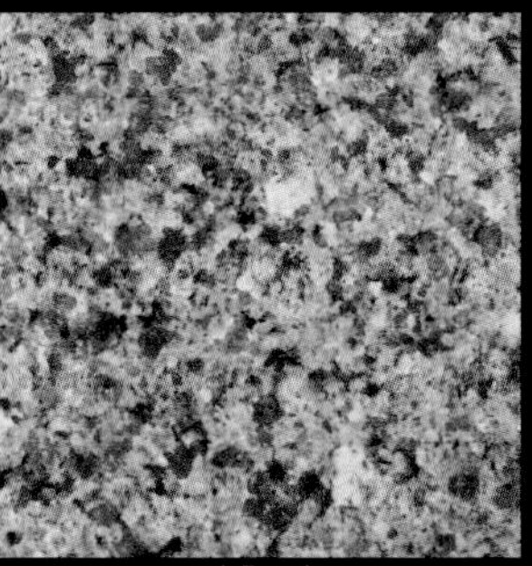
Azul Platina

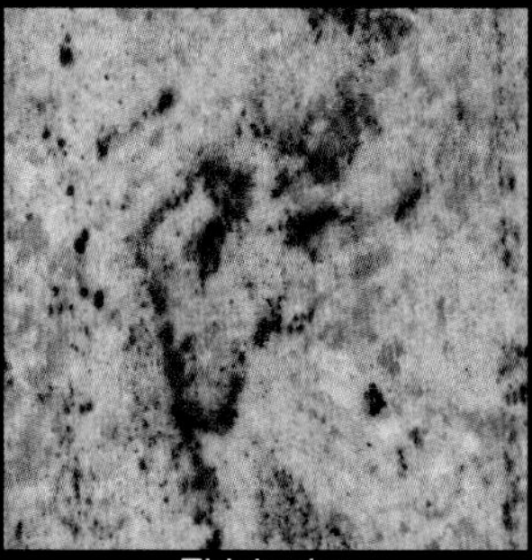
Eidelweiss

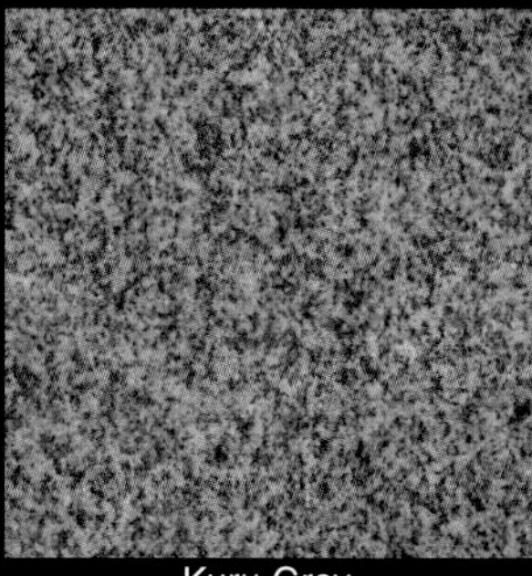
Kuru Grey

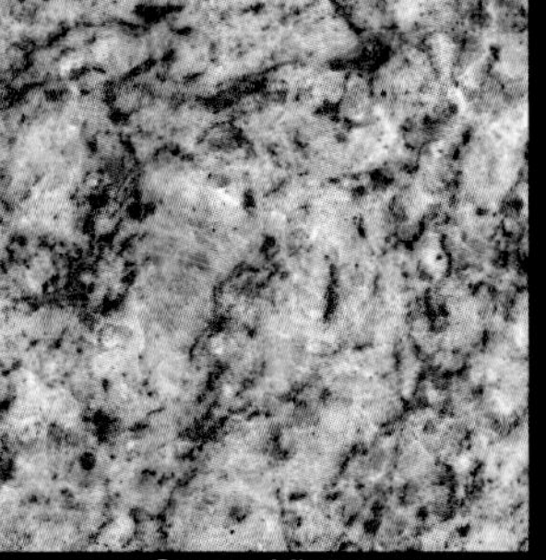
Cream Violet

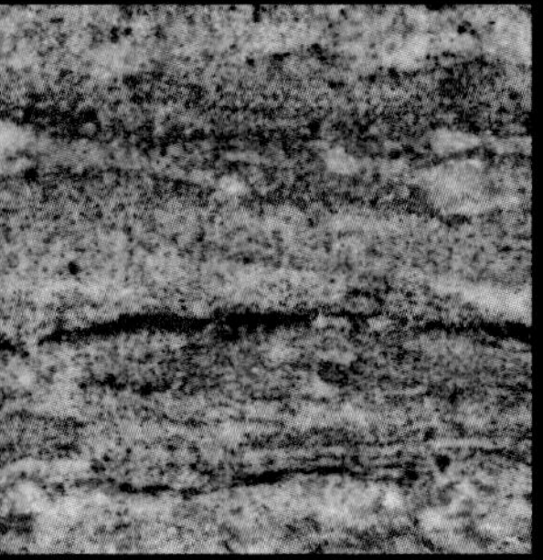
Bianco Piracena

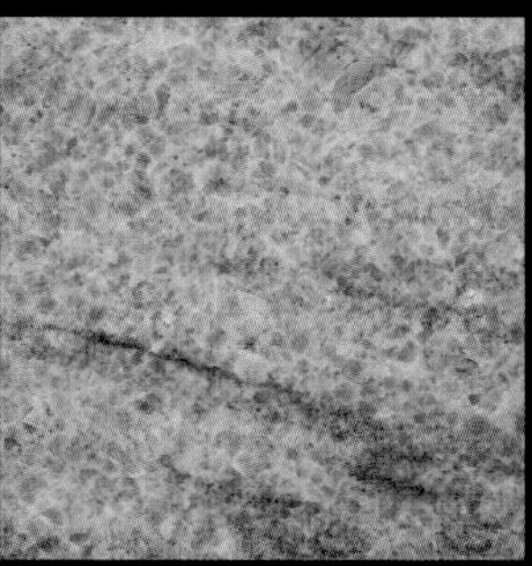

Astir

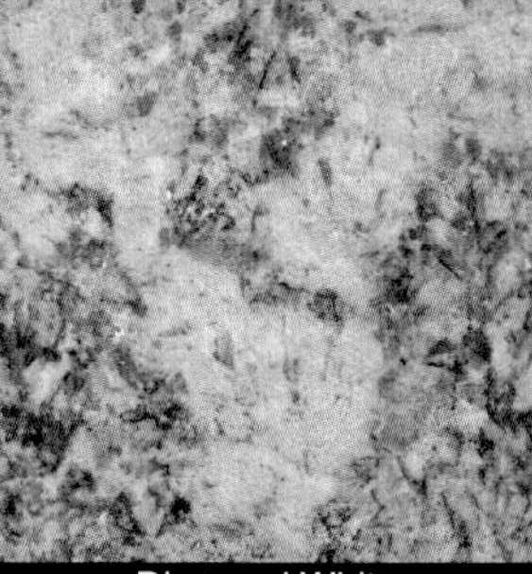
Diamond White

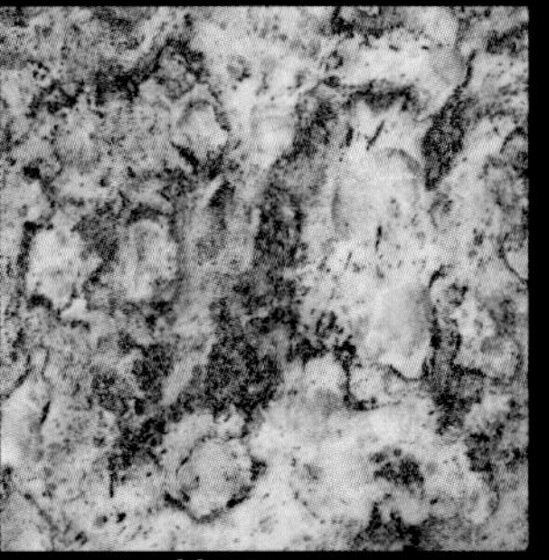
Monterosa

Padang TG33

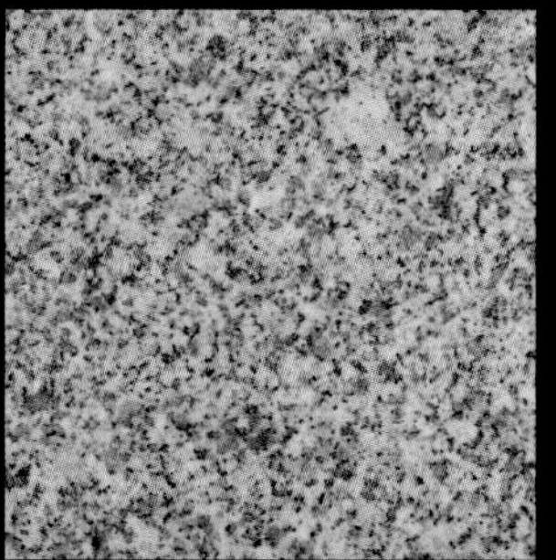
Padang TG34

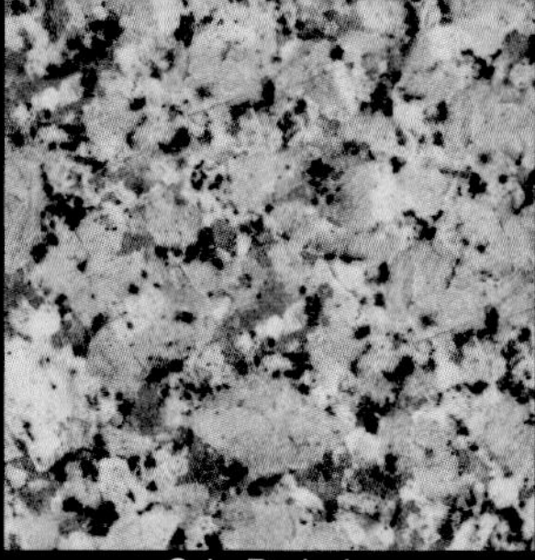
Gris Perlado

Quarrying location: Brazil
Availability: Limited
Compressive strength: 1514/kg cm^2
After freezing: 1450/kg cm^2
Ultimate tensile strength: 93/kg cm^2
Coef. thermal expansion: 0,0076mm/m°C
Water absorption: 0,18%
Impact test / min. fall height: –
Frictional wear test: –
Bulk density: 2566 kg/m^3

CD file number: 0321

Quarrying location: Brazil
Availability: Limited
Compressive strength: 1514/kg cm^2
After freezing: 1450/kg cm^2
Ultimate tensile strength: 93/kg cm^2
Coef. thermal expansion: 0,0076mm/m°C
Water absorption: 0,18%
Impact test / min. fall height: –
Frictional wear test: –
Bulk density: 2566 kg/m^3

CD file number: 0322

Quarrying location: Brazil
Availability: Limited
Compressive strength: 1514/kg cm^2
After freezing: 1450/kg cm^2
Ultimate tensile strength: 93/kg cm^2
Coef. thermal expansion: 0,0076mm/m°C
Water absorption: 0,18%
Impact test / min. fall height: –
Frictional wear test: –
Bulk density: 2566 kg/m^3

CD file number: 0323

Quarrying location: Brazil
Availability: Medium
Compressive strength: 1578/kg cm^2
After freezing: 1599/kg cm^2
Ultimate tensile strength: 104/kg cm^2
Coef. thermal expansion: 0,0013mm/m°C
Water absorption: 0,38 %
Impact test / min. fall height: 41 cm
Frictional wear test: –
Bulk density: 2682 kg/m^3

CD file number: 0324

Juparana

Quarrying location: Brazil
Availability: Medium
Compressive strength: 1578/kg cm^2
After freezing: 1599/kg cm^2
Ultimate tensile strength: 104/kg cm^2
Coef. thermal expansion: 0,0013mm/m°C
Water absorption: 0,38 %
Impact test / min. fall height: 41 cm
Frictional wear test: –
Bulk density: 2682 kg/m^3

CD file number: 0325

Juparana Giallo Veneziano

Quarrying location: India
Availability: Medium
Compressive strength: 1578/kg cm^2
After freezing: 1599/kg cm^2
Ultimate tensile strength: 104/kg cm^2
Coef. thermal expansion: 0,0013mm/m°C
Water absorption: 0,38 %
Impact test / min. fall height: 41 cm
Frictional wear test: –
Bulk density: 2682 kg/m^3

CD file number: 0326

Juparana Giallo Veneziano Gold

Quarrying location: Brazil
Availability: Medium
Compressive strength: 1578/kg cm^2
After freezing: 1599/kg cm^2
Ultimate tensile strength: 104/kg cm^2
Coef. thermal expansion: 0,0013mm/m°C
Water absorption: 0,38 %
Impact test / min. fall height: 41 cm
Frictional wear test: –
Bulk density: 2682 kg/m^3

CD file number: 0327

Juparana Santa Cecilia

Quarrying location: Brazil
Availability: Medium
Compressive strength: 1578/kg cm^2
After freezing: 1599/kg cm^2
Ultimate tensile strength: 104/kg cm^2
Coef. thermal expansion: 0,0013mm/m°C
Water absorption: 0,38 %
Impact test / min. fall height: 41 cm
Frictional wear test: –
Bulk density: 2682 kg/m^3

CD file number: 0328

Juparana Diadema

Quarrying location: Brazil
Availability: Limited
Compressive strength: 1514/kg cm^2
After freezing: 1450/kg cm^2
Ultimate tensile strength: 93/kg cm^2
Coef. thermal expansion: 0,0076mm/m°C
Water absorption: 0,18%
Impact test / min. fall height: –
Frictional wear test: –
Bulk density: 2566 kg/m^3

CD file number: 0329

Juparana Golden Vyara

Quarrying location: India
Availability: Medium
Compressive strength: 1578/kg cm^2
After freezing: 1599/kg cm^2
Ultimate tensile strength: 104/kg cm^2
Coef. thermal expansion: 0,0013mm/m°C
Water absorption: 0,38 %
Impact test / min. fall height: 41 cm
Frictional wear test: –
Bulk density: 2682 kg/m^3

CD file number: 0330

Juparana Fantastico

Quarrying location: Brazil
Availability: Limited
Compressive strength: 1514/kg cm^2
After freezing: 1450/kg cm^2
Ultimate tensile strength: 93/kg cm^2
Coef. thermal expansion: 0,0076mm/m°C
Water absorption: 0,18%
Impact test / min. fall height: –
Frictional wear test: –
Bulk density: 2566 kg/m^3

CD file number: 0331

Juparana California

Quarrying location: India
Availability: Medium
Compressive strength: 1578/kg cm^2
After freezing: 1599/kg cm^2
Ultimate tensile strength: 104/kg cm^2
Coef. thermal expansion: 0,0013mm/m°C
Water absorption: 0,38 %
Impact test / min. fall height: 41 cm
Frictional wear test: –
Bulk density: 2682 kg/m^3

CD file number: 0332

Juparana Classico

Quarrying location: Brazil
Availability: Limited
Compressive strength: 1514/kg cm^2
After freezing: 1450/kg cm^2
Ultimate tensile strength: 93/kg cm^2
Coef. thermal expansion: 0,0076mm/m°C
Water absorption: 0,18%
Impact test / min. fall height: –
Frictional wear test: –
Bulk density: 2566 kg/m^3

CD file number: 0333

Juparana Colombo

Quarrying location: India
Availability: Medium
Compressive strength: 1578/kg cm^2
After freezing: 1599/kg cm^2
Ultimate tensile strength: 104/kg cm^2
Coef. thermal expansion: 0,0013mm/m°C
Water absorption: 0,38 %
Impact test / min. fall height: 41 cm
Frictional wear test: –
Bulk density: 2682 kg/m^3

CD file number: 0334

Juparana Champagne

Quarrying location: India
Availability: Medium
Compressive strength: 1578/kg cm^2
After freezing: 1599/kg cm^2
Ultimate tensile strength: 104/kg cm^2
Coef. thermal expansion: 0,0013mm/m°C
Water absorption: 0,38 %
Impact test / min. fall height: 41 cm
Frictional wear test: –
Bulk density: 2682 kg/m^3

CD file number: 0335

Ivory Brown

Quarrying location: India
Availability: Medium
Compressive strength: 1578/kg cm^2
After freezing: 1599/kg cm^2
Ultimate tensile strength: 104/kg cm^2
Coef. thermal expansion: 0,0013mm/m°C
Water absorption: 0,38 %
Impact test / min. fall height: 41 cm
Frictional wear test: –
Bulk density: 2682 kg/m^3

CD file number: 0336

Amendoa

Golden Beach

Golden Oak

Golden Moon

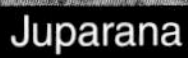
Juparana

Juparana Giallo Veneziano

Juparana Giallo Veneziano Gold

Juparana Santa Cecilia

Juparana Diadema

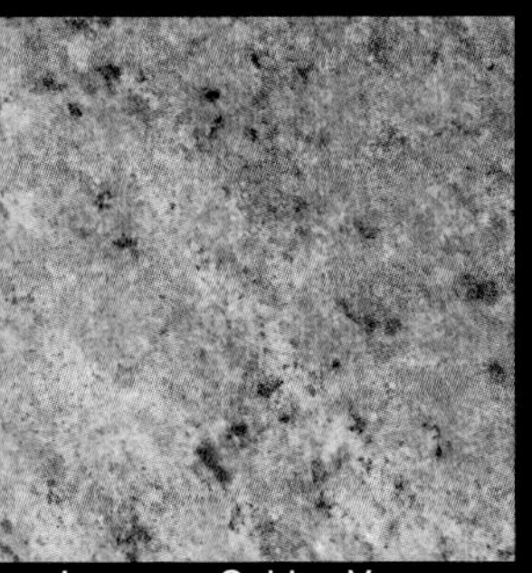
Juparana Golden Vyara

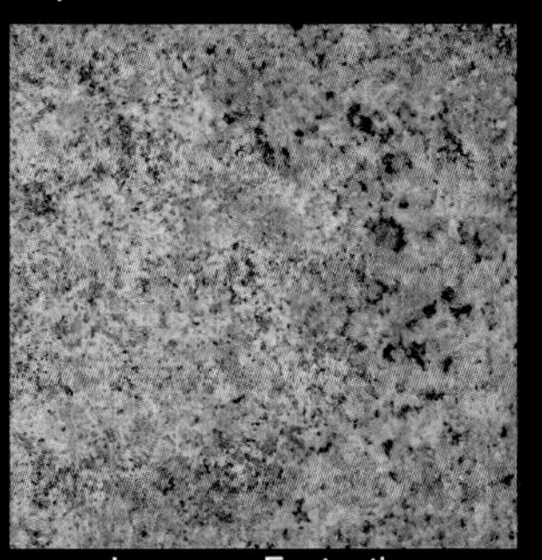
Juparana Fantastico

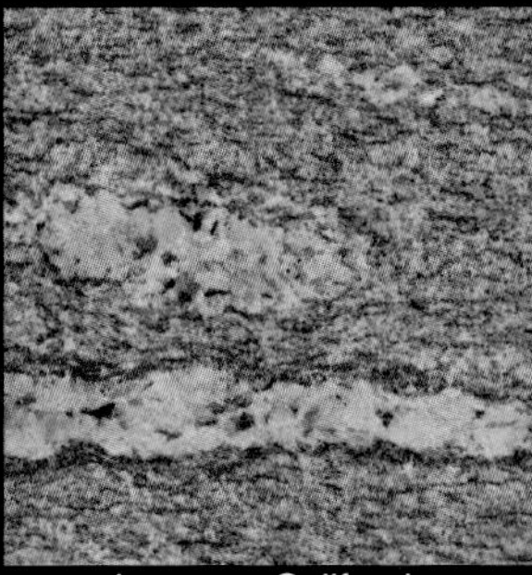
Juparana California

Juparana Classico

Juparana Colombo

Juparana Champagne

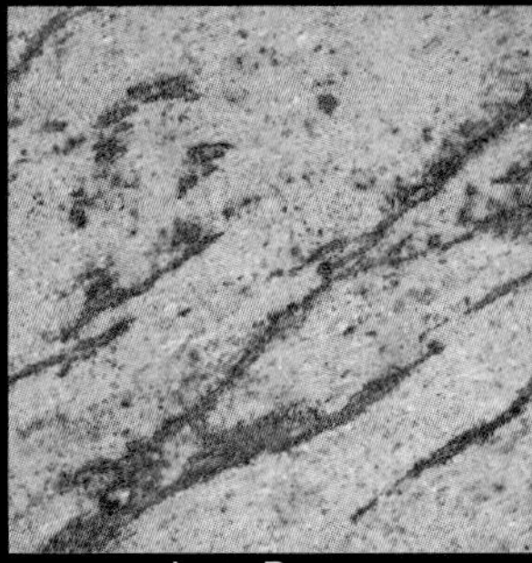
Ivory Brown

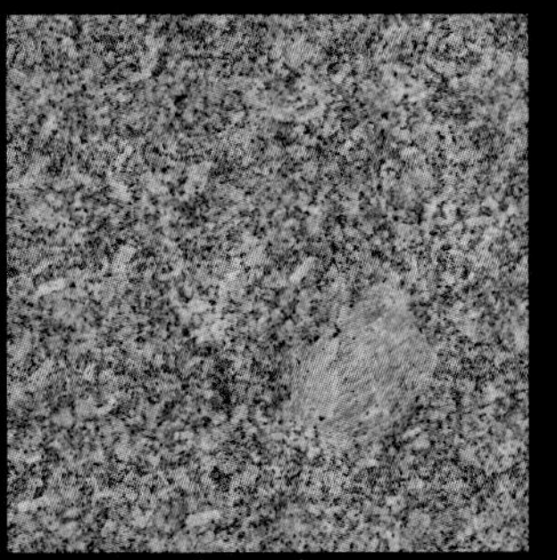
Amendoa

Golden Beach

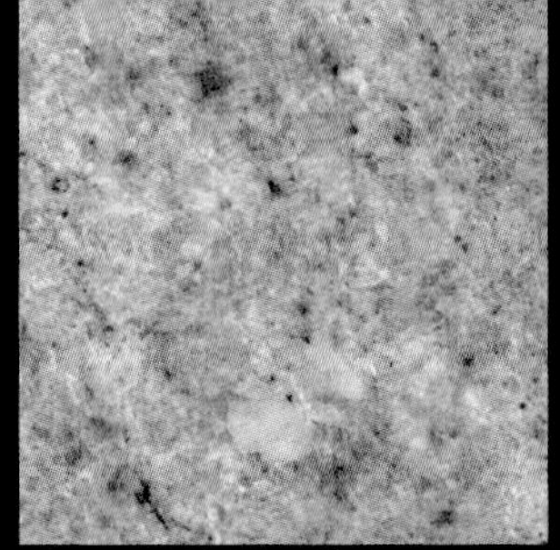
Golden Oak

Golden Moon

Availability: Medium
Compressive strength: 1514/kg cm^2
After freezing: 1450/kg cm^2
Ultimate tensile strength: 93/kg cm^2
Coef. thermal expansion: 0,0076mm/m°C
Water absorption: 0,18%
Impact test / min. fall height: –
Frictional wear test: –
Bulk density: 2566 kg/m^3

CD file number: 0337

Availability: Medium
Compressive strength: 1578/kg cm^2
After freezing: 1599/kg cm^2
Ultimate tensile strength: 104/kg cm^2
Coef. thermal expansion: 0,0013mm/m°C
Water absorption: 0,38 %
Impact test / min. fall height: 41 cm
Frictional wear test: –
Bulk density: 2682 kg/m^3

CD file number: 0338

Availability: Limited
Compressive strength: 1514/kg cm^2
After freezing: 1450/kg cm^2
Ultimate tensile strength: 93/kg cm^2
Coef. thermal expansion: 0,0076mm/m°C
Water absorption: 0,18%
Impact test / min. fall height: –
Frictional wear test: –
Bulk density: 2566 kg/m^3

CD file number: 0339

Availability: Limitec
Compressive strength: 1136/kg cm
After freezing: 1078/kg cm
Ultimate tensile strength: 96/kg cm
Coef. thermal expansion: 0,0085mm/m°C
Water absorption: 0,35%
Impact test / min. fall height: –
Frictional wear test: –
Bulk density: 2621 kg/m

CD file number: 0340

Giallo Duna

Quarrying location: Brazil
Availability: Limited
Compressive strength: 1514/kg cm^2
After freezing: 1450/kg cm^2
Ultimate tensile strength: 93/kg cm^2
Coef. thermal expansion: 0,0076mm/m°C
Water absorption: 0,18%
Impact test / min. fall height: –
Frictional wear test: –
Bulk density: 2566 kg/m^3

CD file number: 0341

Giallo Topazio

Quarrying location: India
Availability: Medium
Compressive strength: 1578/kg cm^2
After freezing: 1599/kg cm^2
Ultimate tensile strength: 104/kg cm^2
Coef. thermal expansion: 0,0013mm/m°C
Water absorption: 0,38 %
Impact test / min. fall height: 41 cm
Frictional wear test: –
Bulk density: 2682 kg/m^3

CD file number: 0342

Giallo Partenon

Quarrying location: Brazil
Availability: Medium
Compressive strength: 1578/kg cm^2
After freezing: 1599/kg cm^2
Ultimate tensile strength: 104/kg cm^2
Coef. thermal expansion: 0,0013mm/m°C
Water absorption: 0,38 %
Impact test / min. fall height: 41 cm
Frictional wear test: –
Bulk density: 2682 kg/m^3

CD file number: 0343

Giallo Antico

Quarrying location: Brazi
Availability: Mediun
Compressive strength: 1578/kg cm
After freezing: 1599/kg cm
Ultimate tensile strength: 104/kg cm
Coef. thermal expansion: 0,0013mm/m°C
Water absorption: 0,38 %
Impact test / min. fall height: 41 cm
Frictional wear test: –
Bulk density: 2682 kg/m

CD file number: 0344

Giallo Fiorito

Quarrying location: Brazil
Availability: Medium
Compressive strength: 1578/kg cm^2
After freezing: 1599/kg cm^2
Ultimate tensile strength: 104/kg cm^2
Coef. thermal expansion: 0,0013mm/m°C
Water absorption: 0,38 %
Impact test / min. fall height: 41 cm
Frictional wear test: –
Bulk density: 2682 kg/m^3

CD file number: 0345

Giallo Tigrato

Quarrying location: Brazil
Availability: Medium
Compressive strength: 1136/kg cm^2
After freezing: 1078/kg cm^2
Ultimate tensile strength: 96/kg cm^2
Coef. thermal expansion: 0,0085mm/m°C
Water absorption: 0,35%
Impact test / min. fall height: –
Frictional wear test: –
Bulk density: 2621 kg/m^3

CD file number: 0346

Giallo Florence

Quarrying location: Brazil
Availability: Medium
Compressive strength: 1533/kg cm^2
After freezing: 1556/kg cm^2
Ultimate tensile strength: 150/kg cm^2
Coef. thermal expansion: 0,0080mm/m°C
Water absorption: 0,47 %
Impact test / min. fall height: 69 cm
Frictional wear test: –
Bulk density: 2623 kg/m^3

CD file number: 0347

Giallo Napoleone

Quarrying location: Saudi Arabia
Availability: Mediun
Compressive strength: 1578/kg cm
After freezing: 1599/kg cm
Ultimate tensile strength: 104/kg cm
Coef. thermal expansion: 0,0013mm/m°C
Water absorption: 0,38 %
Impact test / min. fall height: 41 cm
Frictional wear test: –
Bulk density: 2682 kg/m

CD file number: 0348

Giallo San Rafael

Quarrying location: Brazil
Availability: Medium
Compressive strength: 1578/kg cm^2
After freezing: 1599/kg cm^2
Ultimate tensile strength: 104/kg cm^2
Coef. thermal expansion: 0,0013mm/m°C
Water absorption: 0,38 %
Impact test / min. fall height: 41 cm
Frictional wear test: –
Bulk density: 2682 kg/m^3

CD file number: 0349

Amarello Real

Quarrying location: India
Availability: Medium
Compressive strength: 1578/kg cm^2
After freezing: 1599/kg cm^2
Ultimate tensile strength: 104/kg cm^2
Coef. thermal expansion: 0,0013mm/m°C
Water absorption: 0,38 %
Impact test / min. fall height: 41 cm
Frictional wear test: –
Bulk density: 2682 kg/m^3

CD file number: 0350

Padang TG 39

Quarrying location: India
Availability: Medium
Compressive strength: 1578/kg cm^2
After freezing: 1599/kg cm^2
Ultimate tensile strength: 104/kg cm^2
Coef. thermal expansion: 0,0013mm/m°C
Water absorption: 0,38 %
Impact test / min. fall height: 41 cm
Frictional wear test: –
Bulk density: 2682 kg/m^3

CD file number: 0351

Charme

Quarrying location: India
Availability: Limitec
Compressive strength: 1514/kg cm
After freezing: 1450/kg cm
Ultimate tensile strength: 93/kg cm
Coef. thermal expansion: 0,0076mm/m°C
Water absorption: 0,18%
Impact test / min. fall height: –
Frictional wear test: –
Bulk density: 2566 kg/m

CD file number: 0352

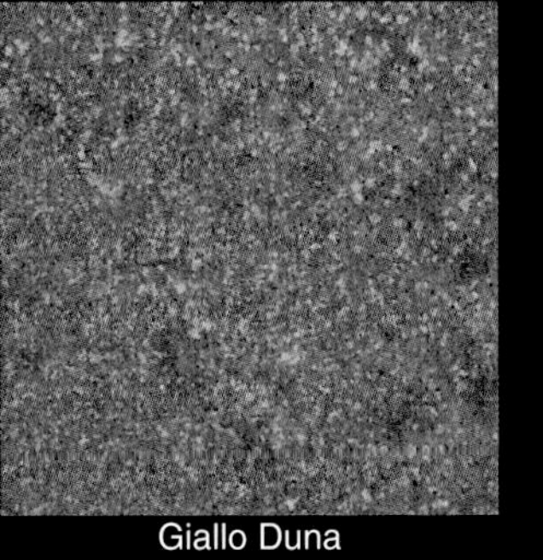

Giallo Duna

Giallo Topazio

Giallo Partenon

Giallo Antico

Giallo Fiorito

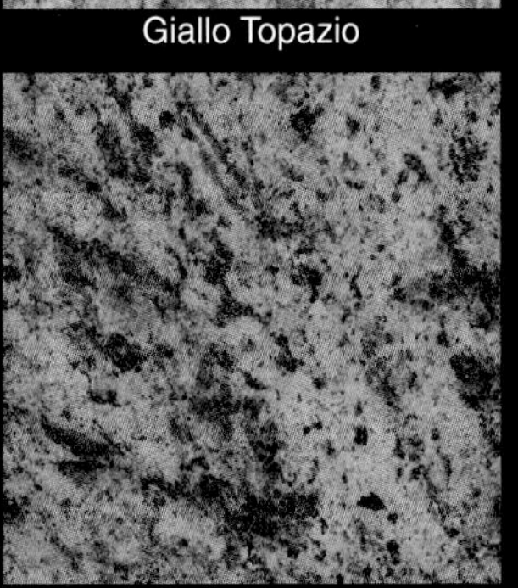

Giallo Tigrato

Giallo Florence

Giallo Napoleone

Giallo San Rafael

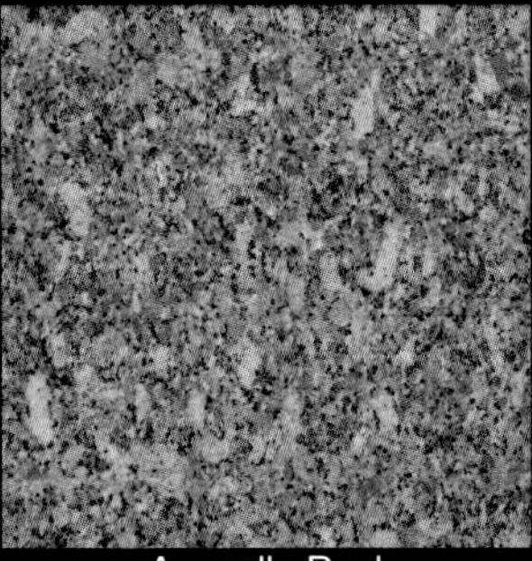

Amarello Real

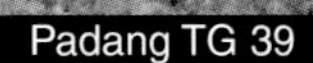

Padang TG 39

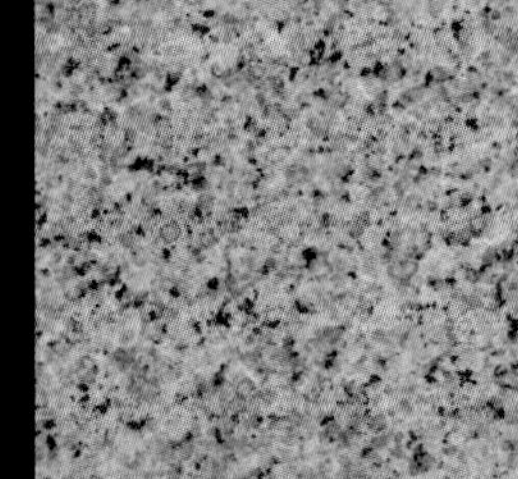

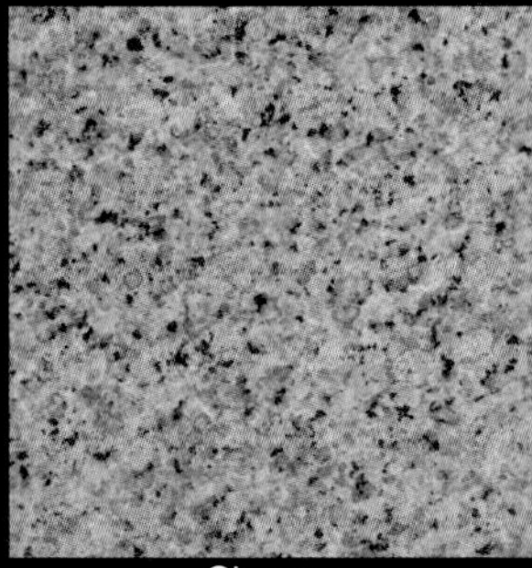

Charme

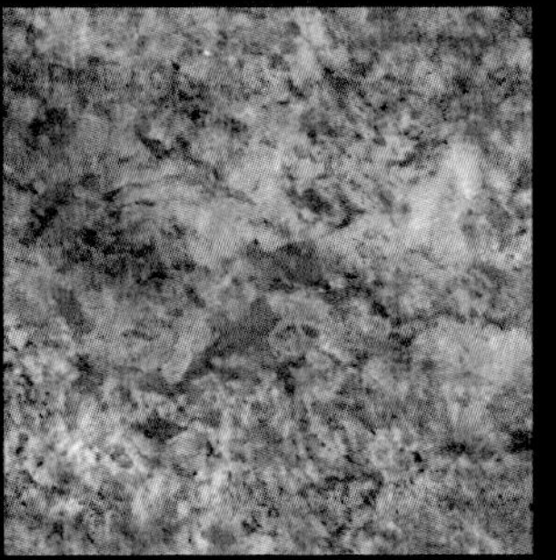

Juparana Florenca

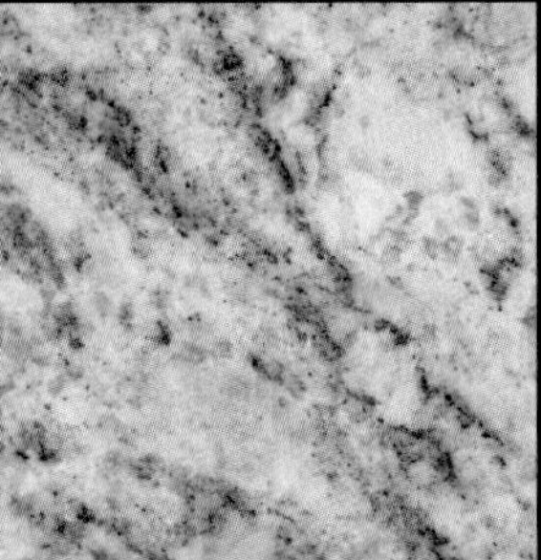

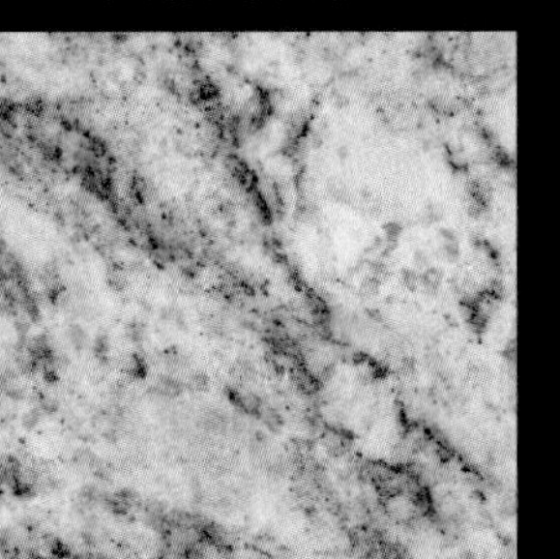

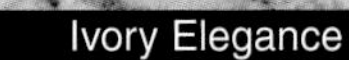

Ivory Elegance

Color Reef

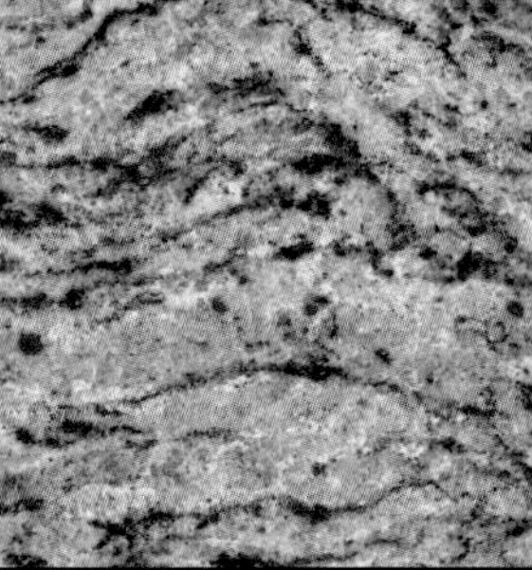

Tiger Skin

Quarrying location: Egypt
Availability: Medium
Compressive strength: 1928/kg cm^2
After freezing: 1784/kg cm^2
Ultimate tensile strength: 158/kg cm^2
Coef. thermal expansion: 0,0084mm/m°C
Water absorption: 0,18 %
Impact test / min. fall height: 50 cm
Frictional wear test: –
Bulk density: 2625 kg/m^3

CD file number: 0353

Red Royal

Quarrying location: Brazil
Availability: Medium
Compressive strength: 1928/kg cm^2
After freezing: 1784/kg cm^2
Ultimate tensile strength: 158/kg cm^2
Coef. thermal expansion: 0,0084mm/m°C
Water absorption: 0,18 %
Impact test / min. fall height: 50 cm
Frictional wear test: –
Bulk density: 2625 kg/m^3

CD file number: 0357

Capao Bonito

Quarrying location: India
Availability: Limited
Compressive strength: 1928/kg cm^2
After freezing: 1784/kg cm^2
Ultimate tensile strength: 158/kg cm^2
Coef. thermal expansion: 0,0084mm/m°C
Water absorption: 0,18 %
Impact test / min. fall height: 50 cm
Frictional wear test: –
Bulk density: 2625 kg/m^3

CD file number: 0361

New Rubin

Quarrying location: Brazil
Availability: Medium
Compressive strength: 1578/kg cm^2
After freezing: 1599/kg cm^2
Ultimate tensile strength: 104/kg cm^2
Coef. thermal expansion: 0,0013mm/m°C
Water absorption: 0,38 %
Impact test / min. fall height: 41 cm
Frictional wear test: –
Bulk density: 2682 kg/m^3

CD file number: 0365

Juparana Red Florenca

Quarrying location: Finland
Availability: Medium
Compressive strength: 1928/kg cm^2
After freezing: 1784/kg cm^2
Ultimate tensile strength: 158/kg cm^2
Coef. thermal expansion: 0,0084mm/m°C
Water absorption: 0,18 %
Impact test / min. fall height: 50 cm
Frictional wear test: –
Bulk density: 2625 kg/m^3

CD file number: 0354

Balmoral Red FG

Quarrying location: Ghana
Availability: Medium
Compressive strength: 1790/kg cm^2
After freezing: 1668/kg cm^2
Ultimate tensile strength: 133/kg cm^2
Coef. thermal expansion: 0,0086mm/m°C
Water absorption: 0,31 %
Impact test / min. fall height: –
Frictional wear test: –
Bulk density: 2660 kg/m^3

CD file number: 0358

Red Bongo

Quarrying location: India
Availability: Good
Compressive strength: 1928/kg cm^2
After freezing: 1784/kg cm^2
Ultimate tensile strength: 158/kg cm^2
Coef. thermal expansion: 0,0084mm/m°C
Water absorption: 0,18 %
Impact test / min. fall height: 50 cm
Frictional wear test: –
Bulk density: 2625 kg/m^3

CD file number: 0362

New Imperial

Quarrying location: Egypt
Availability: Medium
Compressive strength: 1978/kg cm^2
After freezing: 1904/kg cm^2
Ultimate tensile strength: 137/kg cm^2
Coef. thermal expansion: 0,0060mm/m°C
Water absorption: 0,17 %
Impact test / min. fall height: 53 cm
Frictional wear test: –
Bulk density: 2645 kg/m^3

CD file number: 0366

Aswan Red

Quarrying location: Finland
Availability: Medium
Compressive strength: 1928/kg cm^2
After freezing: 1784/kg cm^2
Ultimate tensile strength: 158/kg cm^2
Coef. thermal expansion: 0,0084mm/m°C
Water absorption: 0,18 %
Impact test / min. fall height: 50 cm
Frictional wear test: –
Bulk density: 2625 kg/m^3

CD file number: 0355

Balmoral Red CG

Quarrying location: Sweden
Availability: Medium
Compressive strength: 1928/kg cm^2
After freezing: 1784/kg cm^2
Ultimate tensile strength: 158/kg cm^2
Coef. thermal expansion: 0,0084mm/m°C
Water absorption: 0,18 %
Impact test / min. fall height: 50 cm
Frictional wear test: –
Bulk density: 2625 kg/m^3

CD file number: 0359

Tranas Red

Quarrying location: Sweden
Availability: Limited
Compressive strength: 1928/kg cm^2
After freezing: 1784/kg cm^2
Ultimate tensile strength: 158/kg cm^2
Coef. thermal expansion: 0,0084mm/m°C
Water absorption: 0,18 %
Impact test / min. fall height: 50 cm
Frictional wear test: –
Bulk density: 2625 kg/m^3

CD file number: 0363

Imperial Red

Quarrying location: India
Availability: Medium
Compressive strength: 1978/kg cm^2
After freezing: 1904/kg cm^2
Ultimate tensile strength: 137/kg cm^2
Coef. thermal expansion: 0,0060mm/m°C
Water absorption: 0,17 %
Impact test / min. fall height: 53 cm
Frictional wear test: –
Bulk density: 2645 kg/m^3

CD file number: 0367

Goa Red

Quarrying location: Finland
Availability: Medium
Compressive strength: 1928/kg cm^2
After freezing: 1784/kg cm^2
Ultimate tensile strength: 158/kg cm^2
Coef. thermal expansion: 0,0084mm/m°C
Water absorption: 0,18 %
Impact test / min. fall height: 50 cm
Frictional wear test: –
Bulk density: 2625 kg/m^3

CD file number: 0356

Carmen Red

Quarrying location: India
Availability: Medium
Compressive strength: 1790/kg cm^2
After freezing: 1668/kg cm^2
Ultimate tensile strength: 133/kg cm^2
Coef. thermal expansion: 0,0086mm/m°C
Water absorption: 0,31 %
Impact test / min. fall height: –
Frictional wear test: –
Bulk density: 2660 kg/m^3

CD file number: 0360

Red Itaipu

Quarrying location: South Africa
Availability: Good
Compressive strength: 1928/kg cm^2
After freezing: 1784/kg cm^2
Ultimate tensile strength: 158/kg cm^2
Coef. thermal expansion: 0,0084mm/m°C
Water absorption: 0,18 %
Impact test / min. fall height: 50 cm
Frictional wear test: –
Bulk density: 2625 kg/m^3

CD file number: 0364

African Red

Quarrying location: Ukraina
Availability: Medium
Compressive strength: 1978/kg cm^2
After freezing: 1904/kg cm^2
Ultimate tensile strength: 137/kg cm^2
Coef. thermal expansion: 0,0060mm/m°C
Water absorption: 0,17 %
Impact test / min. fall height: 53 cm
Frictional wear test: –
Bulk density: 2645 kg/m^3

CD file number: 0368

Rosso Santiago

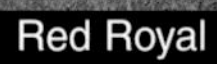
Red Royal

Balmoral Red FG

Balmoral Red CG

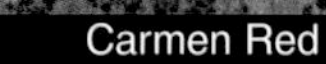
Carmen Red

Capao Bonito

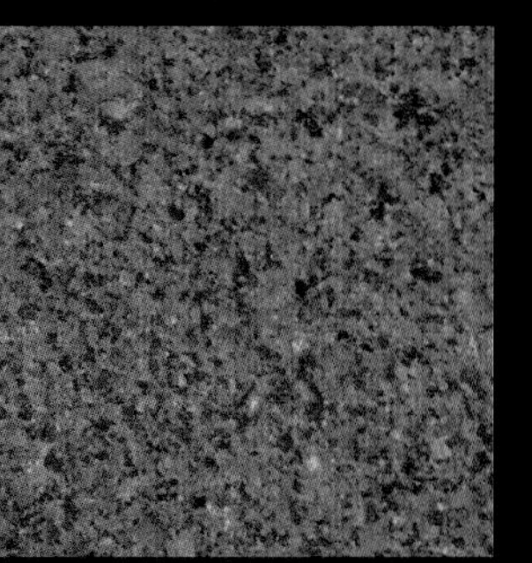
Red Bongo

Tranas Red

Red Itaipu

New Rubin

New Imperial

Imperial Red

African Red

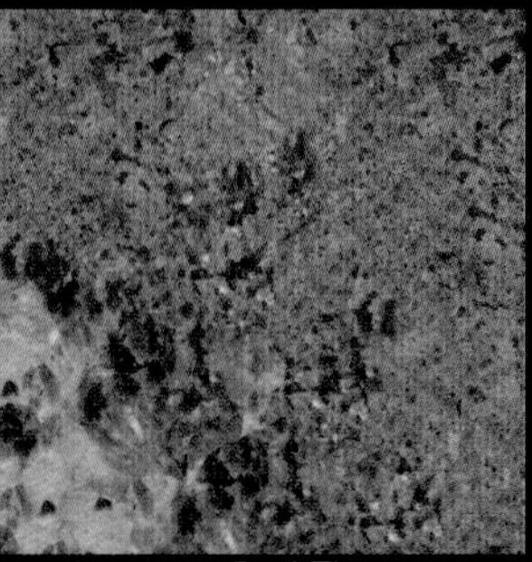
Juparana Red Florenca

Aswan Red

Goa Red

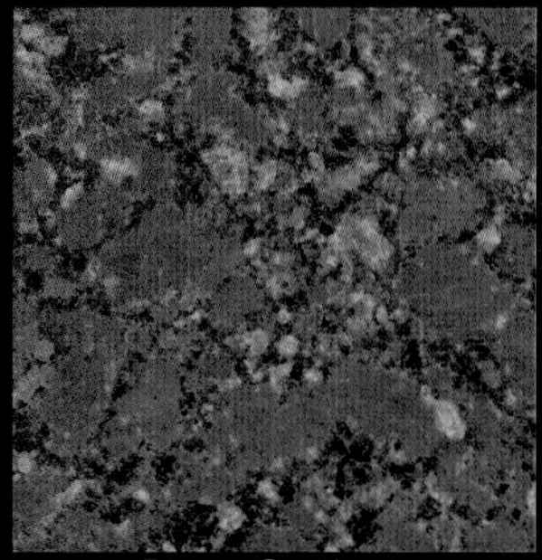
Rosso Santiago

Quarrying location: India
Availability: Good
Compressive strength: 1790/kg cm^2
After freezing: 1668/kg cm^2
Ultimate tensile strength: 133/kg cm^2
Coef. thermal expansion: 0,0086mm/m°C
Water absorption: 0,31 %
Impact test / min. fall height: –
Frictional wear test: –
Bulk density: 2660 kg/m^3

CD file number: 0369

Quarrying location: Brazil
Availability: Good
Compressive strength: 1790/kg cm^2
After freezing: 1668/kg cm^2
Ultimate tensile strength: 133/kg cm^2
Coef. thermal expansion: 0,0086mm/m°C
Water absorption: 0,31 %
Impact test / min. fall height: –
Frictional wear test: –
Bulk density: 2660 kg/m^3

CD file number: 0370

Quarrying location: Brazil
Availability: Limited
Compressive strength: 1790/kg cm^2
After freezing: 1668/kg cm^2
Ultimate tensile strength: 133/kg cm^2
Coef. thermal expansion: 0,0086mm/m°C
Water absorption: 0,31 %
Impact test / min. fall height: –
Frictional wear test: –
Bulk density: 2660 kg/m^3

CD file number: 0371

Quarrying location: Brazil
Availability: Limited
Compressive strength: 1790/kg cm^2
After freezing: 1668/kg cm^2
Ultimate tensile strength: 133/kg cm^2
Coef. thermal expansion: 0,0086mm/m°C
Water absorption: 0,31 %
Impact test / min. fall height: –
Frictional wear test: –
Bulk density: 2660 kg/m^3

CD file number: 0372

Multicolor Red India

Quarrying location: India
Availability: Medium
Compressive strength: 1790/kg cm^2
After freezing: 1668/kg cm^2
Ultimate tensile strength: 133/kg cm^2
Coef. thermal expansion: 0,0086mm/m°C
Water absorption: 0,31 %
Impact test / min. fall height: –
Frictional wear test: –
Bulk density: 2660 kg/m^3

CD file number: 0373

Multicolor Red Brasil

Quarrying location: India
Availability: Medium
Compressive strength: 1790/kg cm^2
After freezing: 1668/kg cm^2
Ultimate tensile strength: 133/kg cm^2
Coef. thermal expansion: 0,0086mm/m°C
Water absorption: 0,31 %
Impact test / min. fall height: –
Frictional wear test: –
Bulk density: 2660 kg/m^3

CD file number: 0374

Jacaranda

Quarrying location: Brazil
Availability: Limited
Compressive strength: 1790/kg cm^2
After freezing: 1668/kg cm^2
Ultimate tensile strength: 133/kg cm^2
Coef. thermal expansion: 0,0086mm/m°C
Water absorption: 0,31 %
Impact test / min. fall height: –
Frictional wear test: –
Bulk density: 2660 kg/m^3

CD file number: 0375

Jacaranda Bahia

Quarrying location: Brazil
Availability: Limited
Compressive strength: 1790/kg cm^2
After freezing: 1668/kg cm^2
Ultimate tensile strength: 133/kg cm^2
Coef. thermal expansion: 0,0086mm/m°C
Water absorption: 0,31 %
Impact test / min. fall height: –
Frictional wear test: –
Bulk density: 2660 kg/m^3

CD file number: 0376

Rainbow

Quarrying location: Brazil
Availability: Medium
Compressive strength: 1790/kg cm^2
After freezing: 1668/kg cm^2
Ultimate tensile strength: 133/kg cm^2
Coef. thermal expansion: 0,0086mm/m°C
Water absorption: 0,31 %
Impact test / min. fall height: –
Frictional wear test: –
Bulk density: 2660 kg/m^3

CD file number: 0377

Red Tiger

Quarrying location: India
Availability: Medium
Compressive strength: 1790/kg cm^2
After freezing: 1668/kg cm^2
Ultimate tensile strength: 133/kg cm^2
Coef. thermal expansion: 0,0086mm/m°C
Water absorption: 0,31 %
Impact test / min. fall height: –
Frictional wear test: –
Bulk density: 2660 kg/m^3

CD file number: 0378

Tupim

Quarrying location: Brazil
Availability: Limited
Compressive strength: 1790/kg cm^2
After freezing: 1668/kg cm^2
Ultimate tensile strength: 133/kg cm^2
Coef. thermal expansion: 0,0086mm/m°C
Water absorption: 0,31 %
Impact test / min. fall height: –
Frictional wear test: –
Bulk density: 2660 kg/m^3

CD file number: 0379

Funil

Quarrying location: India
Availability: Medium
Compressive strength: 1790/kg cm^2
After freezing: 1668/kg cm^2
Ultimate tensile strength: 133/kg cm^2
Coef. thermal expansion: 0,0086mm/m°C
Water absorption: 0,31 %
Impact test / min. fall height: –
Frictional wear test: –
Bulk density: 2660 kg/m^3

CD file number: 0380

Creme Caramel

Quarrying location: Sweden
Availability: Limited
Compressive strength: 1978/kg cm^2
After freezing: 1904/kg cm^2
Ultimate tensile strength: 137/kg cm^2
Coef. thermal expansion: 0,0060mm/m°C
Water absorption: 0,17 %
Impact test / min. fall height: 53 cm
Frictional wear test: –
Bulk density: 2645 kg/m^3

CD file number: 0381

Rosa Incas

Quarrying location: India
Availability: Medium
Compressive strength: 1790/kg cm^2
After freezing: 1668/kg cm^2
Ultimate tensile strength: 133/kg cm^2
Coef. thermal expansion: 0,0086mm/m°C
Water absorption: 0,31 %
Impact test / min. fall height: –
Frictional wear test: –
Bulk density: 2660 kg/m^3

CD file number: 0382

Cobra

Quarrying location: Brazil
Availability: Medium
Compressive strength: 1920/kg cm^2
After freezing: 1810/kg cm^2
Ultimate tensile strength: –
Coef. thermal expansion: –
Water absorption: 0,15 %
Impact test / min. fall height: –
Frictional wear test: –
Bulk density: 2720 kg/m^3

CD file number: 0383

Rosa Turm

Quarrying location: Brazil
Availability: Medium
Compressive strength: 1920/kg cm^2
After freezing: 1810/kg cm^2
Ultimate tensile strength: –
Coef. thermal expansion: –
Water absorption: 0,15 %
Impact test / min. fall height: –
Frictional wear test: –
Bulk density: 2720 kg/m^3

CD file number: 0384

Vanga Red

Ruweday Pink

Saint Tropez Scuro

Saint Tropez

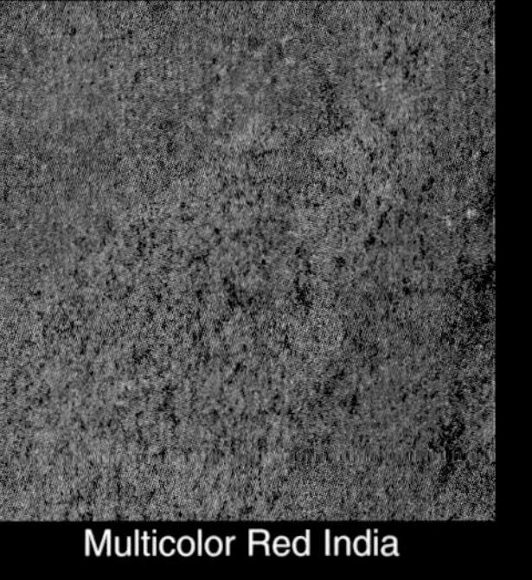

Multicolor Red India

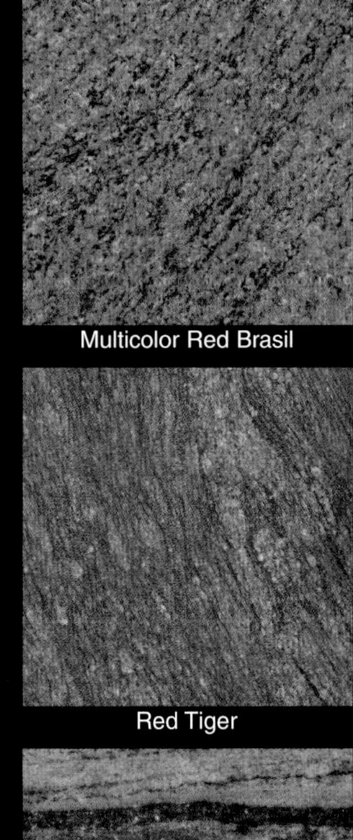

Multicolor Red Brasil

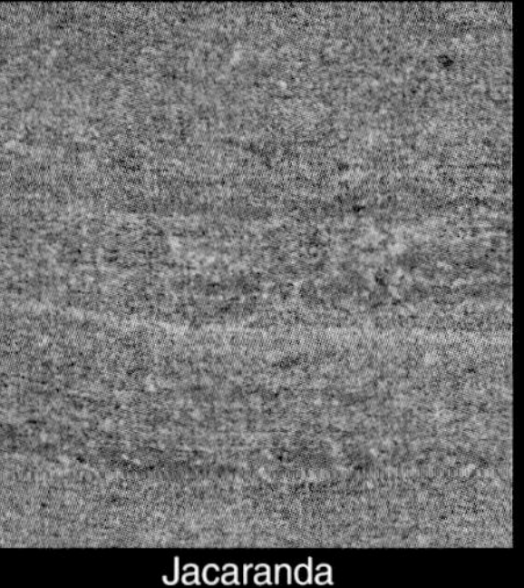

Jacaranda

Jacaranda Bahia

Rainbow

Red Tiger

Tupim

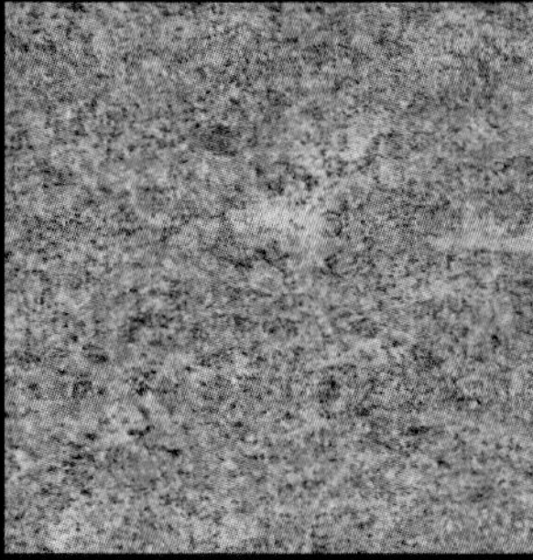

Funil

Creme Caramel

Rosa Incas

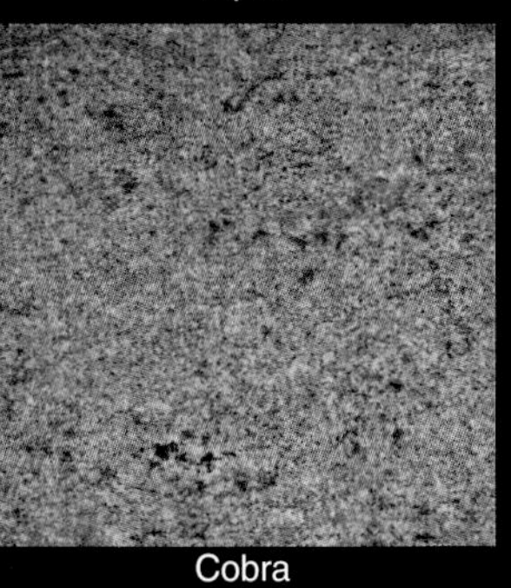

Cobra

Rosa Turm

Vanga Red

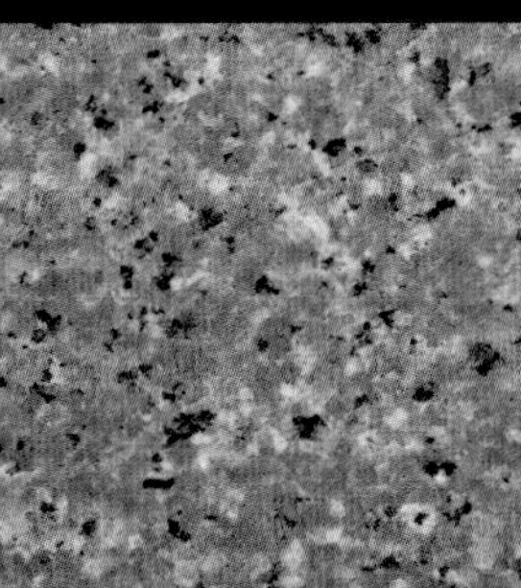

Ruweday Pink

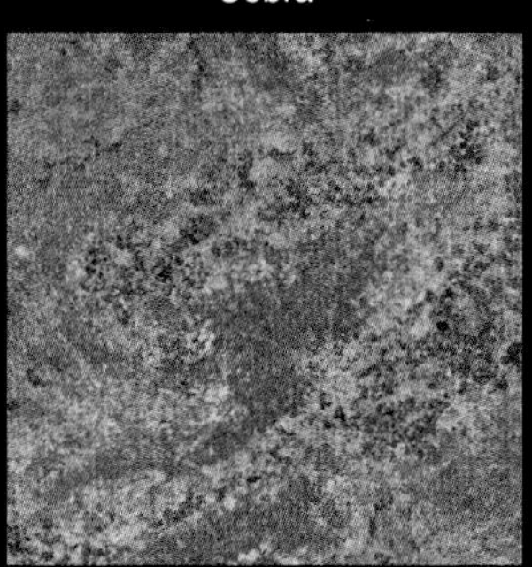

Saint Tropez Scuro

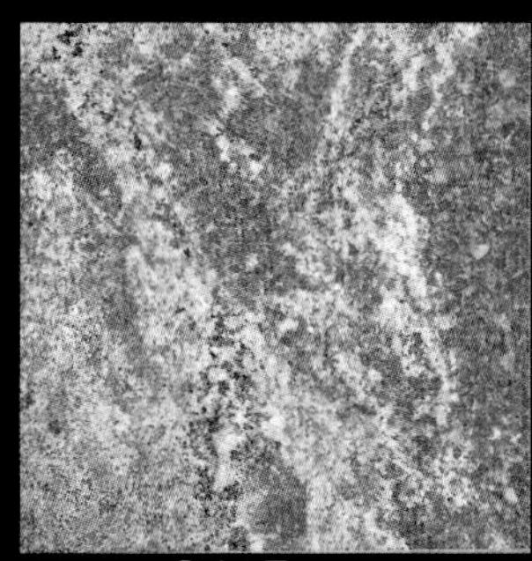

Saint Tropez

Quarrying location: Italy
Availability: Limited
Compressive strength: 2525/kg cm^2
After freezing: –
Ultimate tensile strength: 146/kg cm^2
Coef. thermal expansion: –
Water absorption: 0,26 %
Impact test / min. fall height: 70 cm
Frictional wear test: –
Bulk density: 2636kg/m^3

CD file number: 0385

Quarrying location: Italy
Availability: Limited
Compressive strength: 2525/kg cm^2
After freezing: –
Ultimate tensile strength: 146/kg cm^2
Coef. thermal expansion: –
Water absorption: 0,26 %
Impact test / min. fall height: 70 cm
Frictional wear test: –
Bulk density: 2636kg/m^3

CD file number: 0386

Quarrying location: India
Availability: Medium
Compressive strength: 2525/kg cm^2
After freezing: –
Ultimate tensile strength: 146/kg cm^2
Coef. thermal expansion: –
Water absorption: 0,26 %
Impact test / min. fall height: 70 cm
Frictional wear test: –
Bulk density: 2636kg/m^3

CD file number: 0387

Quarrying location: India
Availability: Medium
Compressive strength: 2300/kg cm^2
After freezing: 1970/kg cm^2
Ultimate tensile strength: 115/kg cm^2
Coef. thermal expansion: –
Water absorption: 0,25 %
Impact test / min. fall height: –
Frictional wear test: –
Bulk density: 2730 kg/m^3

CD file number: 0388

Verde Mergozzo Chiaro

Quarrying location: Italy
Availability: Limited
Compressive strength: 2525/kg cm^2
After freezing: –
Ultimate tensile strength: 146/kg cm^2
Coef. thermal expansion: –
Water absorption: 0,26 %
Impact test / min. fall height: 70 cm
Frictional wear test: –
Bulk density: 2636kg/m^3

CD file number: 0389

Verde Mergozzo Scuro

Quarrying location: India
Availability: Medium
Compressive strength: 2300/kg cm^2
After freezing: 1970/kg cm^2
Ultimate tensile strength: 115/kg cm^2
Coef. thermal expansion: –
Water absorption: 0,25 %
Impact test / min. fall height: –
Frictional wear test: –
Bulk density: 2730 kg/m^3

CD file number: 0390

Green Rose

Quarrying location: Brazil
Availability: Good
Compressive strength: 2240/kg cm^2
After freezing: –
Ultimate tensile strength: 160/kg cm^2
Coef. thermal expansion: –
Water absorption: 0,16 %
Impact test / min. fall height: 52 cm
Frictional wear test: –
Bulk density: 2735 kg/m^3

CD file number: 0391

Andeer

Quarrying location: Brazil
Availability: Good
Compressive strength: 2240/kg cm^2
After freezing: –
Ultimate tensile strength: 160/kg cm^2
Coef. thermal expansion: –
Water absorption: 0,16 %
Impact test / min. fall height: 52 cm
Frictional wear test: –
Bulk density: 2735 kg/m^3

CD file number: 0392

Verde Argento

Quarrying location: Brazil
Availability: Good
Compressive strength: 2240/kg cm^2
After freezing: –
Ultimate tensile strength: 160/kg cm^2
Coef. thermal expansion: –
Water absorption: 0,16 %
Impact test / min. fall height: 52 cm
Frictional wear test: –
Bulk density: 2735 kg/m^3

CD file number: 0393

Verde Marina

Quarrying location: Canada
Availability: Medium
Compressive strength: 2240/kg cm^2
After freezing: –
Ultimate tensile strength: 160/kg cm^2
Coef. thermal expansion: –
Water absorption: 0,16 %
Impact test / min. fall height: 52 cm
Frictional wear test: –
Bulk density: 2735 kg/m^3

CD file number: 0394

Verde Eucalipto

Quarrying location: Brazil
Availability: Medium
Compressive strength: 2607/kg cm^2
After freezing: 1973/kg cm^2
Ultimate tensile strength: 134/kg cm^2
Coef. thermal expansion: –
Water absorption: 0,23 %
Impact test / min. fall height: –
Frictional wear test: –
Bulk density: 2751 kg/m^3

CD file number: 0395

Verde New Eucalipto

Quarrying location: Brazil
Availability: Medium
Compressive strength: 2607/kg cm^2
After freezing: 1973/kg cm^2
Ultimate tensile strength: 134/kg cm^2
Coef. thermal expansion: –
Water absorption: 0,23 %
Impact test / min. fall height: –
Frictional wear test: –
Bulk density: 2751 kg/m^3

CD file number: 0396

Cougan Green

Quarrying location: Brazil
Availability: Medium
Compressive strength: 2607/kg cm^2
After freezing: 1973/kg cm^2
Ultimate tensile strength: 134/kg cm^2
Coef. thermal expansion: –
Water absorption: 0,23 %
Impact test / min. fall height: –
Frictional wear test: –
Bulk density: 2751 kg/m^3

CD file number: 0397

Verde Dorato

Quarrying location: Brazil
Availability: Limited
Compressive strength: 2607/kg cm^2
After freezing: 1973/kg cm^2
Ultimate tensile strength: 134/kg cm^2
Coef. thermal expansion: –
Water absorption: 0,23 %
Impact test / min. fall height: –
Frictional wear test: –
Bulk density: 2751 kg/m^3

CD file number: 0398

Jurassic Green

Quarrying location: Norway
Availability: Medium
Compressive strength: 2607/kg cm^2
After freezing: 1973/kg cm^2
Ultimate tensile strength: 134/kg cm^2
Coef. thermal expansion: –
Water absorption: 0,23 %
Impact test / min. fall height: –
Frictional wear test: –
Bulk density: 2751 kg/m^3

CD file number: 0399

Verde San Francisco

Quarrying location: Brazil
Availability: Medium
Compressive strength: 1920/kg cm^2
After freezing: 1810/kg cm^2
Ultimate tensile strength: –
Coef. thermal expansion: –
Water absorption: 0,15 %
Impact test / min. fall height: –
Frictional wear test: –
Bulk density: 2720 kg/m^3

CD file number: 0400

Verde Maritaca

Verde Maritaca Imperiale

Iceland Green

Tropical Green

Verde Mergozzo Chiaro

Verde Mergozzo Scuro

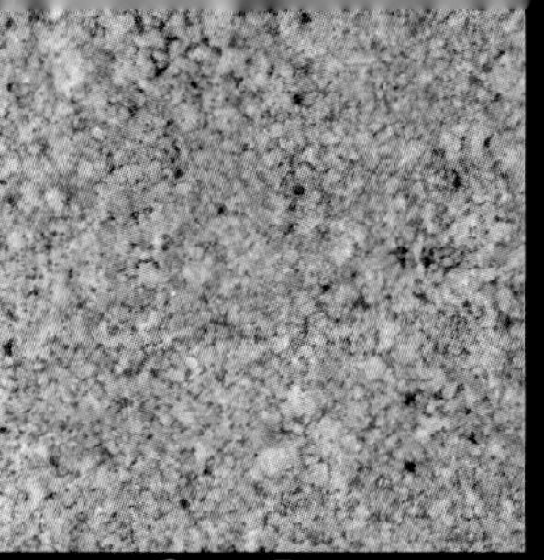

Green Rose

Andeer

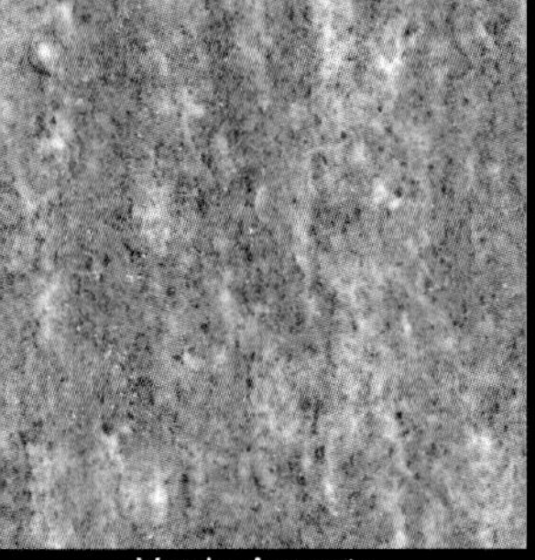

Verde Argento

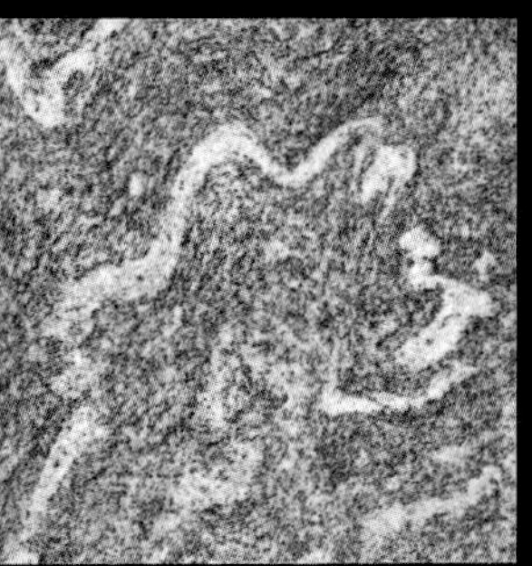

Verde Marina

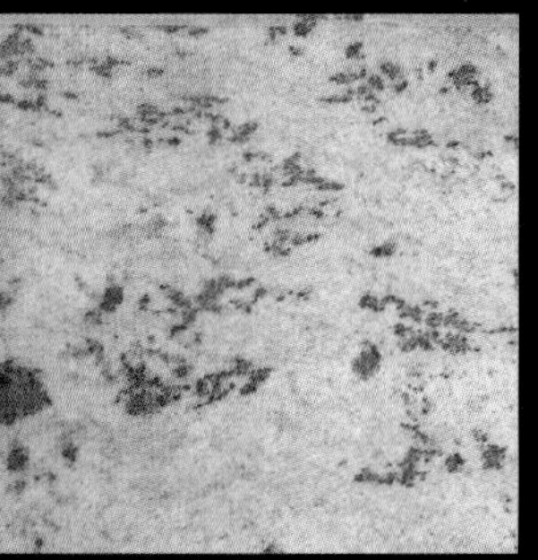

Verde Eucalipto

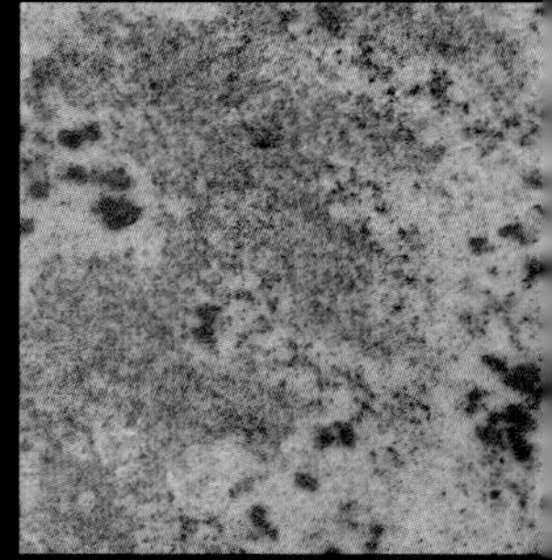

Verde New Eucalipto

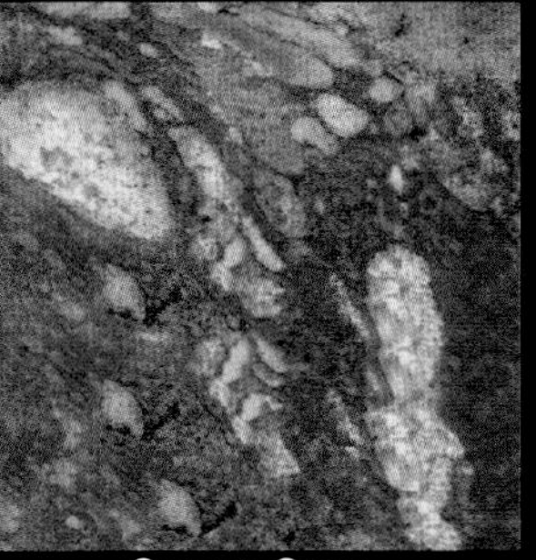

Cougan Green

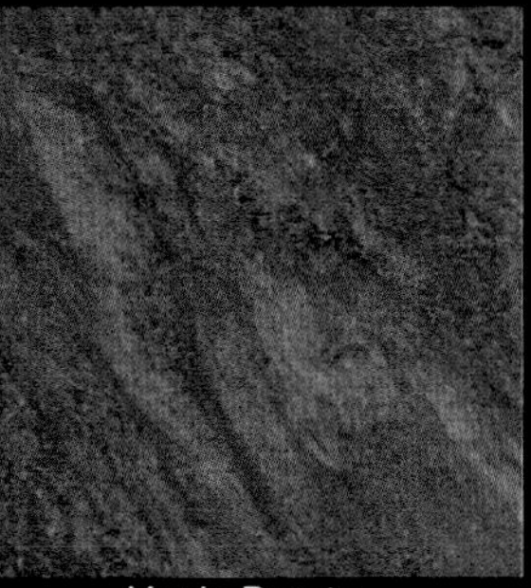

Verde Dorato

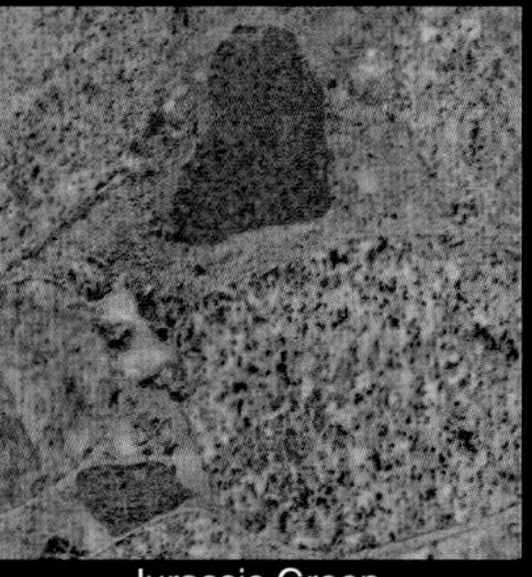

Jurassic Green

Verde San Francisco

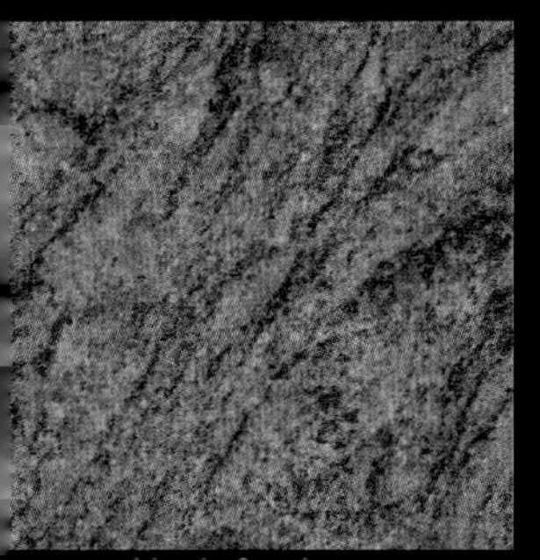

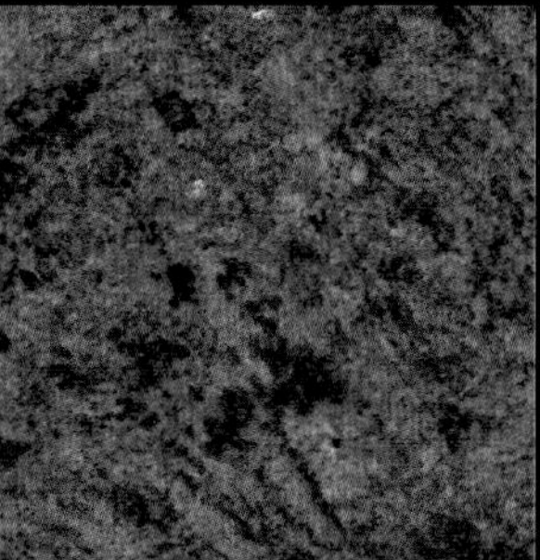

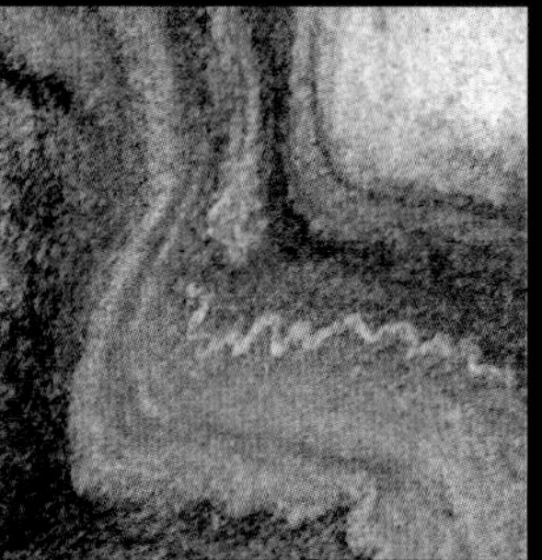

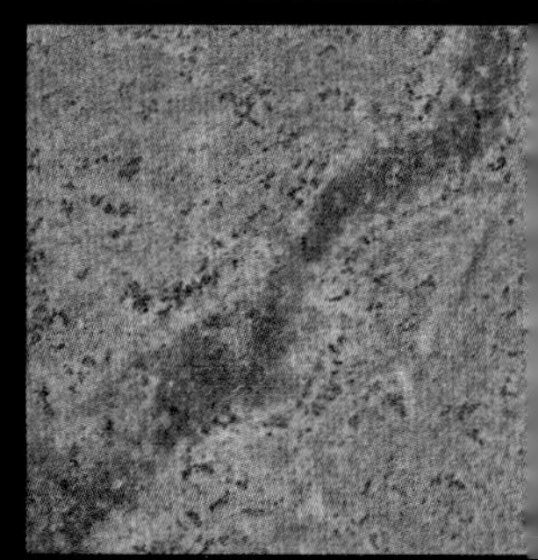

Quarrying location: India
Availability: Medium
Compressive strength: 1790/kg cm^2
After freezing: 1668/kg cm^2
Ultimate tensile strength: 133/kg cm^2
Coef. thermal expansion: 0,0086mm/m°C
Water absorption: 0,31 %
Impact test / min. fall height: –
Frictional wear test: –
Bulk density: 2660 kg/m^3

CD file number: 0401

Quarrying location: Brazil
Availability: Medium
Compressive strength: 2607/kg cm^2
After freezing: 1973/kg cm^2
Ultimate tensile strength: 134/kg cm^2
Coef. thermal expansion: –
Water absorption: 0,23 %
Impact test / min. fall height: –
Frictional wear test: –
Bulk density: 2751 kg/m^3

CD file number: 0402

Quarrying location: Brazil
Availability: Medium
Compressive strength: 2607/kg cm^2
After freezing: 1973/kg cm^2
Ultimate tensile strength: 134/kg cm^2
Coef. thermal expansion: –
Water absorption: 0,23 %
Impact test / min. fall height: –
Frictional wear test: –
Bulk density: 2751 kg/m^3

CD file number: 0403

Quarrying location: Brazil
Availability: Medium
Compressive strength: 2607/kg cm^2
After freezing: 1973/kg cm^2
Ultimate tensile strength: 134/kg cm^2
Coef. thermal expansion: –
Water absorption: 0,23 %
Impact test / min. fall height: –
Frictional wear test: –
Bulk density: 2751 kg/m^3

CD file number: 0404

Oriental Green

Quarrying location: Brazil
Availability: Medium
Compressive strength: 2607/kg cm^2
After freezing: 1973/kg cm^2
Ultimate tensile strength: 134/kg cm^2
Coef. thermal expansion: –
Water absorption: 0,23 %
Impact test / min. fall height: –
Frictional wear test: –
Bulk density: 2751 kg/m^3

CD file number: 0405

Verde Butterfly

Quarrying location: South Africa
Availability: Good
Compressive strength: 1920/kg cm^2
After freezing: 1822/kg cm^2
Ultimate tensile strength: 200/kg cm^2
Coef. thermal expansion: –
Water absorption: 0,14 %
Impact test / min. fall height: –
Frictional wear test: –
Bulk density: 2700 kg/m^3

CD file number: 0406

Verde Veneziano

Quarrying location: South Africa
Availability: Good
Compressive strength: 1920/kg cm^2
After freezing: 1822/kg cm^2
Ultimate tensile strength: 200/kg cm^2
Coef. thermal expansion: –
Water absorption: 0,14 %
Impact test / min. fall height: –
Frictional wear test: –
Bulk density: 2700 kg/m^3

CD file number: 0407

Verde Lavras

Quarrying location: Brazil
Availability: Medium
Compressive strength: 2607/kg cm^2
After freezing: 1973/kg cm^2
Ultimate tensile strength: 134/kg cm^2
Coef. thermal expansion: –
Water absorption: 0,23 %
Impact test / min. fall height: –
Frictional wear test: –
Bulk density: 2751 kg/m^3

CD file number: 0408

Forest Green

Quarrying location: Brazil
Availability: Medium
Compressive strength: 2607/kg cm^2
After freezing: 1973/kg cm^2
Ultimate tensile strength: 134/kg cm^2
Coef. thermal expansion: –
Water absorption: 0,23 %
Impact test / min. fall height: –
Frictional wear test: –
Bulk density: 2751 kg/m^3

CD file number: 0409

Fountaine Green

Quarrying location: India
Availability: Good
Compressive strength: 2240/kg cm^2
After freezing: –
Ultimate tensile strength: 160/kg cm^2
Coef. thermal expansion: –
Water absorption: 0,16 %
Impact test / min. fall height: 52 cm
Frictional wear test: –
Bulk density: 2735 kg/m^3

CD file number: 0410

Verde Mare

Quarrying location: Brazil
Availability: Medium
Compressive strength: 1920/kg cm^2
After freezing: 1810/kg cm^2
Ultimate tensile strength: –
Coef. thermal expansion: –
Water absorption: 0,15 %
Impact test / min. fall height: –
Frictional wear test: –
Bulk density: 2720 kg/m^3

CD file number: 0411

Olive Green

Quarrying location: Brazil
Availability: Medium
Compressive strength: 1920/kg cm^2
After freezing: 1810/kg cm^2
Ultimate tensile strength: –
Coef. thermal expansion: –
Water absorption: 0,15 %
Impact test / min. fall height: –
Frictional wear test: –
Bulk density: 2720 kg/m^3

CD file number: 0412

New Tunas Green

Quarrying location: Brazil
Availability: Medium
Compressive strength: 2607/kg cm^2
After freezing: 1973/kg cm^2
Ultimate tensile strength: 134/kg cm^2
Coef. thermal expansion: –
Water absorption: 0,23 %
Impact test / min. fall height: –
Frictional wear test: –
Bulk density: 2751 kg/m^3

CD file number: 0413

Verde Star

Quarrying location: Brazil
Availability: Medium
Compressive strength: 2607/kg cm^2
After freezing: 1973/kg cm^2
Ultimate tensile strength: 134/kg cm^2
Coef. thermal expansion: –
Water absorption: 0,23 %
Impact test / min. fall height: –
Frictional wear test: –
Bulk density: 2751 kg/m^3

CD file number: 0414

Marinace Verde

Quarrying location: Brazil
Availability: Limited
Compressive strength: 2607/kg cm^2
After freezing: 1973/kg cm^2
Ultimate tensile strength: 134/kg cm^2
Coef. thermal expansion: –
Water absorption: 0,23 %
Impact test / min. fall height: –
Frictional wear test: –
Bulk density: 2751 kg/m^3

CD file number: 0415

Marinace

Quarrying location: Brazil
Availability: Limited
Compressive strength: 2607/kg cm^2
After freezing: 1973/kg cm^2
Ultimate tensile strength: 134/kg cm^2
Coef. thermal expansion: –
Water absorption: 0,23 %
Impact test / min. fall height: –
Frictional wear test: –
Bulk density: 2751 kg/m^3

CD file number: 0416

Atlantic Green

Verde Esmeralda

Verde Ubatuba

Verde Ubatuba Scuro

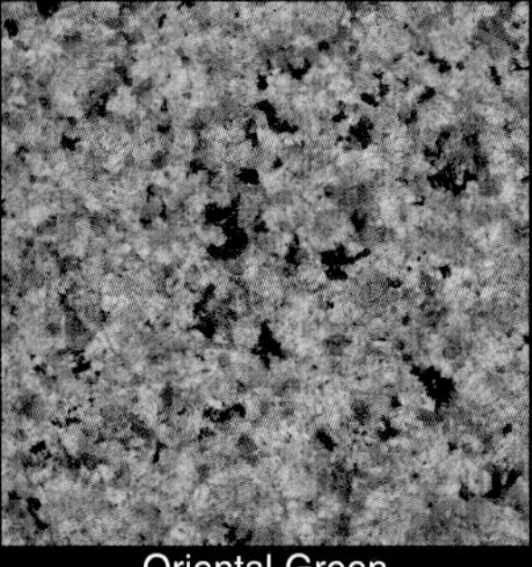
Oriental Green

Verde Butterfly

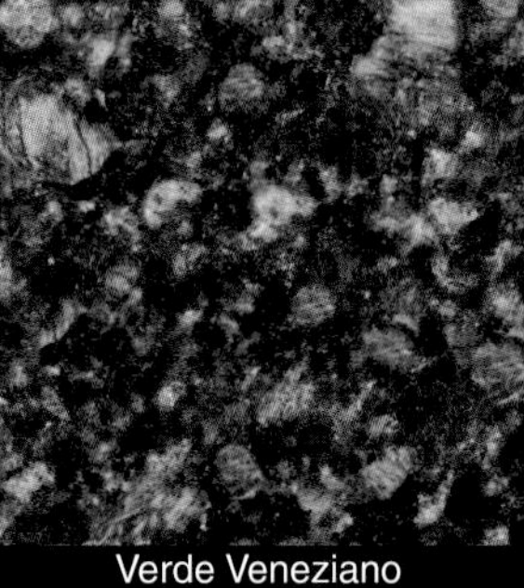
Verde Veneziano

Verde Lavras

Forest Green

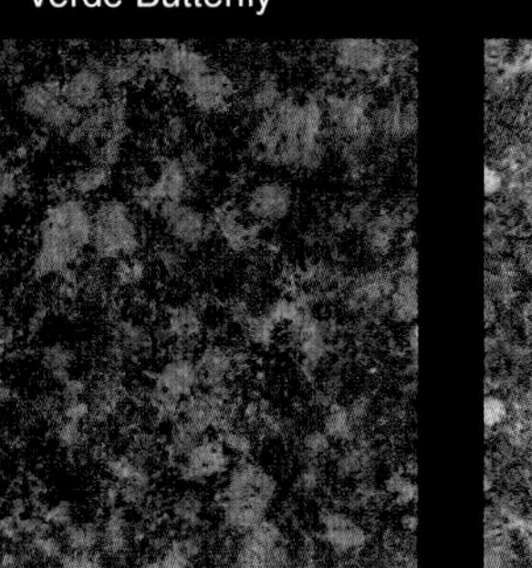
Fountaine Green

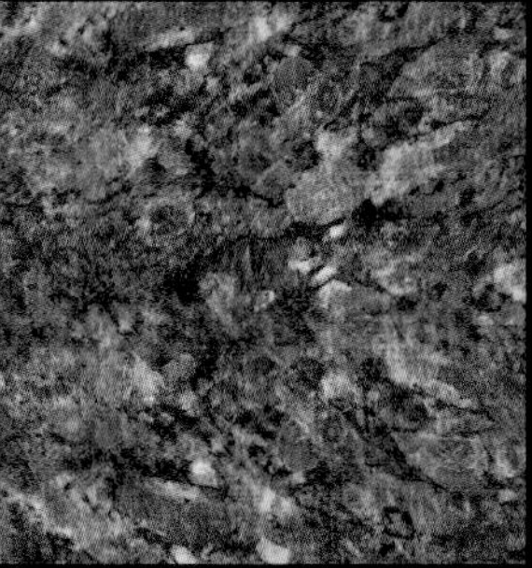
Verde Mare

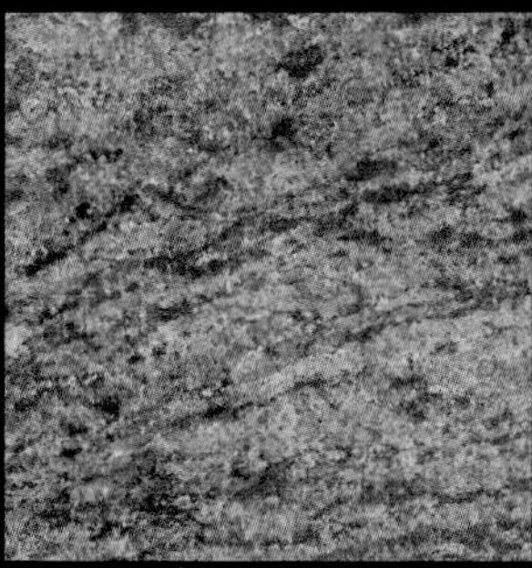
Olive Green

New Tunas Green

Verde Star

Marinace Verde

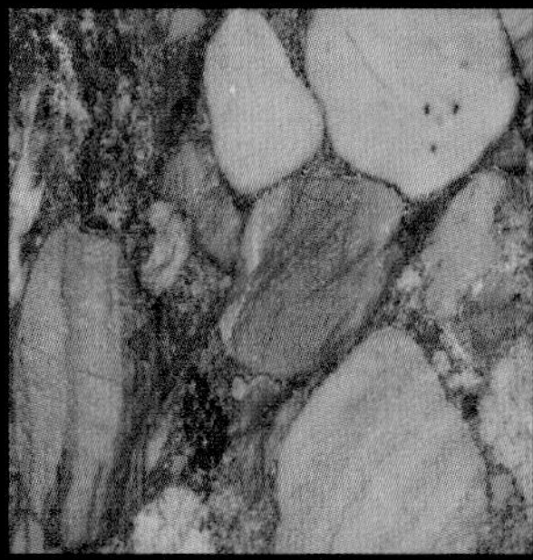
Marinace

Atlantic Green

Verde Esmeralda

Verde Ubatuba

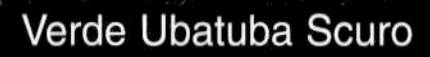
Verde Ubatuba Scuro

Quarrying location: Soth Africa
Availability: Limited
Compressive strength: 1790/kg cm^2
After freezing: 1668/kg cm^2
Ultimate tensile strength: 133/kg cm^2
Coef. thermal expansion: 0,0086mm/m°C
Water absorption: 0,31 %
Impact test / min. fall height: –
Frictional wear test: –
Bulk density: 2660 kg/m^3

CD file number: 0417

Juparana Africa

Quarrying location: Soth Africa
Availability: Limited
Compressive strength: 1790/kg cm^2
After freezing: 1668/kg cm^2
Ultimate tensile strength: 133/kg cm^2
Coef. thermal expansion: 0,0086mm/m°C
Water absorption: 0,31 %
Impact test / min. fall height: –
Frictional wear test: –
Bulk density: 2660 kg/m^3

CD file number: 0418

African Lillac

Quarrying location: Italy
Availability: Good
Compressive strength: 1719/kg cm^2
After freezing: 1653/kg cm^2
Ultimate tensile strength: 115/kg cm^2
Coef. thermal expansion: 0,0072mm/m°C
Water absorption: 0,31 %
Impact test / min. fall height: 61 cm
Frictional wear test: –
Bulk density: 2583 kg/m^3

CD file number: 0419

Ghiandone Limbara

Quarrying location: Italy
Availability: Good
Compressive strength: 1719/kg cm^2
After freezing: 1653/kg cm^2
Ultimate tensile strength: 115/kg cm^2
Coef. thermal expansion: 0,0072mm/m°C
Water absorption: 0,31 %
Impact test / min. fall height: 61 cm
Frictional wear test: –
Bulk density: 2583 kg/m^3

CD file number: 0420

Ghiandone Rosato

Quarrying location: Italy
Availability: Limited
Compressive strength: 1719/kg cm^2
After freezing: 1653/kg cm^2
Ultimate tensile strength: 115/kg cm^2
Coef. thermal expansion: 0,0072mm/m°C
Water absorption: 0,31 %
Impact test / min. fall height: 61 cm
Frictional wear test: –
Bulk density: 2583 kg/m^3

CD file number: 0421

Rosa Baveno

Quarrying location: Spain
Availability: Good
Compressive strength: 1719/kg cm^2
After freezing: 1653/kg cm^2
Ultimate tensile strength: 115/kg cm^2
Coef. thermal expansion: 0,0072mm/m°C
Water absorption: 0,31 %
Impact test / min. fall height: 61 cm
Frictional wear test: –
Bulk density: 2583 kg/m^3

CD file number: 0422

Rosa Porrino

Quarrying location: Italy
Availability: Medium
Compressive strength: 1719/kg cm^2
After freezing: 1653/kg cm^2
Ultimate tensile strength: 115/kg cm^2
Coef. thermal expansion: 0,0072mm/m°C
Water absorption: 0,31 %
Impact test / min. fall height: 61 cm
Frictional wear test: –
Bulk density: 2583 kg/m^3

CD file number: 0423

Rosa Sardo

Quarrying location: Italy
Availability: Medium
Compressive strength: 1719/kg cm^2
After freezing: 1653/kg cm^2
Ultimate tensile strength: 115/kg cm^2
Coef. thermal expansion: 0,0072mm/m°C
Water absorption: 0,31 %
Impact test / min. fall height: 61 cm
Frictional wear test: –
Bulk density: 2583 kg/m^3

CD file number: 0424

Rosa Sardo Champagne

Quarrying location: Italy
Availability: Limited
Compressive strength: 1719/kg cm^2
After freezing: 1653/kg cm^2
Ultimate tensile strength: 115/kg cm^2
Coef. thermal expansion: 0,0072mm/m°C
Water absorption: 0,31 %
Impact test / min. fall height: 61 cm
Frictional wear test: –
Bulk density: 2583 kg/m^3

CD file number: 0425

Rosa Nule

Quarrying location: Egypt
Availability: Good
Compressive strength: 1719/kg cm^2
After freezing: 1653/kg cm^2
Ultimate tensile strength: 115/kg cm^2
Coef. thermal expansion: 0,0072mm/m°C
Water absorption: 0,31 %
Impact test / min. fall height: 61 cm
Frictional wear test: –
Bulk density: 2583 kg/m^3

CD file number: 0426

Rosa Kali

Quarrying location: India
Availability: Good
Compressive strength: 1811/kg cm^2
After freezing: –
Ultimate tensile strength: 161/kg cm^2
Coef. thermal expansion: 0,0080mm/m°C
Water absorption: 0,28 %
Impact test / min. fall height: 80 cm
Frictional wear test: –
Bulk density: 2580 kg/m^3

CD file number: 0427

Juparana India

Quarrying location: USA
Availability: Medium
Compressive strength: 1811/kg cm^2
After freezing: –
Ultimate tensile strength: 161/kg cm^2
Coef. thermal expansion: 0,0080mm/m°C
Water absorption: 0,28 %
Impact test / min. fall height: 80 cm
Frictional wear test: –
Bulk density: 2580 kg/m^3

CD file number: 0428

Salisbury Pink

Quarrying location: India
Availability: Limited
Compressive strength: 1415/kg cm^2
After freezing: 1450/kg cm^2
Ultimate tensile strength: 93 /kg cm^2
Coef. thermal expansion: 0,0086mm/m°C
Water absorption: 0,31 %
Impact test / min. fall height: –
Frictional wear test: –
Bulk density: 2660 kg/m^3

CD file number: 0429

Shiwakashi

Quarrying location: India
Availability: Limited
Compressive strength: 1415/kg cm^2
After freezing: 1450/kg cm^2
Ultimate tensile strength: 93 /kg cm^2
Coef. thermal expansion: 0,0086mm/m°C
Water absorption: 0,31 %
Impact test / min. fall height: –
Frictional wear test: –
Bulk density: 2660 kg/m^3

CD file number: 0430

Shiwakashi Chiaro

Quarrying location: India
Availability: Limited
Compressive strength: 1415/kg cm^2
After freezing: 1450/kg cm^2
Ultimate tensile strength: 93 /kg cm^2
Coef. thermal expansion: 0,0086mm/m°C
Water absorption: 0,31 %
Impact test / min. fall height: –
Frictional wear test: –
Bulk density: 2660 kg/m^3

CD file number: 0431

Shiwakashi Cream

Quarrying location: India
Availability: Good
Compressive strength: 1811/kg cm^2
After freezing: –
Ultimate tensile strength: 161/kg cm^2
Coef. thermal expansion: 0,0080mm/m°C
Water absorption: 0,28 %
Impact test / min. fall height: 80 cm
Frictional wear test: –
Bulk density: 2580 kg/m^3

CD file number: 0432

Imperial Rose

Juparana Africa

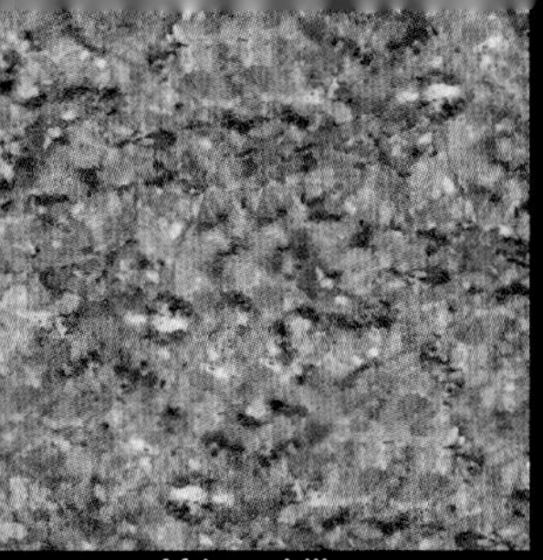

African Lillac

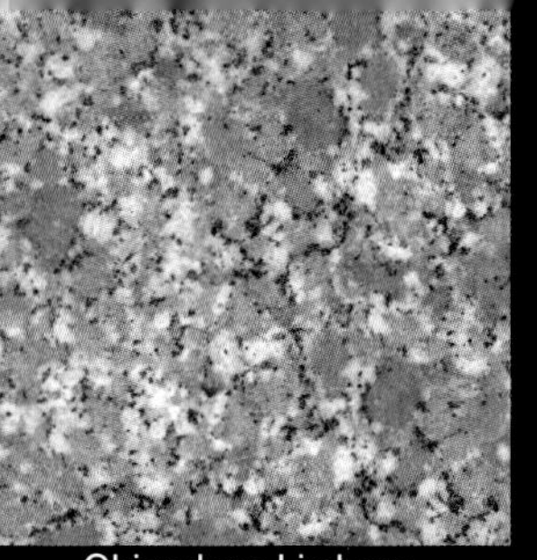

Ghiandone Limbara

Ghiandone Rosato

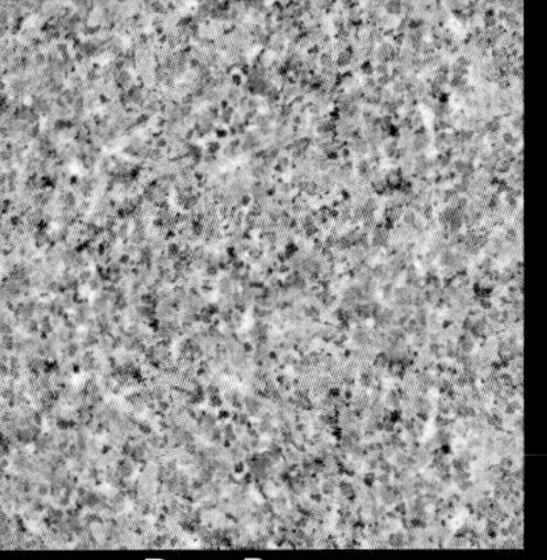

Rosa Baveno

Rosa Porrino

Rosa Sardo

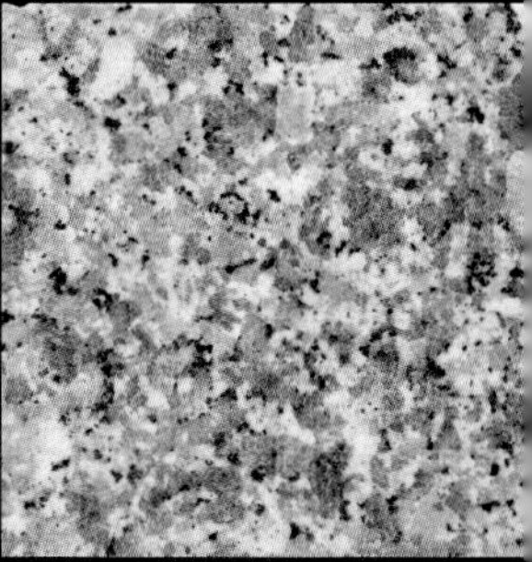

Rosa Sardo Champagne

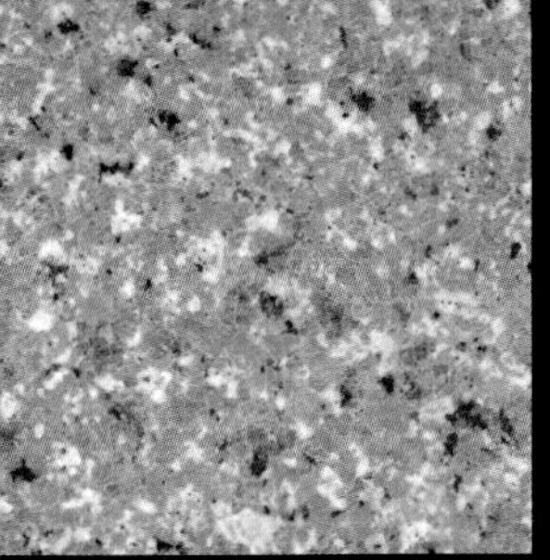

Rosa Nule

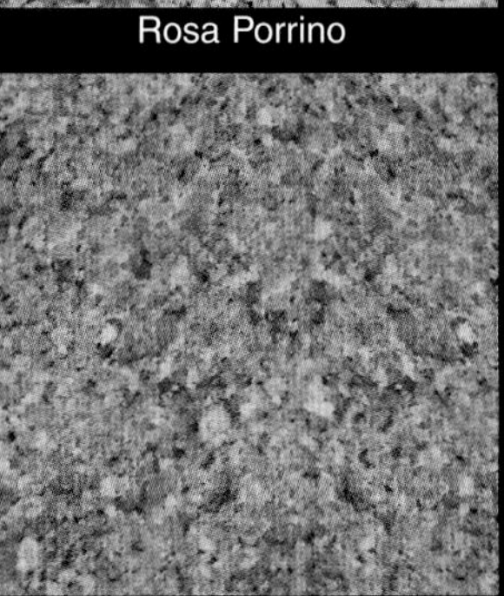

Rosa Kali

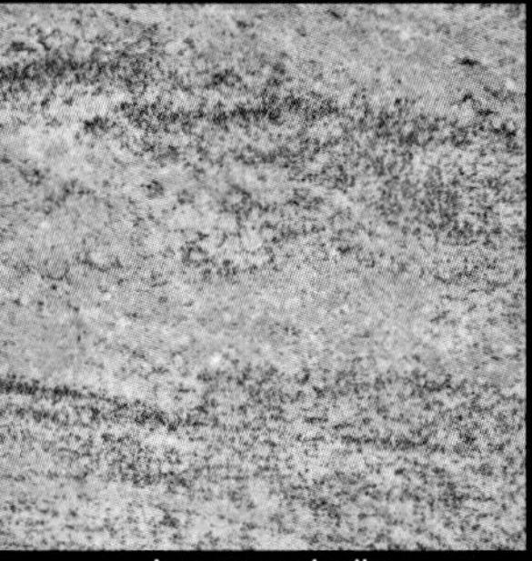

Juparana India

Salisbury Pink

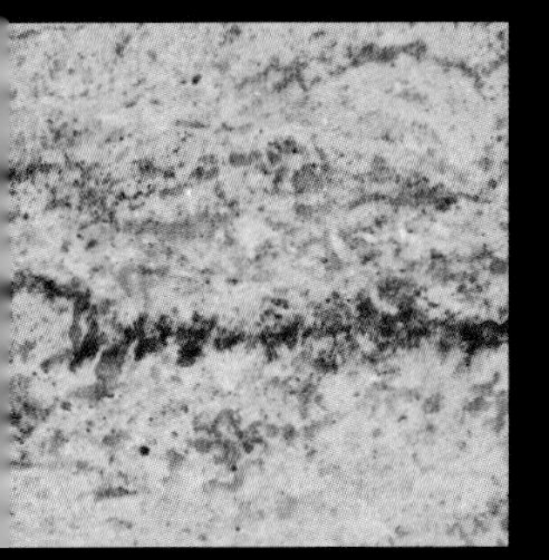

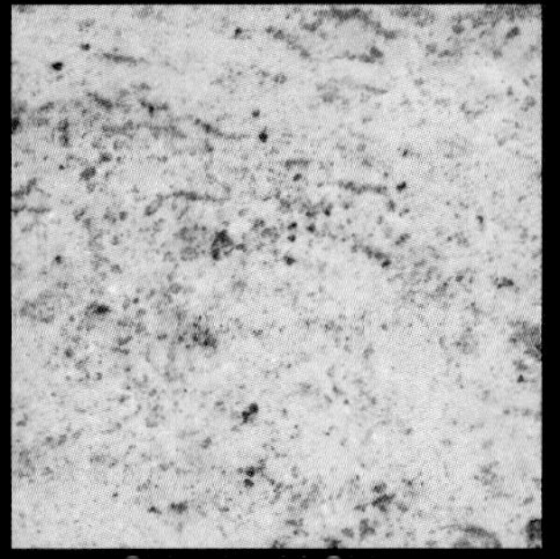

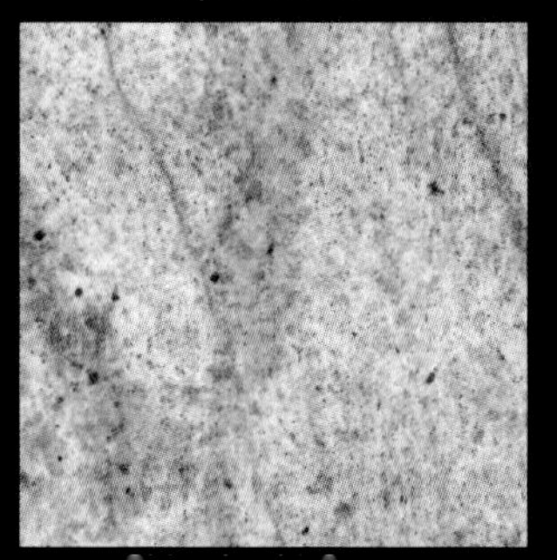

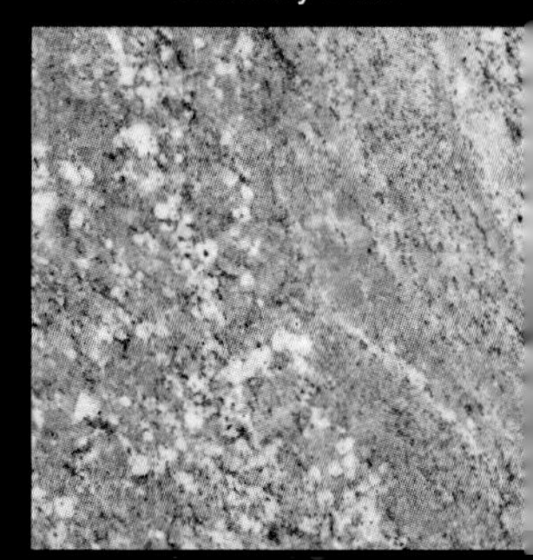

Quarrying location: Brazil
Availability: Medium
Compressive strength: 1776/kg cm^2
After freezing: 1610/kg cm^2
Ultimate tensile strength: 152/kg cm^2
Coef. thermal expansion: 0,0073mm/m°C
Water absorption: 0,23 %
Impact test / min. fall height: –
Frictional wear test: –
Bulk density: 2621 kg/m^3

CD file number: 0433

Quarrying location: Brazil
Availability: Medium
Compressive strength: 1776/kg cm^2
After freezing: 1610/kg cm^2
Ultimate tensile strength: 152/kg cm^2
Coef. thermal expansion: 0,0073mm/m°C
Water absorption: 0,23 %
Impact test / min. fall height: –
Frictional wear test: –
Bulk density: 2621 kg/m^3

CD file number: 0434

Quarrying location: India
Availability: Medium
Compressive strength: 1776/kg cm^2
After freezing: 1610/kg cm^2
Ultimate tensile strength: 152/kg cm^2
Coef. thermal expansion: 0,0073mm/m°C
Water absorption: 0,23 %
Impact test / min. fall height: –
Frictional wear test: –
Bulk density: 2621 kg/m^3

CD file number: 0435

Quarrying location: India
Availability: Medium
Compressive strength: 1776/kg cm^2
After freezing: 1610/kg cm^2
Ultimate tensile strength: 152/kg cm^2
Coef. thermal expansion: 0,0073mm/m°C
Water absorption: 0,23 %
Impact test / min. fall height: –
Frictional wear test: –
Bulk density: 2621 kg/m^3

CD file number: 0436

Lilla Gerais

Quarrying location: Brazil
Availability: Medium
Compressive strength: 1776/kg cm^2
After freezing: 1610/kg cm^2
Ultimate tensile strength: 152/kg cm^2
Coef. thermal expansion: 0,0073mm/m°C
Water absorption: 0,23 %
Impact test / min. fall height: –
Frictional wear test: –
Bulk density: 2621 kg/m^3

CD file number: 0437

Rosa Raissa

Quarrying location: Brazil
Availability: Medium
Compressive strength: 1776/kg cm^2
After freezing: 1610/kg cm^2
Ultimate tensile strength: 152/kg cm^2
Coef. thermal expansion: 0,0073mm/m°C
Water absorption: 0,23 %
Impact test / min. fall height: –
Frictional wear test: –
Bulk density: 2621 kg/m^3

CD file number: 0438

Raw Silk

Quarrying location: Brazil
Availability: Medium
Compressive strength: 1776/kg cm^2
After freezing: 1610/kg cm^2
Ultimate tensile strength: 152/kg cm^2
Coef. thermal expansion: 0,0073mm/m°C
Water absorption: 0,23 %
Impact test / min. fall height: –
Frictional wear test: –
Bulk density: 2621 kg/m^3

CD file number: 0439

Sunny

Quarrying location: Brazil
Availability: Medium
Compressive strength: 1776/kg cm^2
After freezing: 1610/kg cm^2
Ultimate tensile strength: 152/kg cm^2
Coef. thermal expansion: 0,0073mm/m°C
Water absorption: 0,23 %
Impact test / min. fall height: –
Frictional wear test: –
Bulk density: 2621 kg/m^3

CD file number: 0440

Kinawa

Quarrying location: Sweden
Availability: Medium
Compressive strength: 1894/kg cm^2
After freezing: 1742/kg cm^2
Ultimate tensile strength: 168/kg cm^2
Coef. thermal expansion: 0,0083mm/m°C
Water absorption: 0,38 %
Impact test / min. fall height: 48 cm
Frictional wear test: –
Bulk density: 2839 kg/m^3

CD file number: 0441

Kinawa Classico

Quarrying location: USA
Availability: Medium
Compressive strength: 1894/kg cm^2
After freezing: 1742/kg cm^2
Ultimate tensile strength: 168/kg cm^2
Coef. thermal expansion: 0,0083mm/m°C
Water absorption: 0,38 %
Impact test / min. fall height: 48 cm
Frictional wear test: –
Bulk density: 2839 kg/m^3

CD file number: 0442

Himalayan Blu

Quarrying location: Brazil
Availability: Medium
Compressive strength: 1920/kg cm^2
After freezing: 1810/kg cm^2
Ultimate tensile strength: –
Coef. thermal expansion: –
Water absorption: 0,15 %
Impact test / min. fall height: –
Frictional wear test: –
Bulk density: 2720 kg/m^3

CD file number: 0443

Ita Green

Quarrying location: China
Availability: Good
Compressive strength: 1776/kg cm^2
After freezing: 1610/kg cm^2
Ultimate tensile strength: 152/kg cm^2
Coef. thermal expansion: –
Water absorption: 0,23 %
Impact test / min. fall height: –
Frictional wear test: –
Bulk density: 2621 kg/m^3

CD file number: 0444

Royal Mahogany

Quarrying location: Brazil
Availability: Medium
Compressive strength: 1920/kg cm^2
After freezing: 1810/kg cm^2
Ultimate tensile strength: –
Coef. thermal expansion: –
Water absorption: 0,15 %
Impact test / min. fall height: –
Frictional wear test: –
Bulk density: 2720 kg/m^3

CD file number: 0445

Dakota Mahogany

Quarrying location: Brazil
Availability: Medium
Compressive strength: 1920/kg cm^2
After freezing: 1810/kg cm^2
Ultimate tensile strength: –
Coef. thermal expansion: –
Water absorption: 0,15 %
Impact test / min. fall height: –
Frictional wear test: –
Bulk density: 2720 kg/m^3

CD file number: 0446

Gran Violet

Quarrying location: Brazil
Availability: GOOD
Compressive strength: 1776/kg cm^2
After freezing: 1610/kg cm^2
Ultimate tensile strength: 152/kg cm^2
Coef. thermal expansion: 0,0073mm/m°C
Water absorption: 0,23 %
Impact test / min. fall height: –
Frictional wear test: –
Bulk density: 2621 kg/m^3

CD file number: 0447

Almond Mauve

Quarrying location: Brazil
Availability: Medium
Compressive strength: 1900/kg cm^2
After freezing: 1830/kg cm^2
Ultimate tensile strength: 190/kg cm^2
Coef. thermal expansion: –
Water absorption: –
Impact test / min. fall height: –
Frictional wear test: –
Bulk density: 2700 kg/m^3

CD file number: 0448

Mozart

Palladio

Shangri-la

Royal Celadon

Lilla Gerais

Rosa Raissa

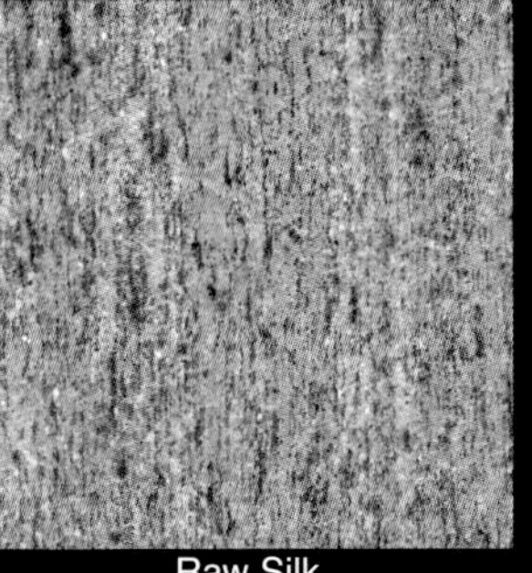
Raw Silk

Sunny

Kinawa

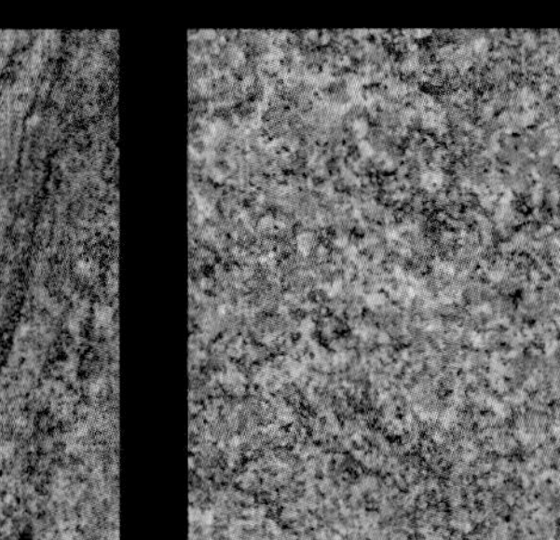
Kinawa Classico

Himalayan Blu

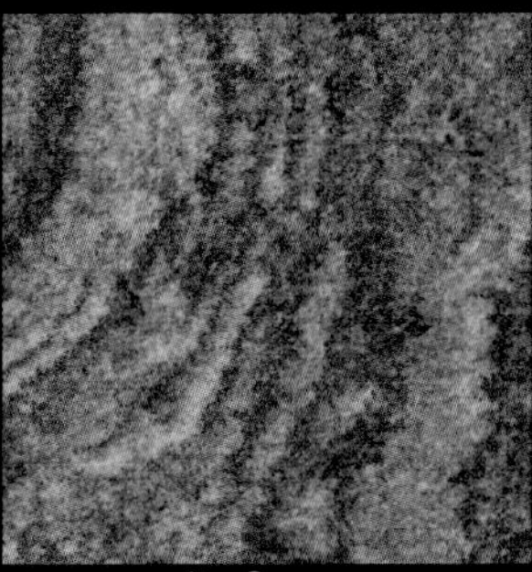
Ita Green

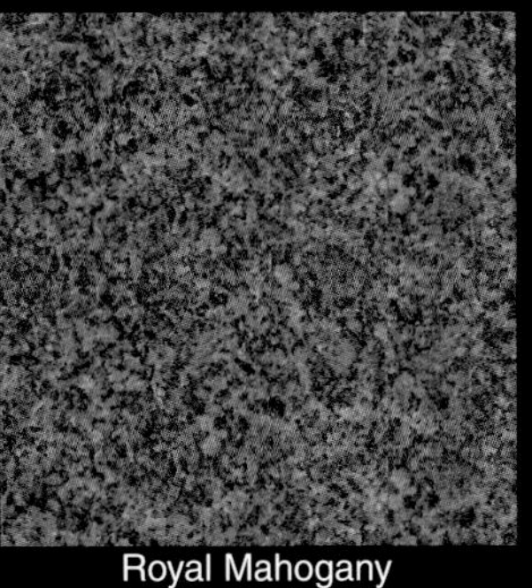
Royal Mahogany

Dakota Mahogany

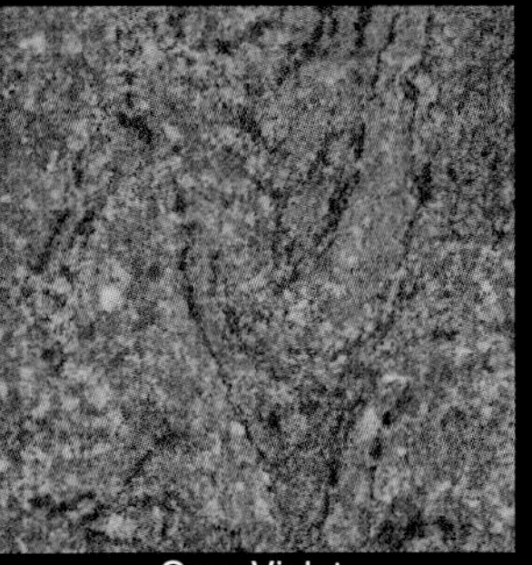
Gran Violet

Almond Mauve

Mozart

Palladio

Shangri-la

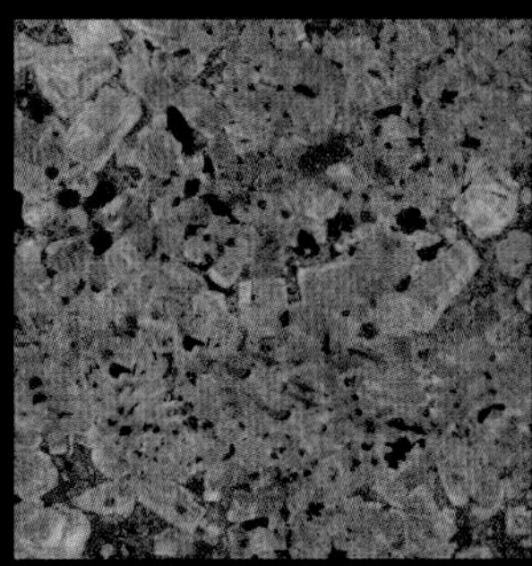
Royal Celadon

Quarrying location:	Finland
Availability:	Good
Compressive strength:	1986/kg cm^2
After freezing:	1777/kg cm^2
Ultimate tensile strength:	118/kg cm^2
Coef. thermal expansion:	0,0070mm/m°C
Water absorption:	0,20 %
Impact test / min. fall height:	62 cm
Frictional wear test:	–
Bulk density:	2640 kg/m^3

CD file number: 0449

Baltic Brown

Quarrying location:	Brazil
Availability:	Limited
Compressive strength:	1570/kg cm^2
After freezing:	1465/kg cm^2
Ultimate tensile strength:	53/kg cm^2
Coef. thermal expansion:	0,0040mm/m°C
Water absorption:	0,12 %
Impact test / min. fall height:	58 cm
Frictional wear test:	0,7 mm
Bulk density:	2540 kg/m^3

CD file number: 0450

Marron Guaiba

Quarrying location:	Brazil
Availability:	Medium
Compressive strength:	1570/kg cm^2
After freezing:	1465/kg cm^2
Ultimate tensile strength:	53/kg cm^2
Coef. thermal expansion:	0,0040mm/m°C
Water absorption:	0,12 %
Impact test / min. fall height:	58 cm
Frictional wear test:	0,7 mm
Bulk density:	2540 kg/m^3

CD file number: 0451

Marron Caffé

Quarrying location:	Brazil
Availability:	Medium
Compressive strength:	2326/kg cm^2
After freezing:	2181/kg cm^2
Ultimate tensile strength:	143/kg cm^2
Coef. thermal expansion:	0,0050mm/m°C
Water absorption:	0,13 %
Impact test / min. fall height:	72 cm
Frictional wear test:	1,80 mm
Bulk density:	2706 kg/m^3

CD file number: 0452

Marron Bahia

Quarrying location:	South Africa
Availability:	Medium
Compressive strength:	1640/kg cm^2
After freezing:	–
Ultimate tensile strength:	118/kg cm^2
Coef. thermal expansion:	0,0090mm/m°C
Water absorption:	0,22 %
Impact test / min. fall height:	50 cm
Frictional wear test:	0,70 mm
Bulk density:	2732 kg/m^3

CD file number: 0453

Crystal Brown

Quarrying location:	Norway
Availability:	Medium
Compressive strength:	1640/kg cm^2
After freezing:	–
Ultimate tensile strength:	118/kg cm^2
Coef. thermal expansion:	0,0090mm/m°C
Water absorption:	0,22 %
Impact test / min. fall height:	50 cm
Frictional wear test:	0,70 mm
Bulk density:	2732 kg/m^3

CD file number: 0454

Labrador Antique Scuro

Quarrying location:	Norway
Availability:	Medium
Compressive strength:	1640/kg cm^2
After freezing:	–
Ultimate tensile strength:	118/kg cm^2
Coef. thermal expansion:	0,0090mm/m°C
Water absorption:	0,22 %
Impact test / min. fall height:	50 cm
Frictional wear test:	0,70 mm
Bulk density:	2732 kg/m^3

CD file number: 0455

Labrador Antique

Quarrying location:	Brazil
Availability:	Medium
Compressive strength:	2326/kg cm^2
After freezing:	2181/kg cm^2
Ultimate tensile strength:	143/kg cm^2
Coef. thermal expansion:	0,0050mm/m°C
Water absorption:	0,13 %
Impact test / min. fall height:	72 cm
Frictional wear test:	1,80 mm
Bulk density:	2706 kg/m^3

CD file number: 0456

Imperial Brown

Quarrying location:	Canada
Availability:	Medium
Compressive strength:	2326/kg cm^2
After freezing:	2181/kg cm^2
Ultimate tensile strength:	143/kg cm^2
Coef. thermal expansion:	0,0050mm/m°C
Water absorption:	0,13 %
Impact test / min. fall height:	72 cm
Frictional wear test:	1,80 mm
Bulk density:	2706 kg/m^3

CD file number: 0457

Polichrome

Quarrying location:	Canada
Availability:	Medium
Compressive strength:	2326/kg cm^2
After freezing:	2181/kg cm^2
Ultimate tensile strength:	143/kg cm^2
Coef. thermal expansion:	0,0050mm/m°C
Water absorption:	0,13 %
Impact test / min. fall height:	72 cm
Frictional wear test:	1,80 mm
Bulk density:	2706 kg/m^3

CD file number: 0458

New Caledonia

Quarrying location:	Brazil
Availability:	Medium
Compressive strength:	2326/kg cm^2
After freezing:	2181/kg cm^2
Ultimate tensile strength:	143/kg cm^2
Coef. thermal expansion:	0,0050mm/m°C
Water absorption:	0,13 %
Impact test / min. fall height:	72 cm
Frictional wear test:	1,80 mm
Bulk density:	2706 kg/m^3

CD file number: 0459

Zeta Brown

Quarrying location:	Brazil
Availability:	Medium
Compressive strength:	1570/kg cm^2
After freezing:	1465/kg cm^2
Ultimate tensile strength:	53/kg cm^2
Coef. thermal expansion:	0,0040mm/m°C
Water absorption:	0,12 %
Impact test / min. fall height:	58 cm
Frictional wear test:	0,7 mm
Bulk density:	2540 kg/m^3

CD file number: 0460

Tropic Brown

Quarrying location:	Saudi Arabia
Availability:	Medium
Compressive strength:	2326/kg cm^2
After freezing:	2181/kg cm^2
Ultimate tensile strength:	143/kg cm^2
Coef. thermal expansion:	0,0050mm/m°C
Water absorption:	0,13 %
Impact test / min. fall height:	72 cm
Frictional wear test:	1,80 mm
Bulk density:	2706 kg/m^3

CD file number: 0461

Najran Brown

Quarrying location:	Brazil
Availability:	Medium
Compressive strength:	1570/kg cm^2
After freezing:	1465/kg cm^2
Ultimate tensile strength:	53/kg cm^2
Coef. thermal expansion:	0,0040mm/m°C
Water absorption:	0,12 %
Impact test / min. fall height:	58 cm
Frictional wear test:	0,7 mm
Bulk density:	2540 kg/m^3

CD file number: 0462

Brown Leather

Quarrying location:	India
Availability:	Medium
Compressive strength:	2364/kg cm^2
After freezing:	2228/kg cm^2
Ultimate tensile strength:	312/kg cm^2
Coef. thermal expansion:	–
Water absorption:	0,18 %
Impact test / min. fall height:	–
Frictional wear test:	–
Bulk density:	2680 kg/m^3

CD file number: 0463

Saphire Brown

Quarrying location:	Saudi Arabia
Availability:	Limited
Compressive strength:	1900/kg cm^2
After freezing:	1830/kg cm^2
Ultimate tensile strength:	190/kg cm^2
Coef. thermal expansion:	–
Water absorption:	–
Impact test / min. fall height:	–
Frictional wear test:	–
Bulk density:	2700 kg/m^3

CD file number: 0464

Violetta

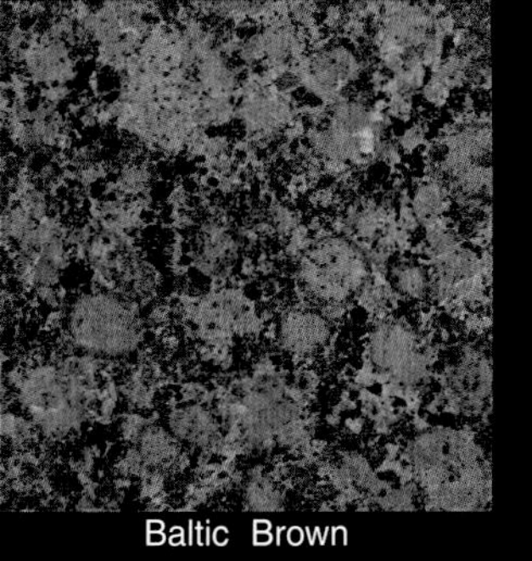

Baltic Brown

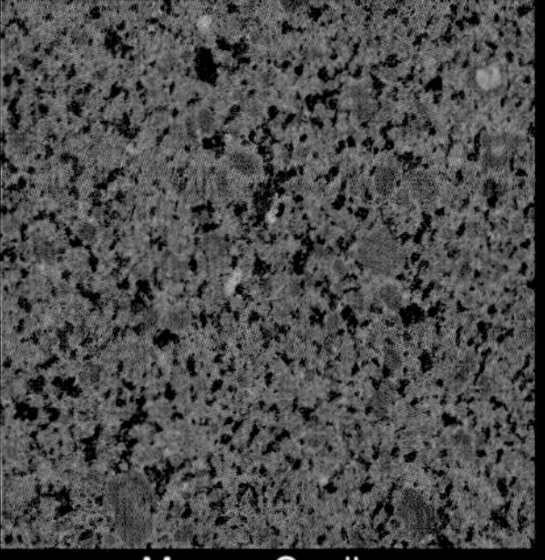

Marron Guaiba

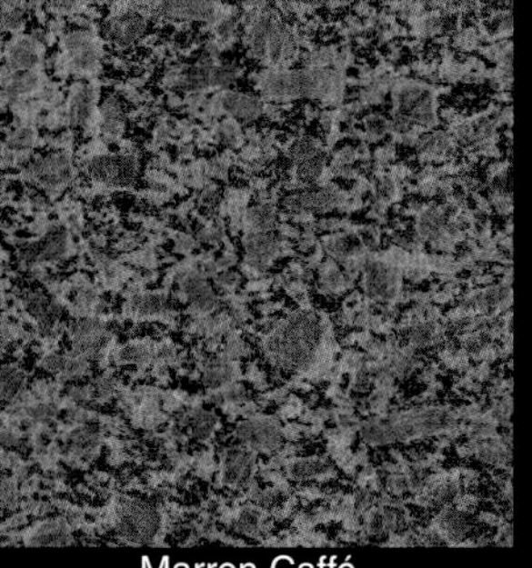

Marron Caffé

Marron Bahia

Crystal Brown

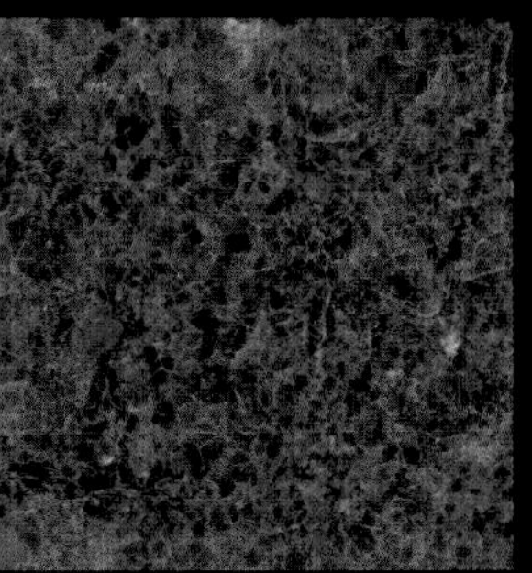

Labrador Antique Scuro

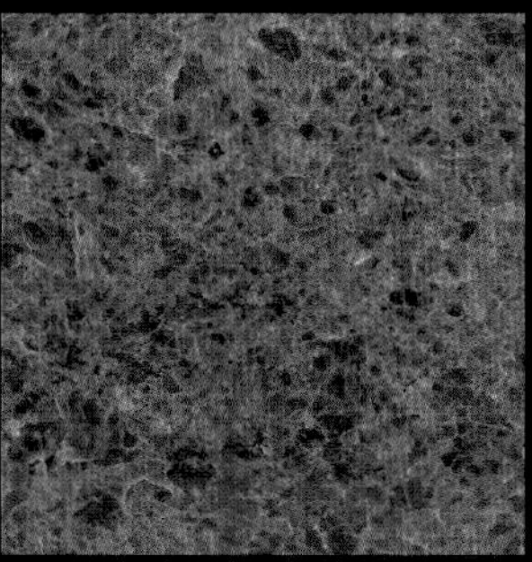

Labrador Antique

Imperial Brown

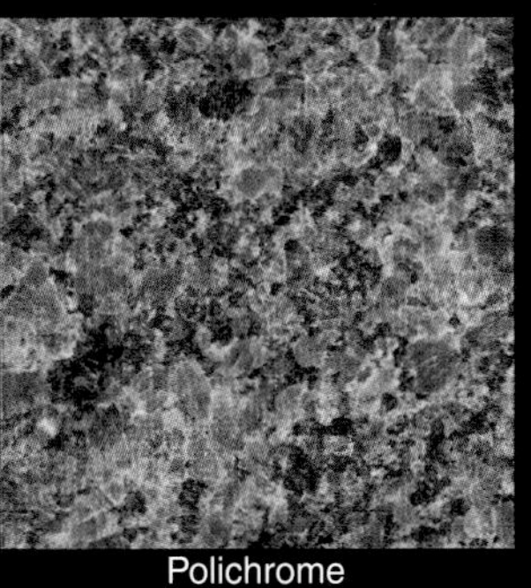

Polichrome

New Caledonia

Zeta Brown

Tropic Brown

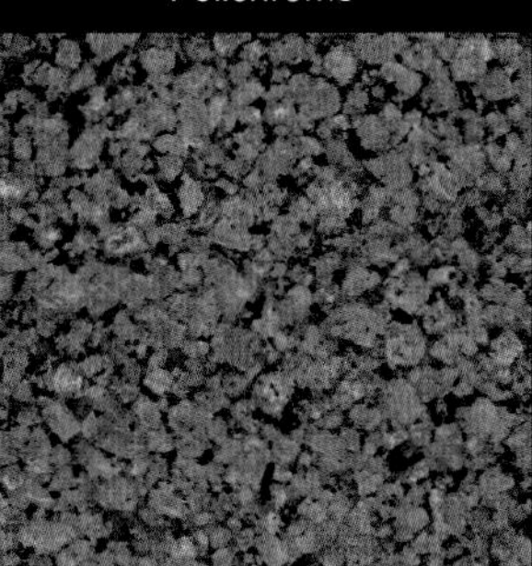

Najran Brown

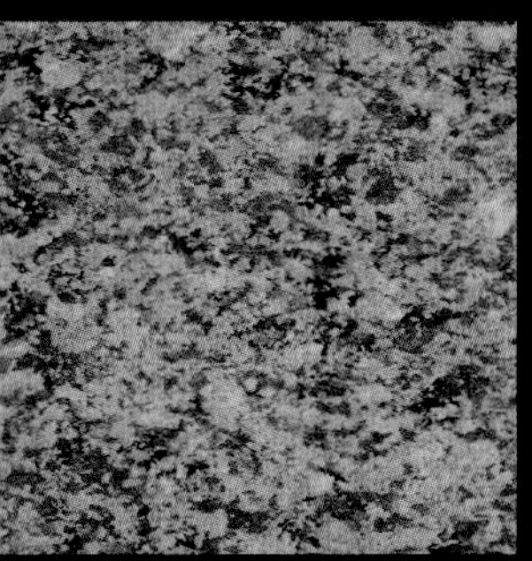

Brown Leather

Saphire Brown

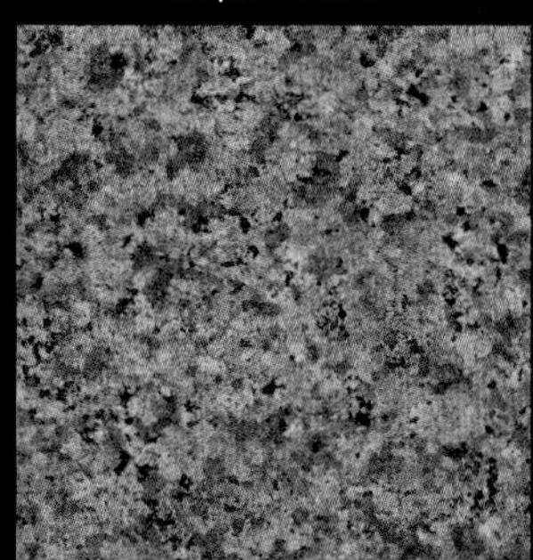

Violetta

Quarrying location:	Brazil
Availability:	Limited
Compressive strength:	1776/kg cm^2
After freezing:	–
Ultimate tensile strength:	165/kg cm^2
Coef. thermal expansion:	0,0012mm/m°C
Water absorption:	–
Impact test / min. fall height:	40 cm
Frictional wear test:	–
Bulk density:	2553 kg/m^3

CD file number: 0465

Quarrying location:	Zambia
Availability:	Limited
Compressive strength:	1776/kg cm^2
After freezing:	–
Ultimate tensile strength:	165/kg cm^2
Coef. thermal expansion:	0,0012mm/m°C
Water absorption:	–
Impact test / min. fall height:	40 cm
Frictional wear test:	–
Bulk density:	2553 kg/m^3

CD file number: 0466

Quarrying location:	Brazil
Availability:	Limited
Compressive strength:	1776 /kg cm^2
After freezing:	–
Ultimate tensile strength:	165/kg cm^2
Coef. thermal expansion:	0,0012mm/m°C
Water absorption:	–
Impact test / min. fall height:	40 cm
Frictional wear test:	–
Bulk density:	2553 kg/m^3

CD file number: 0467

Quarrying location:	India
Availability:	Medium
Compressive strength:	1993 /kg cm^2
After freezing:	1590 /kg cm^2
Ultimate tensile strength:	111/kg cm^2
Coef. thermal expansion:	–
Water absorption:	0,22 %
Impact test / min. fall height:	–
Frictional wear test:	–
Bulk density:	2623 kg/m^3

CD file number: 0468

Azul Bahia

Quarrying location:	India
Availability:	Medium
Compressive strength:	1993 /kg cm^2
After freezing:	1590 /kg cm^2
Ultimate tensile strength:	111/kg cm^2
Coef. thermal expansion:	–
Water absorption:	0,22 %
Impact test / min. fall height:	–
Frictional wear test:	–
Bulk density:	2623 kg/m^3

CD file number: 0469

Blu King

Quarrying location:	India
Availability:	Medium
Compressive strength:	1993 /kg cm^2
After freezing:	1590 /kg cm^2
Ultimate tensile strength:	111/kg cm^2
Coef. thermal expansion:	–
Water absorption:	0,22 %
Impact test / min. fall height:	–
Frictional wear test:	–
Bulk density:	2623 kg/m^3

CD file number: 0470

Guanabara Blu

Quarrying location:	India
Availability:	Medium
Compressive strength:	1993 /kg cm^2
After freezing:	1590 /kg cm^2
Ultimate tensile strength:	111/kg cm^2
Coef. thermal expansion:	–
Water absorption:	0,22 %
Impact test / min. fall height:	–
Frictional wear test:	–
Bulk density:	2623 kg/m^3

CD file number: 0471

Orissa Blu

Quarrying location:	India
Availability:	Good
Compressive strength:	1993 /kg cm^2
After freezing:	1590 /kg cm^2
Ultimate tensile strength:	111/kg cm^2
Coef. thermal expansion:	–
Water absorption:	0,22 %
Impact test / min. fall height:	–
Frictional wear test:	–
Bulk density:	2623 kg/m^3

CD file number: 0472

Samantha Blu

Quarrying location:	Norway
Availability:	Good
Compressive strength:	2250 /kg cm^2
After freezing:	1969 /kg cm^2
Ultimate tensile strength:	201/kg cm^2
Coef. thermal expansion:	–
Water absorption:	–
Impact test / min. fall height:	46 cm
Frictional wear test:	–
Bulk density:	2740 kg/m^3

CD file number: 0473

Paradiso Blu

Quarrying location:	Norway
Availability:	Good
Compressive strength:	2250 /kg cm^2
After freezing:	1969 /kg cm^2
Ultimate tensile strength:	201/kg cm^2
Coef. thermal expansion:	–
Water absorption:	–
Impact test / min. fall height:	46 cm
Frictional wear test:	–
Bulk density:	2740 kg/m^3

CD file number: 0474

Bahama Blu

Quarrying location:	Norway
Availability:	Limited
Compressive strength:	2250 /kg cm^2
After freezing:	1969 /kg cm^2
Ultimate tensile strength:	201/kg cm^2
Coef. thermal expansion:	–
Water absorption:	–
Impact test / min. fall height:	46 cm
Frictional wear test:	–
Bulk density:	2740 kg/m^3

CD file number: 0475

Vizag

Quarrying location:	Norway
Availability:	Good
Compressive strength:	2250 /kg cm^2
After freezing:	1969 /kg cm^2
Ultimate tensile strength:	201/kg cm^2
Coef. thermal expansion:	–
Water absorption:	–
Impact test / min. fall height:	46 cm
Frictional wear test:	–
Bulk density:	2740 kg/m^3

CD file number: 0476

Blu Pearl

Quarrying location:	Canada
Availability:	Medium
Compressive strength:	1993 /kg cm^2
After freezing:	1590 /kg cm^2
Ultimate tensile strength:	111/kg cm^2
Coef. thermal expansion:	–
Water absorption:	0,22 %
Impact test / min. fall height:	–
Frictional wear test:	–
Bulk density:	2623 kg/m^3

CD file number: 0477

Emerald Pearl

Quarrying location:	Canada
Availability:	Medium
Compressive strength:	1993 /kg cm^2
After freezing:	1590 /kg cm^2
Ultimate tensile strength:	111/kg cm^2
Coef. thermal expansion:	–
Water absorption:	0,22 %
Impact test / min. fall height:	–
Frictional wear test:	–
Bulk density:	2623 kg/m^3

CD file number: 0478

Marina Pearl

Quarrying location:	Ukraine
Availability:	Medium
Compressive strength:	1993 /kg cm^2
After freezing:	1590 /kg cm^2
Ultimate tensile strength:	111/kg cm^2
Coef. thermal expansion:	–
Water absorption:	0,22 %
Impact test / min. fall height:	–
Frictional wear test:	–
Bulk density:	2623 kg/m^3

CD file number: 0479

Gran Pearl

Quarrying location:	India
Availability:	Medium
Compressive strength:	1993 /kg cm^2
After freezing:	1590 /kg cm^2
Ultimate tensile strength:	111/kg cm^2
Coef. thermal expansion:	–
Water absorption:	0,22 %
Impact test / min. fall height:	–
Frictional wear test:	–
Bulk density:	2623 kg/m^3

CD file number: 0480

Blu Eyes Chiaro

Blu Eyes

Volga Blu

Tropical Green

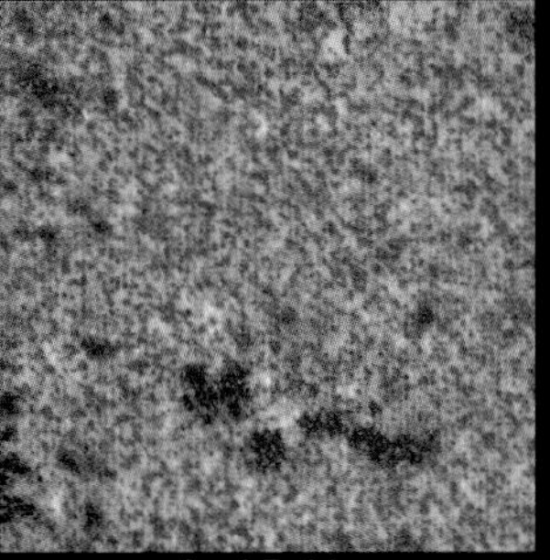

Azul Bahia

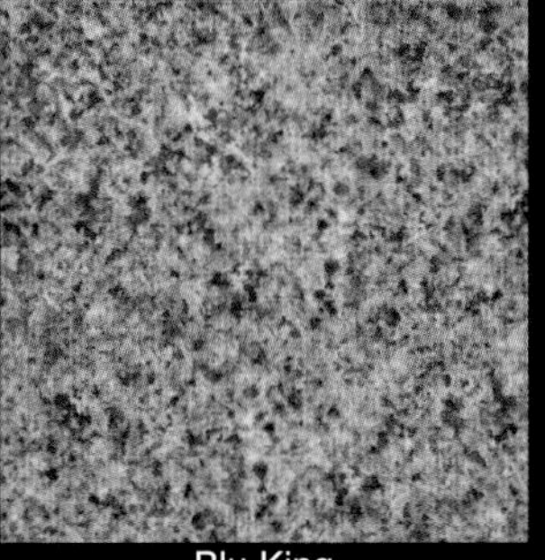

Blu King

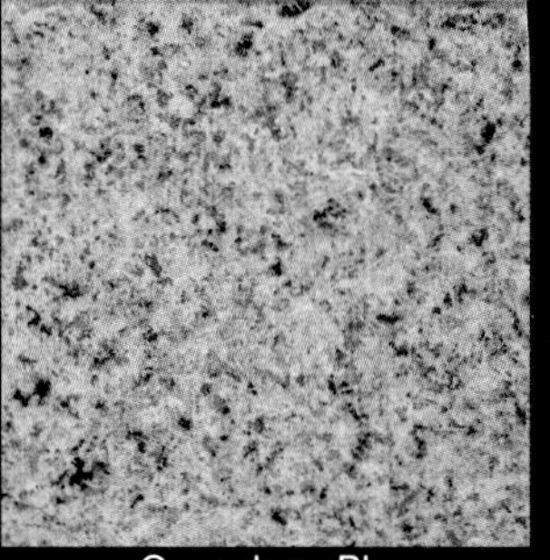

Guanabara Blu

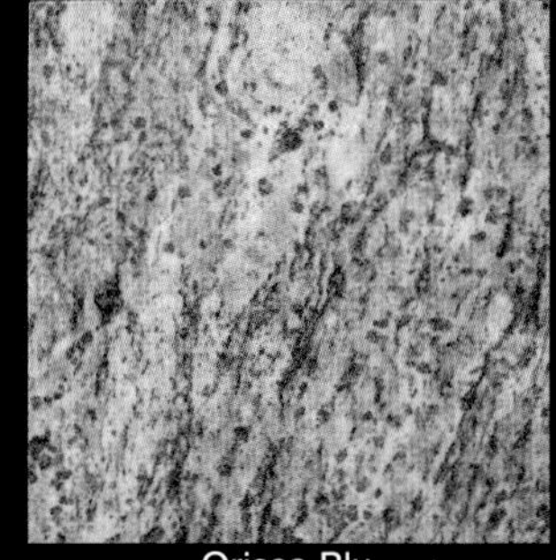

Orissa Blu

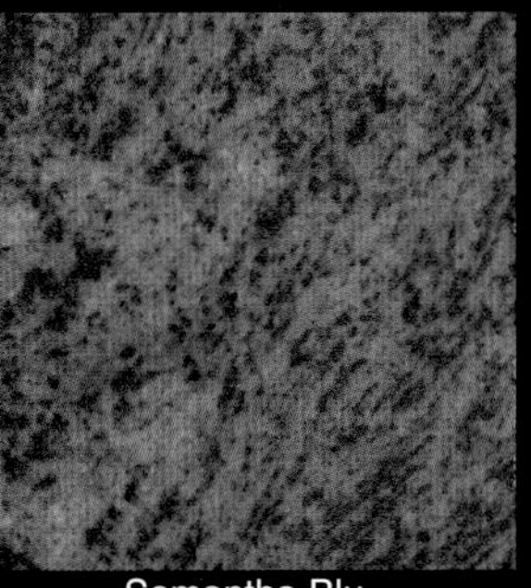

Samantha Blu

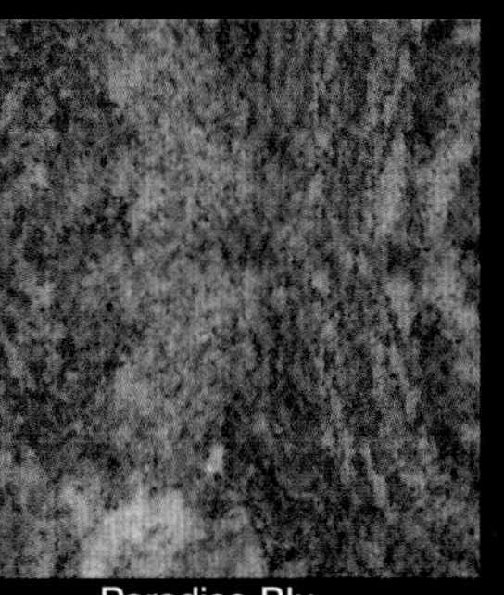

Paradiso Blu

Bahama Blu

Vizag

Blu Pearl

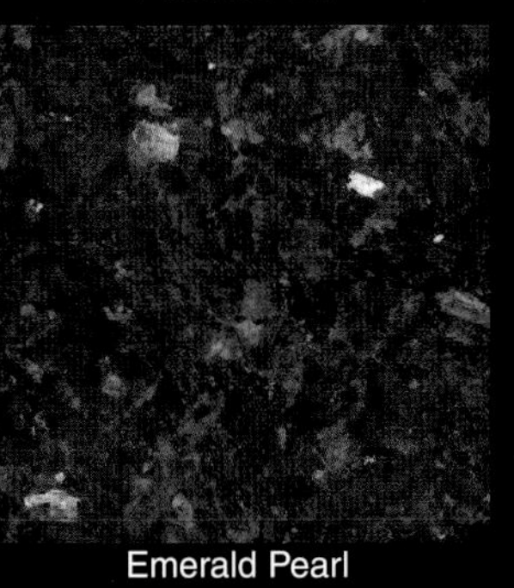

Emerald Pearl

Marina Pearl

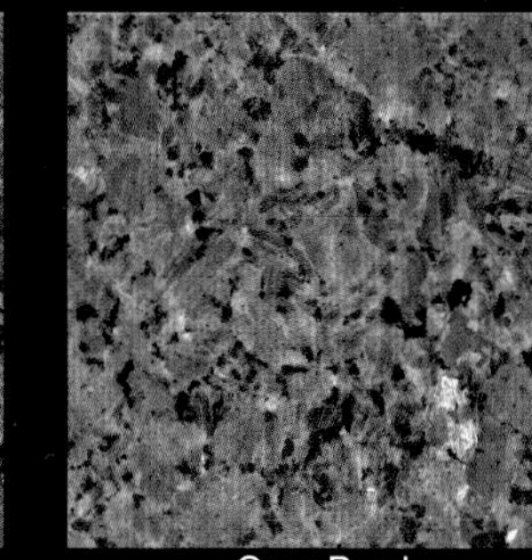

Gran Pearl

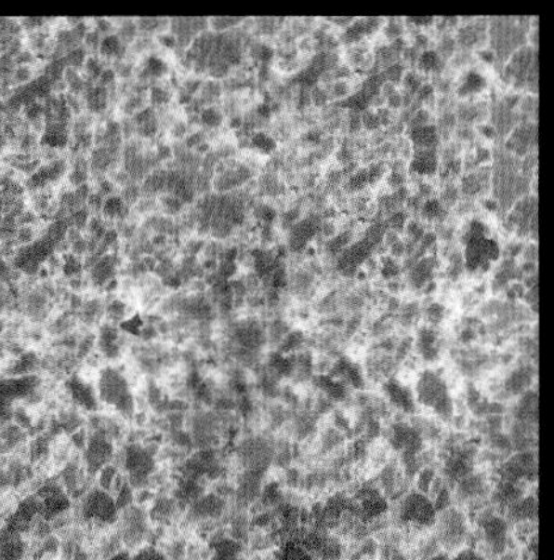

Blu Eyes Chiaro

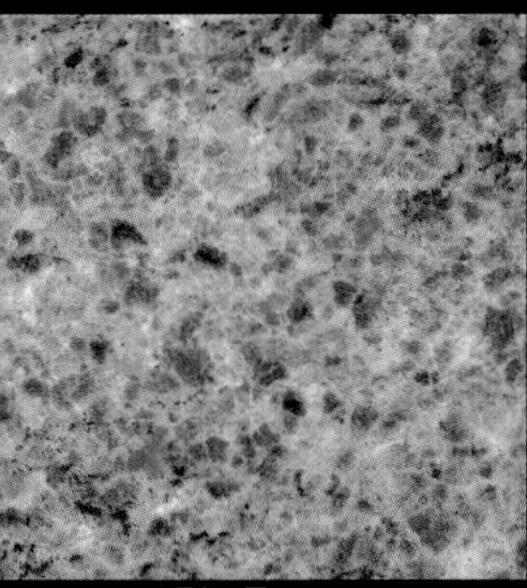

Blu Eyes

Volga Blu

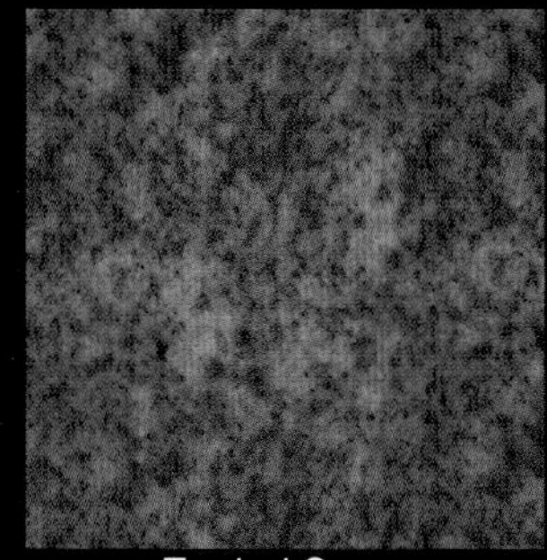

Tropical Green

Quarrying location: India
Availability: Good
Compressive strength: 1899 /kg cm^2
After freezing: 1745 /kg cm^2
Ultimate tensile strength: –
Coef. thermal expansion: 0,0063mm/m°C
Water absorption: –
Impact test / min. fall height: –
Frictional wear test: –
Bulk density: 2641 kg/m^3

CD file number: 0481

Quarrying location: India
Availability: Good
Compressive strength: 1899 /kg cm^2
After freezing: 1745 /kg cm^2
Ultimate tensile strength: –
Coef. thermal expansion: 0,0063mm/m°C
Water absorption: –
Impact test / min. fall height: –
Frictional wear test: –
Bulk density: 2641 kg/m^3

CD file number: 0482

Quarrying location: India
Availability: Good
Compressive strength: 1899 /kg cm^2
After freezing: 1745 /kg cm^2
Ultimate tensile strength: –
Coef. thermal expansion: 0,0063mm/m°C
Water absorption: –
Impact test / min. fall height: –
Frictional wear test: –
Bulk density: 2641 kg/m^3

CD file number: 0483

Quarrying location: Portugal
Availability: Medium
Compressive strength: 1720/kg cm^2
After freezing: 1664/kg cm^2
Ultimate tensile strength: 139/kg cm^2
Coef. thermal expansion: 0,0050mm/m°C
Water absorption: 0,32%
Impact test / min. fall height: 86 cm
Frictional wear test: –
Bulk density: 2661 kg/m^3

CD file number: 0484

Paradiso Bash

Quarrying location: Porto Rose
Availability: Limited
Compressive strength: 1900/kg cm^2
After freezing: 1830/kg cm^2
Ultimate tensile strength: 190/kg cm^2
Coef. thermal expansion: –
Water absorption: –
Impact test / min. fall height: –
Frictional wear test: –
Bulk density: 2700 kg/m^3

CD file number: 0485

Paradiso Chiaro

Quarrying location: Brazil
Availability: Medium
Compressive strength: 2364/kg cm^2
After freezing: 2228/kg cm^2
Ultimate tensile strength: 312/kg cm^2
Coef. thermal expansion: –
Water absorption: 0,18 %
Impact test / min. fall height: –
Frictional wear test: –
Bulk density: 2680 kg/m^3

CD file number: 0486

Paradiso Scuro

Quarrying location: Brazil
Availability: Medium
Compressive strength: 1920/kg cm^2
After freezing: 1810/kg cm^2
Ultimate tensile strength: –
Coef. thermal expansion: –
Water absorption: 0,15 %
Impact test / min. fall height: –
Frictional wear test: –
Bulk density: 2720 kg/m^3

CD file number: 0487

Saint Louis

Quarrying location: China
Availability: Medium
Compressive strength: 1720/kg cm^2
After freezing: 1664/kg cm^2
Ultimate tensile strength: 139/kg cm^2
Coef. thermal expansion: 0,0050mm/m°C
Water absorption: 0,32%
Impact test / min. fall height: 86 cm
Frictional wear test: –
Bulk density: 2661 kg/m^3

CD file number: 0488

Porto Rose

Quarrying location: Norway
Availability: Medium
Compressive strength: 2250 /kg cm^2
After freezing: 1969 /kg cm^2
Ultimate tensile strength: 201/kg cm^2
Coef. thermal expansion: –
Water absorption: –
Impact test / min. fall height: 46 cm
Frictional wear test: –
Bulk density: 2740 kg/m^3

CD file number: 0489

Sucurù

Quarrying location: India
Availability: Medium
Compressive strength: 2080 /kg cm^2
After freezing: 1990 /kg cm^2
Ultimate tensile strength: 275/kg cm2
Coef. thermal expansion: 0,0065mm/m°C
Water absorption: 0,02 %
Impact test / min. fall height: –
Frictional wear test: –
Bulk density: 2930 kg/m^3

CD file number: 0490

Temprest Black

Quarrying location: Sierra Leone
Availability: Medium
Compressive strength: 3011 /kg cm^2
After freezing: 2636 /kg cm^2
Ultimate tensile strength: 280 /kg cm2
Coef. thermal expansion: –
Water absorption: 0,01 %
Impact test / min. fall height: 69 cm
Frictional wear test: –
Bulk density: 2989 kg/m^3

CD file number: 0491

Padang TG 36

Quarrying location: South Africa
Availability: Limited
Compressive strength: 3011 /kg cm^2
After freezing: 2636 /kg cm^2
Ultimate tensile strength: 280 /kg cm2
Coef. thermal expansion: –
Water absorption: 0,01 %
Impact test / min. fall height: 69 cm
Frictional wear test: –
Bulk density: 2989 kg/m^3

CD file number: 0492

Labrador Black

Quarrying location: South Africa
Availability: Good
Compressive strength: 2823 /kg cm^2
After freezing: 2636 /kg cm^2
Ultimate tensile strength: 280/kg cm2
Coef. thermal expansion: –
Water absorption: 0,01 %
Impact test / min. fall height: 69 cm
Frictional wear test: –
Bulk density: 2989 kg/m^3

CD file number: 0493

Galaxy Black

Quarrying location: Zimbabwe
Availability: Good
Compressive strength: 3011 /kg cm^2
After freezing: 2636 /kg cm^2
Ultimate tensile strength: 280 /kg cm2
Coef. thermal expansion: –
Water absorption: 0,01 %
Impact test / min. fall height: 69 cm
Frictional wear test: –
Bulk density: 2989 kg/m^3

CD file number: 0494

Black Sierra

Quarrying location: India
Availability: Medium
Compressive strength: 3011 /kg cm^2
After freezing: 2636 /kg cm^2
Ultimate tensile strength: 280 /kg cm2
Coef. thermal expansion: –
Water absorption: 0,01 %
Impact test / min. fall height: 69 cm
Frictional wear test: –
Bulk density: 2989 kg/m^3

CD file number: 0495

Super Black

Quarrying location: South Africa
Availability: Medium
Compressive strength: 3011 /kg cm^2
After freezing: 2636 /kg cm^2
Ultimate tensile strength: 280 /kg cm2
Coef. thermal expansion: –
Water absorption: 0,01 %
Impact test / min. fall height: 69 cm
Frictional wear test: –
Bulk density: 2989 kg/m^3

CD file number: 0496

Nero Africa

Absolute Black Zimbabwe

Absolute Black India

Absolute Black Belfast

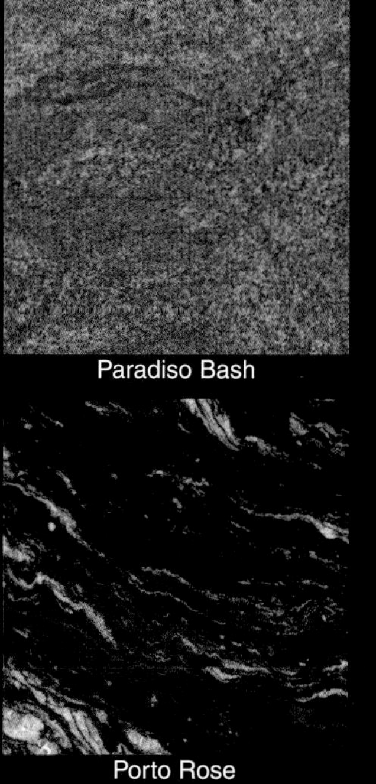

Paradiso Bash

Paradiso Chiaro

Paradiso Scuro

Saint Louis

Porto Rose

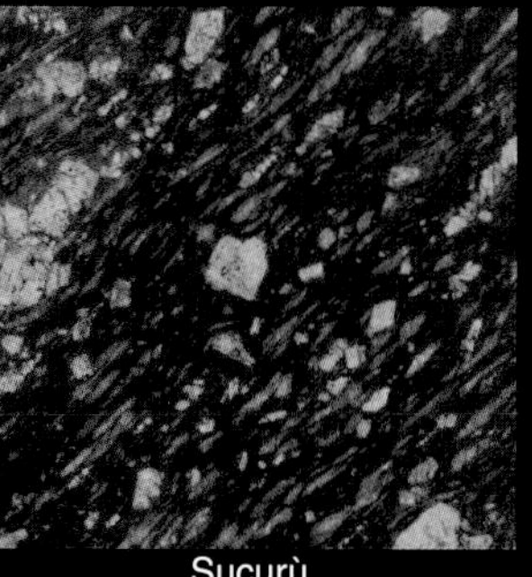

Sucurù

Temprest Black

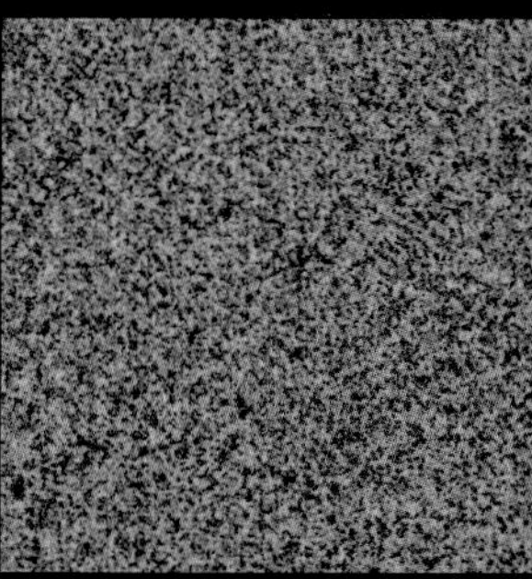

Padang TG 36

Labrador Black

Galaxy Black

Black Sierra

Super Black

Nero Africa

Absolute Black Zimbabwe

Absolute Black India

Absolute Black Belfast

QUARTZITE

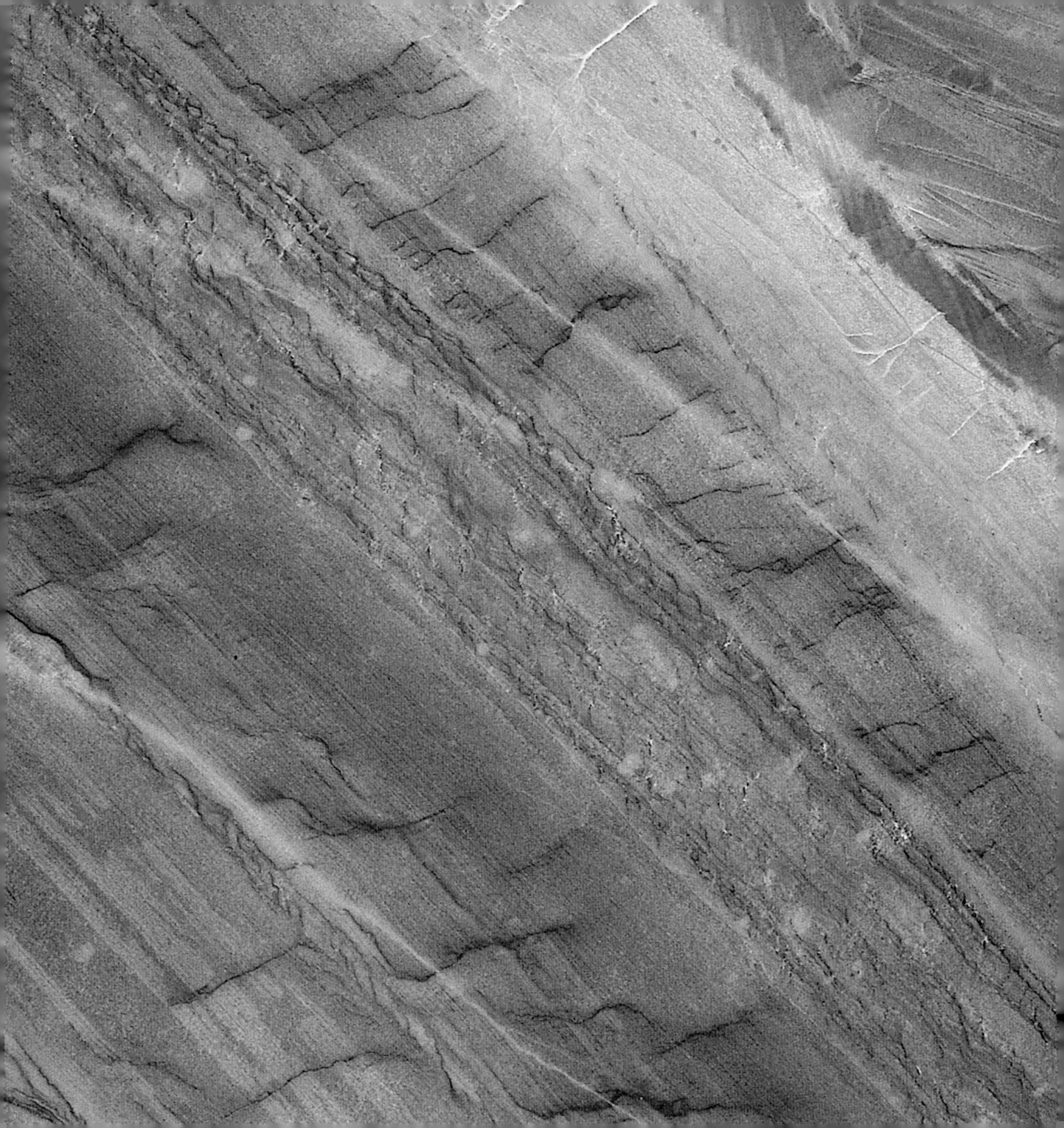

Quarrying location: Brazil
Availability: Good
Compressive strength: 1900/kg cm^2
After freezing: 1720/kg cm^2
Ultimate tensile strength: 202/kg cm^2
Coef. thermal expansion: 0,0016mm/m°C
Water absorption: 0,43%
Impact test / min. fall height: 80 cm
Frictional wear test: 0,47 mm
Bulk density: 2661 kg/m^3

CD file number: 0497

Quarrying location: Brazil
Availability: Good
Compressive strength: 1900/kg cm^2
After freezing: 1720/kg cm^2
Ultimate tensile strength: 202/kg cm^2
Coef. thermal expansion: 0,0016mm/m°C
Water absorption: 0,43%
Impact test / min. fall height: 80 cm
Frictional wear test: 0,47 mm
Bulk density: 2661 kg/m^3

CD file number: 0498

Quarrying location: Brazil
Availability: Good
Compressive strength: 1900/kg cm^2
After freezing: 1720/kg cm^2
Ultimate tensile strength: 202/kg cm^2
Coef. thermal expansion: 0,0016mm/m°C
Water absorption: 0,43%
Impact test / min. fall height: 80 cm
Frictional wear test: 0,47 mm
Bulk density: 2661 kg/m^3

CD file number: 0499

Quarrying location: Brazil
Availability: Medium
Compressive strength: 1900/kg cm^2
After freezing: 1720/kg cm^2
Ultimate tensile strength: 202/kg cm^2
Coef. thermal expansion: 0,0016mm/m°C
Water absorption: 0,43%
Impact test / min. fall height: 80 cm
Frictional wear test: 0,47 mm
Bulk density: 2661 kg/m^3

CD file number: 0500

Quarzite Rosa Chiara

Quarrying location: Brazil
Availability: Medium
Compressive strength: 2130/kg cm^2
After freezing: 2090/kg cm^2
Ultimate tensile strength: 203/kg cm^2
Coef. thermal expansion: 0,0014mm/m°C
Water absorption: 0,11%
Impact test / min. fall height: 81 cm
Frictional wear test: 0,54 mm
Bulk density: 2680 kg/m^3

CD file number: 0501

Quarzite Rosa

Quarrying location: Brazil
Availability: Medium
Compressive strength: 2130/kg cm^2
After freezing: 2090/kg cm^2
Ultimate tensile strength: 203/kg cm^2
Coef. thermal expansion: 0,0014mm/m°C
Water absorption: 0,11%
Impact test / min. fall height: 81 cm
Frictional wear test: 0,54 mm
Bulk density: 2680 kg/m^3

CD file number: 0502

Quarzite Rosa Corallo

Quarrying location: Brazil
Availability: Medium
Compressive strength: 2130/kg cm^2
After freezing: 2090/kg cm^2
Ultimate tensile strength: 203/kg cm^2
Coef. thermal expansion: 0,0014mm/m°C
Water absorption: 0,11%
Impact test / min. fall height: 81 cm
Frictional wear test: 0,54 mm
Bulk density: 2680 kg/m^3

CD file number: 0503

Quarzite Rosa Flamingo

Quarrying location: Brazil
Availability: Medium
Compressive strength: 2130/kg cm^2
After freezing: 2090/kg cm^2
Ultimate tensile strength: 203/kg cm^2
Coef. thermal expansion: 0,0014mm/m°C
Water absorption: 0,11%
Impact test / min. fall height: 81 cm
Frictional wear test: 0,54 mm
Bulk density: 2680 kg/m^3

CD file number: 0504

Azul Imperial

Quarrying location: Brazil
Availability: Limited
Compressive strength: 2130/kg cm^2
After freezing: 2090/kg cm^2
Ultimate tensile strength: 203/kg cm^2
Coef. thermal expansion: 0,0014mm/m°C
Water absorption: 0,11%
Impact test / min. fall height: 81 cm
Frictional wear test: 0,54 mm
Bulk density: 2680 kg/m^3

CD file number: 0505

Azul Imperial Chiaro

Quarrying location: Brazil
Availability: Limited
Compressive strength: 2130/kg cm^2
After freezing: 2090/kg cm^2
Ultimate tensile strength: 203/kg cm^2
Coef. thermal expansion: 0,0014mm/m°C
Water absorption: 0,11%
Impact test / min. fall height: 81 cm
Frictional wear test: 0,54 mm
Bulk density: 2680 kg/m^3

CD file number: 0506

Azul Imperial Scuro

Quarrying location: Brazil
Availability: Limited
Compressive strength: 2130/kg cm^2
After freezing: 2090/kg cm^2
Ultimate tensile strength: 203/kg cm^2
Coef. thermal expansion: 0,0014mm/m°C
Water absorption: 0,11%
Impact test / min. fall height: 81 cm
Frictional wear test: 0,54 mm
Bulk density: 2680 kg/m^3

CD file number: 0507

Azul Imperial Venato

Quarrying location: Brazil
Availability: Limited
Compressive strength: 2130/kg cm^2
After freezing: 2090/kg cm^2
Ultimate tensile strength: 203/kg cm^2
Coef. thermal expansion: 0,0014mm/m°C
Water absorption: 0,11%
Impact test / min. fall height: 81 cm
Frictional wear test: 0,54 mm
Bulk density: 2680 kg/m^3

CD file number: 0508

Azul Macauba Chiaro

Quarrying location: Brazil
Availability: Limited
Compressive strength: 2130/kg cm^2
After freezing: 2090/kg cm^2
Ultimate tensile strength: 203/kg cm^2
Coef. thermal expansion: 0,0014mm/m°C
Water absorption: 0,11%
Impact test / min. fall height: 81 cm
Frictional wear test: 0,54 mm
Bulk density: 2680 kg/m^3

CD file number: 0509

Azul Macauba

Quarrying location: Brazil
Availability: Limited
Compressive strength: 2130/kg cm^2
After freezing: 2090/kg cm^2
Ultimate tensile strength: 203/kg cm^2
Coef. thermal expansion: 0,0014mm/m°C
Water absorption: 0,11%
Impact test / min. fall height: 81 cm
Frictional wear test: 0,54 mm
Bulk density: 2680 kg/m^3

CD file number: 0510

Quarzite Blu Chiara

Quarrying location: Perù
Availability: Limited
Compressive strength: 2130/kg cm^2
After freezing: 2090/kg cm^2
Ultimate tensile strength: 203/kg cm^2
Coef. thermal expansion: 0,0014mm/m°C
Water absorption: 0,11%
Impact test / min. fall height: 81 cm
Frictional wear test: 0,54 mm
Bulk density: 2680 kg/m^3

CD file number: 0511

Quarzite Blu

Quarrying location: Brazil
Availability: Limited
Compressive strength: 2130/kg cm^2
After freezing: 2090/kg cm^2
Ultimate tensile strength: 203/kg cm^2
Coef. thermal expansion: 0,0014mm/m°C
Water absorption: 0,11%
Impact test / min. fall height: 81 cm
Frictional wear test: 0,54 mm
Bulk density: 2680 kg/m^3

CD file number: 0512

Quarzite Rosa Chiara

Quarzite Rosa

Quarzite Rosa Corallo

Quarzite Rosa Flamingo

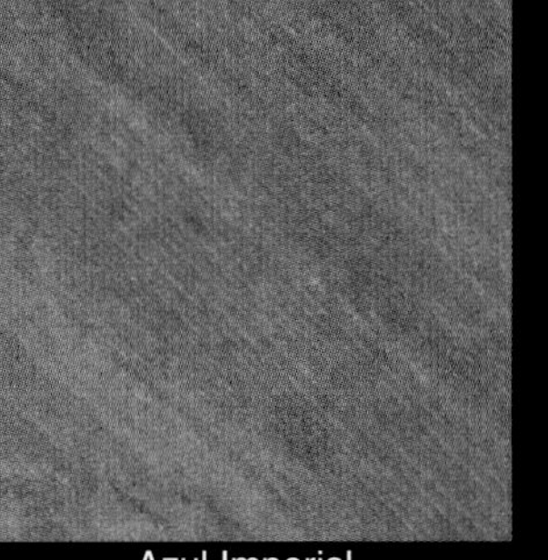

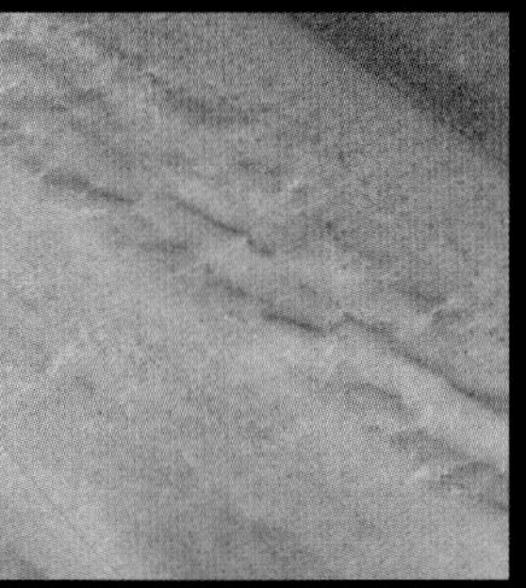

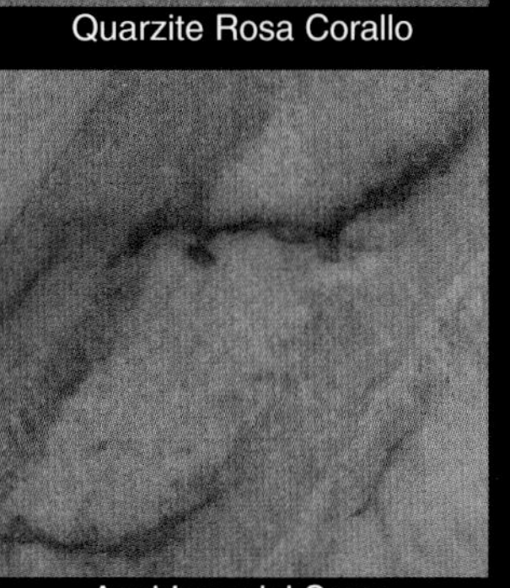

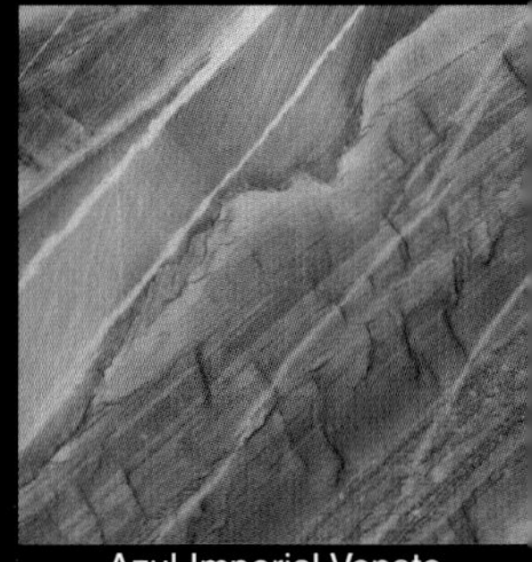

Azul Imperial

Azul Imperial Chiaro

Azul Imperial Scuro

Azul Imperial Venato

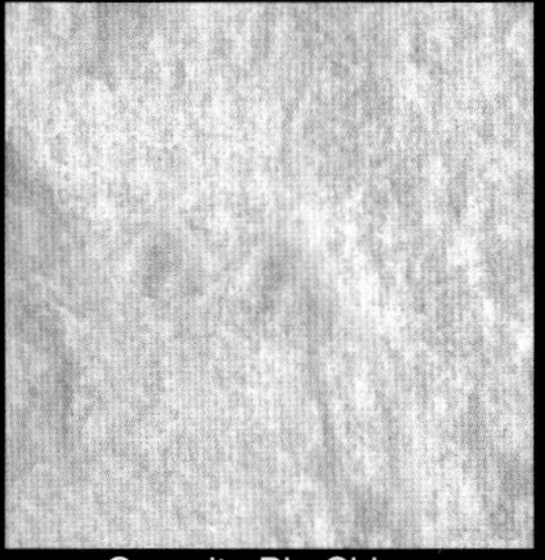

Azul Macauba Chiaro

Azul Macauba

Quarzite Blu Chiara

Quarzite Blu

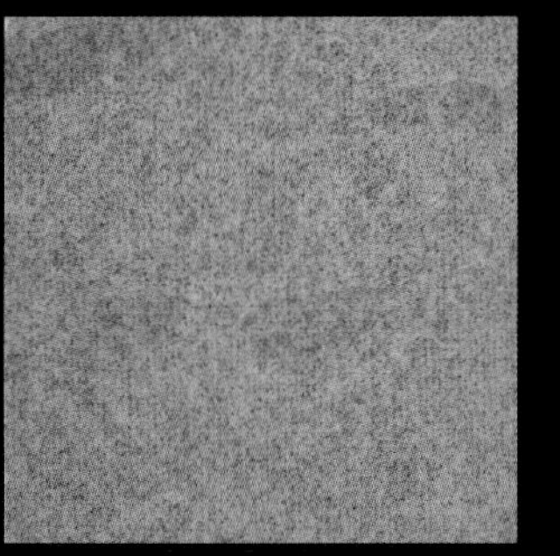

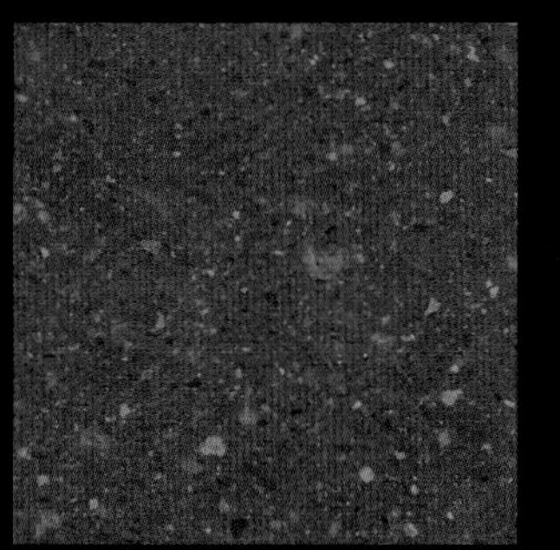

LIMESTONE

Quarrying location: France
Availability: Medium
Compressive strength: 2060/kg cm^2
After freezing: 1879/kg cm^2
Ultimate tensile strength: 155/kg cm^2
Coef. thermal expansion: 0,0040mm/m°C
Water absorption: 0,06%
Impact test / min. fall height: 26 cm
Frictional wear test: –
Bulk density: 2670 kg/m^3

CD file number: 0513

Quarrying location: Portugal
Availability: Medium
Compressive strength: 2060/kg cm^2
After freezing: 1879/kg cm^2
Ultimate tensile strength: 155/kg cm^2
Coef. thermal expansion: 0,0040mm/m°C
Water absorption: 0,06%
Impact test / min. fall height: 26 cm
Frictional wear test: –
Bulk density: 2670 kg/m^3

CD file number: 0514

Quarrying location: France
Availability: Medium
Compressive strength: 2060/kg cm^2
After freezing: 1879/kg cm^2
Ultimate tensile strength: 155/kg cm^2
Coef. thermal expansion: 0,0040mm/m°C
Water absorption: 0,06%
Impact test / min. fall height: 26 cm
Frictional wear test: –
Bulk density: 2670 kg/m^3

CD file number: 0515

Quarrying location: Spain
Availability: Medium
Compressive strength: 2060/kg cm^2
After freezing: 1879/kg cm^2
Ultimate tensile strength: 155/kg cm^2
Coef. thermal expansion: 0,0040mm/m°C
Water absorption: 0,06%
Impact test / min. fall height: 26 cm
Frictional wear test: –
Bulk density: 2670 kg/m^3

CD file number: 0516

Chambroad

Quarrying location: France
Availability: Medium
Compressive strength: 2060/kg cm^2
After freezing: 1879/kg cm^2
Ultimate tensile strength: 155/kg cm^2
Coef. thermal expansion: 0,0040mm/m°C
Water absorption: 0,06%
Impact test / min. fall height: 26 cm
Frictional wear test: –
Bulk density: 2670 kg/m^3

CD file number: 0517

Moleanos

Quarrying location: France
Availability: Medium
Compressive strength: 2060/kg cm^2
After freezing: 1879/kg cm^2
Ultimate tensile strength: 155/kg cm^2
Coef. thermal expansion: 0,0040mm/m°C
Water absorption: 0,06%
Impact test / min. fall height: 26 cm
Frictional wear test: –
Bulk density: 2670 kg/m^3

CD file number: 0518

Champagne

Quarrying location: France
Availability: Medium
Compressive strength: 2060/kg cm^2
After freezing: 1879/kg cm^2
Ultimate tensile strength: 155/kg cm^2
Coef. thermal expansion: 0,0040mm/m°C
Water absorption: 0,06%
Impact test / min. fall height: 26 cm
Frictional wear test: –
Bulk density: 2670 kg/m^3

CD file number: 0519

Durango

Quarrying location: Portugal
Availability: Medium
Compressive strength: 2060/kg cm^2
After freezing: 1879/kg cm^2
Ultimate tensile strength: 155/kg cm^2
Coef. thermal expansion: 0,0040mm/m°C
Water absorption: 0,06%
Impact test / min. fall height: 26 cm
Frictional wear test: –
Bulk density: 2670 kg/m^3

CD file number: 0520

Venezia

Quarrying location: France
Availability: Medium
Compressive strength: 2060/kg cm^2
After freezing: 1879/kg cm^2
Ultimate tensile strength: 155/kg cm^2
Coef. thermal expansion: 0,0040mm/m°C
Water absorption: 0,06%
Impact test / min. fall height: 26 cm
Frictional wear test: –
Bulk density: 2670 kg/m^3

CD file number: 0521

Ancona Beige

Quarrying location: France
Availability: Medium
Compressive strength: 2060/kg cm^2
After freezing: 1879/kg cm^2
Ultimate tensile strength: 155/kg cm^2
Coef. thermal expansion: 0,0040mm/m°C
Water absorption: 0,06%
Impact test / min. fall height: 26 cm
Frictional wear test: –
Bulk density: 2670 kg/m^3

CD file number: 0522

Capri

Quarrying location: France
Availability: Medium
Compressive strength: 2060/kg cm^2
After freezing: 1879/kg cm^2
Ultimate tensile strength: 155/kg cm^2
Coef. thermal expansion: 0,0040mm/m°C
Water absorption: 0,06%
Impact test / min. fall height: 26 cm
Frictional wear test: –
Bulk density: 2670 kg/m^3

CD file number: 0523

Moca Creme

Quarrying location: France
Availability: Medium
Compressive strength: 2060/kg cm^2
After freezing: 1879/kg cm^2
Ultimate tensile strength: 155/kg cm^2
Coef. thermal expansion: 0,0040mm/m°C
Water absorption: 0,06%
Impact test / min. fall height: 26 cm
Frictional wear test: –
Bulk density: 2670 kg/m^3

CD file number: 0524

Beauharnais

Quarrying location: France
Availability: Medium
Compressive strength: 2060/kg cm^2
After freezing: 1879/kg cm^2
Ultimate tensile strength: 155/kg cm^2
Coef. thermal expansion: 0,0040mm/m°C
Water absorption: 0,06%
Impact test / min. fall height: 26 cm
Frictional wear test: –
Bulk density: 2670 kg/m^3

CD file number: 0525

Aztec

Quarrying location: France
Availability: Medium
Compressive strength: 2060/kg cm^2
After freezing: 1879/kg cm^2
Ultimate tensile strength: 155/kg cm^2
Coef. thermal expansion: 0,0040mm/m°C
Water absorption: 0,06%
Impact test / min. fall height: 26 cm
Frictional wear test: –
Bulk density: 2670 kg/m^3

CD file number: 0526

Beaumanière Classic

Quarrying location: France
Availability: Medium
Compressive strength: 2060/kg cm^2
After freezing: 1879/kg cm^2
Ultimate tensile strength: 155/kg cm^2
Coef. thermal expansion: 0,0040mm/m°C
Water absorption: 0,06%
Impact test / min. fall height: 26 cm
Frictional wear test: –
Bulk density: 2670 kg/m^3

CD file number: 0527

Massangis

Quarrying location: France
Availability: Medium
Compressive strength: 2060/kg cm^2
After freezing: 1879/kg cm^2
Ultimate tensile strength: 155/kg cm^2
Coef. thermal expansion: 0,0040mm/m°C
Water absorption: 0,06%
Impact test / min. fall height: 26 cm
Frictional wear test: –
Bulk density: 2670 kg/m^3

CD file number: 0528

Beaurnais

Magny Louvre

Richeval

Fountaine Clare

Chambroad

Moleanos

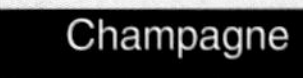
Champagne

Durango

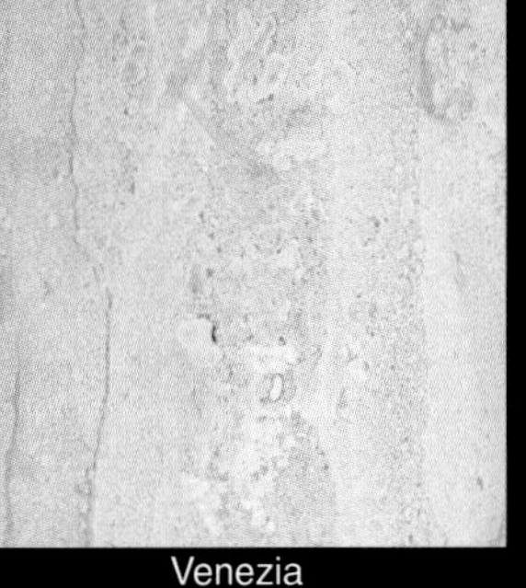
Venezia

Ancona Beige

Capri

Moca Creme

Beauharnais

Aztec

Beaumanière Classic

Massangis

Beaurnais

Magny Louvre

Richeval

Fountaine Clare

Quarrying location: France
Availability: Medium
Compressive strength: 2060/kg cm^2
After freezing: 1879/kg cm^2
Ultimate tensile strength: 155/kg cm^2
Coef. thermal expansion: 0,0040mm/m°C
Water absorption: 0,06%
Impact test / min. fall height: 26 cm
Frictional wear test: –
Bulk density: 2670 kg/m^3

CD file number: 0529

Quarrying location: Spain
Availability: Medium
Compressive strength: 2060/kg cm^2
After freezing: 1879/kg cm^2
Ultimate tensile strength: 155/kg cm^2
Coef. thermal expansion: 0,0040mm/m°C
Water absorption: 0,06%
Impact test / min. fall height: 26 cm
Frictional wear test: –
Bulk density: 2670 kg/m^3

CD file number: 0530

Quarrying location: France
Availability: Medium
Compressive strength: 2060/kg cm^2
After freezing: 1879/kg cm^2
Ultimate tensile strength: 155/kg cm^2
Coef. thermal expansion: 0,0040mm/m°C
Water absorption: 0,06%
Impact test / min. fall height: 26 cm
Frictional wear test: –
Bulk density: 2670 kg/m^3

CD file number: 0531

Quarrying location: France
Availability: Medium
Compressive strength: 2060/kg cm^2
After freezing: 1879/kg cm^2
Ultimate tensile strength: 155/kg cm^2
Coef. thermal expansion: 0,0040mm/m°C
Water absorption: 0,06%
Impact test / min. fall height: 26 cm
Frictional wear test: –
Bulk density: 2670 kg/m^3

CD file number: 0532

Heliodoro

Quarrying location: Spain
Availability: Medium
Compressive strength: 2060/kg cm^2
After freezing: 1879/kg cm^2
Ultimate tensile strength: 155/kg cm^2
Coef. thermal expansion: 0,0040mm/m°C
Water absorption: 0,06%
Impact test / min. fall height: 26 cm
Frictional wear test: –
Bulk density: 2670 kg/m^3

CD file number: 0533

Dore Reale

Quarrying location: Spain
Availability: Medium
Compressive strength: 2060/kg cm^2
After freezing: 1879/kg cm^2
Ultimate tensile strength: 155/kg cm^2
Coef. thermal expansion: 0,0040mm/m°C
Water absorption: 0,06%
Impact test / min. fall height: 26 cm
Frictional wear test: –
Bulk density: 2670 kg/m^3

CD file number: 0534

Heauteville

Quarrying location: France
Availability: Medium
Compressive strength: 2060/kg cm^2
After freezing: 1879/kg cm^2
Ultimate tensile strength: 155/kg cm^2
Coef. thermal expansion: 0,0040mm/m°C
Water absorption: 0,06%
Impact test / min. fall height: 26 cm
Frictional wear test: –
Bulk density: 2670 kg/m^3

CD file number: 0535

Giallo Elena

Quarrying location: France
Availability: Medium
Compressive strength: 2060/kg cm^2
After freezing: 1879/kg cm^2
Ultimate tensile strength: 155/kg cm^2
Coef. thermal expansion: 0,0040mm/m°C
Water absorption: 0,06%
Impact test / min. fall height: 26 cm
Frictional wear test: –
Bulk density: 2670 kg/m^3

CD file number: 0536

Damask Gold

Quarrying location: France
Availability: Medium
Compressive strength: 2060/kg cm^2
After freezing: 1879/kg cm^2
Ultimate tensile strength: 155/kg cm^2
Coef. thermal expansion: 0,0040mm/m°C
Water absorption: 0,06%
Impact test / min. fall height: 26 cm
Frictional wear test: –
Bulk density: 2670 kg/m^3

CD file number: 0537

Damask Gold Flamed

Quarrying location: France
Availability: Medium
Compressive strength: 2060/kg cm^2
After freezing: 1879/kg cm^2
Ultimate tensile strength: 155/kg cm^2
Coef. thermal expansion: 0,0040mm/m°C
Water absorption: 0,06%
Impact test / min. fall height: 26 cm
Frictional wear test: –
Bulk density: 2670 kg/m^3

CD file number: 0538

Rochebelle

Quarrying location: France
Availability: Medium
Compressive strength: 2060/kg cm^2
After freezing: 1879/kg cm^2
Ultimate tensile strength: 155/kg cm^2
Coef. thermal expansion: 0,0040mm/m°C
Water absorption: 0,06%
Impact test / min. fall height: 26 cm
Frictional wear test: –
Bulk density: 2670 kg/m^3

CD file number: 0539

Rochebelle Flamed

Quarrying location: France
Availability: Medium
Compressive strength: 2060/kg cm^2
After freezing: 1879/kg cm^2
Ultimate tensile strength: 155/kg cm^2
Coef. thermal expansion: 0,0040mm/m°C
Water absorption: 0,06%
Impact test / min. fall height: 26 cm
Frictional wear test: –
Bulk density: 2670 kg/m^3

CD file number: 0540

Richeval

Quarrying location: France
Availability: Medium
Compressive strength: 2060/kg cm^2
After freezing: 1879/kg cm^2
Ultimate tensile strength: 155/kg cm^2
Coef. thermal expansion: 0,0040mm/m°C
Water absorption: 0,06%
Impact test / min. fall height: 26 cm
Frictional wear test: –
Bulk density: 2670 kg/m^3

CD file number: 0541

Roc Argent Flamed

Quarrying location: France
Availability: Medium
Compressive strength: 2060/kg cm^2
After freezing: 1879/kg cm^2
Ultimate tensile strength: 155/kg cm^2
Coef. thermal expansion: 0,0040mm/m°C
Water absorption: 0,06%
Impact test / min. fall height: 26 cm
Frictional wear test: –
Bulk density: 2670 kg/m^3

CD file number: 0542

Heauteville Scuro

Quarrying location: France
Availability: Medium
Compressive strength: 2060/kg cm^2
After freezing: 1879/kg cm^2
Ultimate tensile strength: 155/kg cm^2
Coef. thermal expansion: 0,0040mm/m°C
Water absorption: 0,06%
Impact test / min. fall height: 26 cm
Frictional wear test: –
Bulk density: 2670 kg/m^3

CD file number: 0543

Rose Laurents

Quarrying location: Portugal
Availability: Medium
Compressive strength: 2060/kg cm^2
After freezing: 1879/kg cm^2
Ultimate tensile strength: 155/kg cm^2
Coef. thermal expansion: 0,0040mm/m°C
Water absorption: 0,06%
Impact test / min. fall height: 26 cm
Frictional wear test: –
Bulk density: 2670 kg/m^3

CD file number: 0544

Cedar Honed

Cedar Polished

Blu Chevernie

Gascogne Blu

Heliodoro

Dore Reale

Heauteville

Giallo Elena

Damask Gold

Damask Gold Flamed

Rochebelle

Rochebelle Flamed

Richeval

Roc Argent Flamed

Heauteville Scuro

Rose Laurents

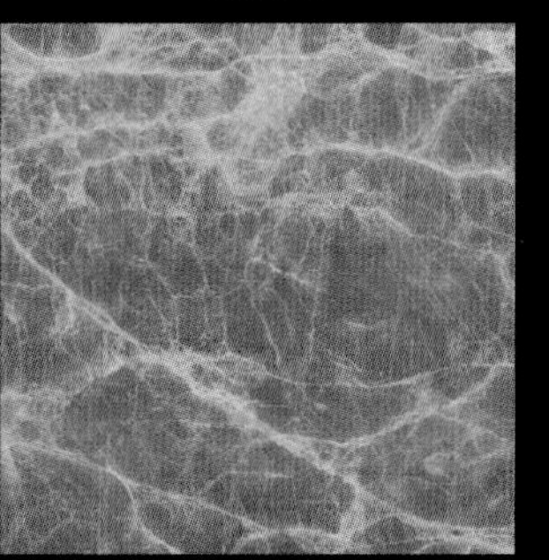
Cedar Honed

Cedar Polished

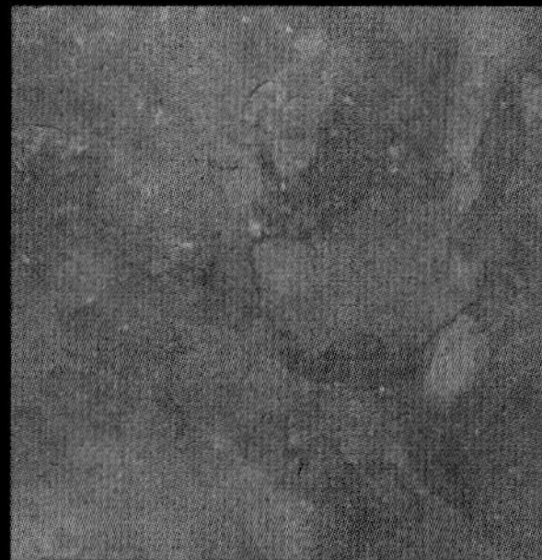
Blu Chevernie

Gascogne Blu

Quarrying location: Italy
Availability: Medium
Compressive strength: 800/kg cm^2
After freezing: 740/kg cm^2
Ultimate tensile strength: –
Coef. thermal expansion: –
Water absorption: –
Impact test / min. fall height: –
Frictional wear test: –
Bulk density: –

CD file number: 0545

Quarrying location: Italy
Availability: Medium
Compressive strength: 800/kg cm^2
After freezing: 740/kg cm^2
Ultimate tensile strength: –
Coef. thermal expansion: –
Water absorption: –
Impact test / min. fall height: –
Frictional wear test: –
Bulk density: –

CD file number: 0546

Quarrying location: Italy
Availability: Medium
Compressive strength: 1214/kg cm^2
After freezing: 1037/kg cm^2
Ultimate tensile strength: –
Coef. thermal expansion: –
Water absorption: 0,06%
Impact test / min. fall height: –
Frictional wear test: 7,2 mm
Bulk density: 2616 kg/m^3

CD file number: 0547

Quarrying location: Italy
Availability: Medium
Compressive strength: 1214/kg cm^2
After freezing: 1037/kg cm^2
Ultimate tensile strength: –
Coef. thermal expansion: –
Water absorption: 0,06%
Impact test / min. fall height: –
Frictional wear test: 7,2 mm
Bulk density: 2616 kg/m^3

CD file number: 0548

Pietra di S. Lucido

Quarrying location: Italy
Availability: Medium
Compressive strength: 1214/kg cm^2
After freezing: 1037/kg cm^2
Ultimate tensile strength: –
Coef. thermal expansion: –
Water absorption: 0,06%
Impact test / min. fall height: –
Frictional wear test: –
Bulk density: 2616 kg/m^3

CD file number: 0549

Pietra Rosa di Mendicino

Quarrying location: Italy
Availability: Medium
Compressive strength: 1214/kg cm^2
After freezing: 1037/kg cm^2
Ultimate tensile strength: –
Coef. thermal expansion: –
Water absorption: 0,06%
Impact test / min. fall height: –
Frictional wear test: –
Bulk density: 2616 kg/m^3

CD file number: 0550

Pietra di Matraia

Quarrying location: Italy
Availability: Medium
Compressive strength: 1214/kg cm^2
After freezing: 1037/kg cm^2
Ultimate tensile strength: –
Coef. thermal expansion: –
Water absorption: 0,06%
Impact test / min. fall height: –
Frictional wear test: 7,2 mm
Bulk density: 2616 kg/m^3

CD file number: 0551

Pietra del Cardoso

Quarrying location: Italy
Availability: Medium
Compressive strength: 1214/kg cm^2
After freezing: 1037/kg cm^2
Ultimate tensile strength: –
Coef. thermal expansion: –
Water absorption: 0,06%
Impact test / min. fall height: –
Frictional wear test: 7,2 mm
Bulk density: 2616 kg/m^3

CD file number: 0552

Pietra Basaltina

Quarrying location: Italy
Availability: Medium
Compressive strength: 1490/kg cm^2
After freezing: 1330/kg cm^2
Ultimate tensile strength: 570/kg cm^2
Coef. thermal expansion: –
Water absorption: 0,32%
Impact test / min. fall height: 94 cm
Frictional wear test: –
Bulk density: 2710 kg/m^3

CD file number: 0553

Pietra di Bedonia

Quarrying location: Italy
Availability: Medium
Compressive strength: 1490/kg cm^2
After freezing: 1330/kg cm^2
Ultimate tensile strength: 570/kg cm^2
Coef. thermal expansion: –
Water absorption: 0,32%
Impact test / min. fall height: 94 cm
Frictional wear test: –
Bulk density: 2710 kg/m^3

CD file number: 0554

Pietra Serena

Quarrying location: Germany
Availability: Medium
Compressive strength: 1490/kg cm^2
After freezing: 1330/kg cm^2
Ultimate tensile strength: 570/kg cm^2
Coef. thermal expansion: –
Water absorption: 0,32%
Impact test / min. fall height: 94 cm
Frictional wear test: –
Bulk density: 2710 kg/m^3

CD file number: 0555

Peperino Grigio

Quarrying location: Germany
Availability: Medium
Compressive strength: 1490/kg cm^2
After freezing: 1330/kg cm^2
Ultimate tensile strength: 570/kg cm^2
Coef. thermal expansion: –
Water absorption: 0,32%
Impact test / min. fall height: 94 cm
Frictional wear test: –
Bulk density: 2710 kg/m^3

CD file number: 0556

Ardesia Nera Honed

Quarrying location: Italy
Availability: Medium
Compressive strength: 1214/kg cm^2
After freezing: 1037/kg cm^2
Ultimate tensile strength: –
Coef. thermal expansion: –
Water absorption: 0,06%
Impact test / min. fall height: –
Frictional wear test: 7,2 mm
Bulk density: 2616 kg/m^3

CD file number: 0557

Ardesia Nera Cleft

Quarrying location: Italy
Availability: Medium
Compressive strength: 1214/kg cm^2
After freezing: 1037/kg cm^2
Ultimate tensile strength: –
Coef. thermal expansion: –
Water absorption: 0,06%
Impact test / min. fall height: –
Frictional wear test: 7,2 mm
Bulk density: 2616 kg/m^3

CD file number: 0558

Ardesia Verde Honed

Quarrying location: Italy
Availability: Medium
Compressive strength: –
After freezing: –
Ultimate tensile strength: –
Coef. thermal expansion: –
Water absorption: –
Impact test / min. fall height: –
Frictional wear test: –
Bulk density: –

CD file number: 0559

Ardesia Verde Cleft

Quarrying location: Italy
Availability: Medium
Compressive strength: –
After freezing: –
Ultimate tensile strength: –
Coef. thermal expansion: –
Water absorption: –
Impact test / min. fall height: –
Frictional wear test: –
Bulk density: –

CD file number: 0560

Pietra di Luserna

Pietra di Courtil

Pietra Dorata

Pietra Dorata Venata

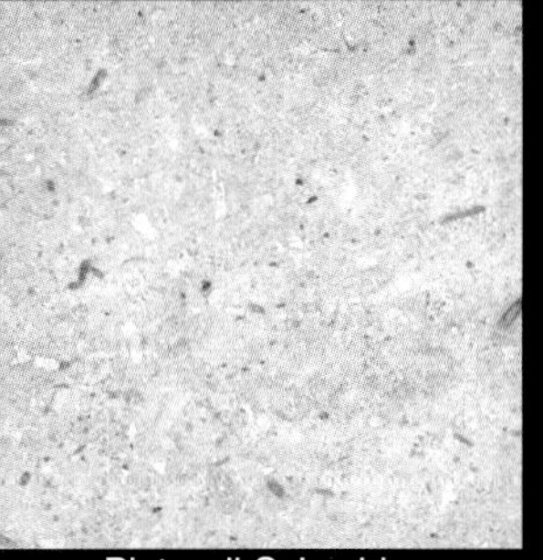

Pietra di S. Lucido

Pietra Rosa di Mendicino

Pietra di Matraia

Pietra del Cardoso

Pietra Basaltina

Pietra di Bedonia

Pietra Serena

Peperino Grigio

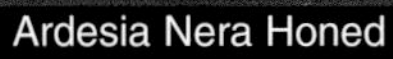

Ardesia Nera Honed

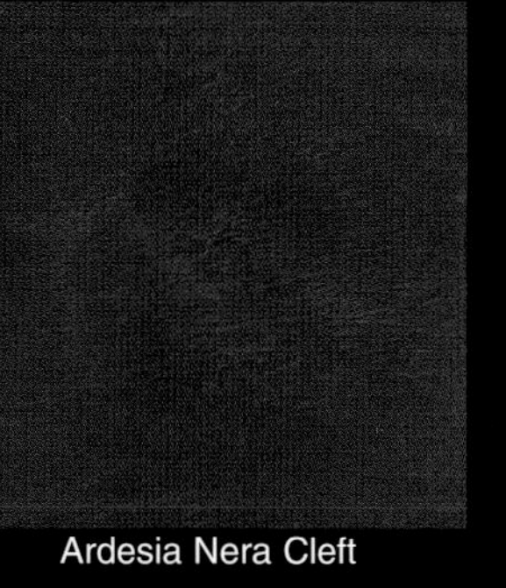

Ardesia Nera Cleft

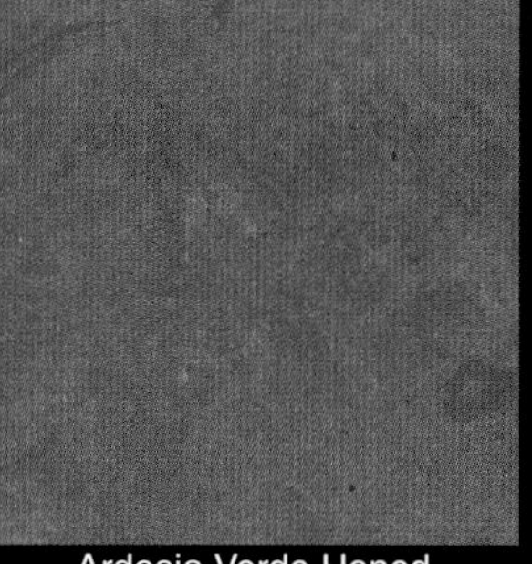

Ardesia Verde Honed

Ardesia Verde Cleft

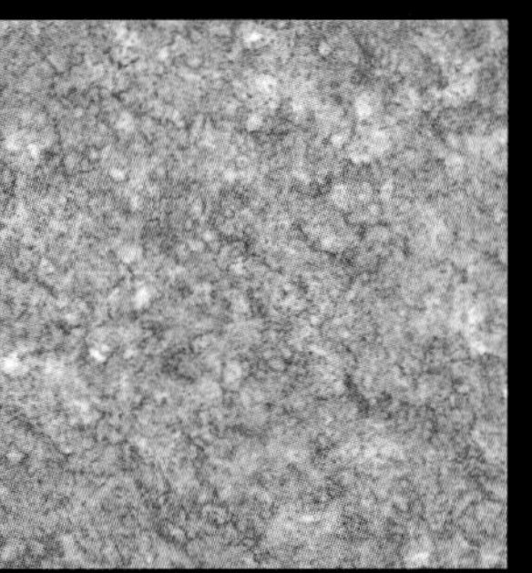

Pietra di Luserna

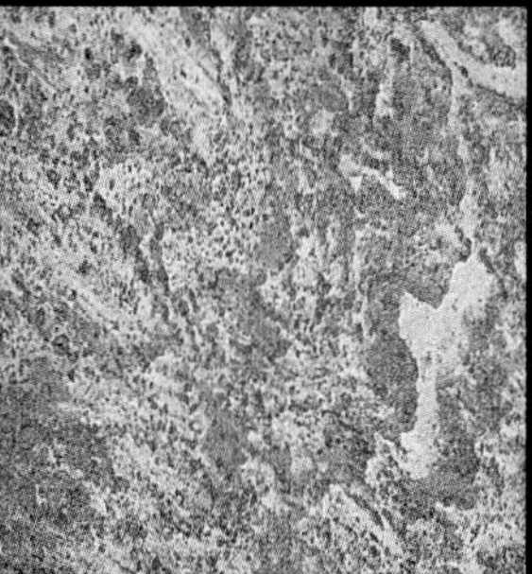

Pietra di Courtil

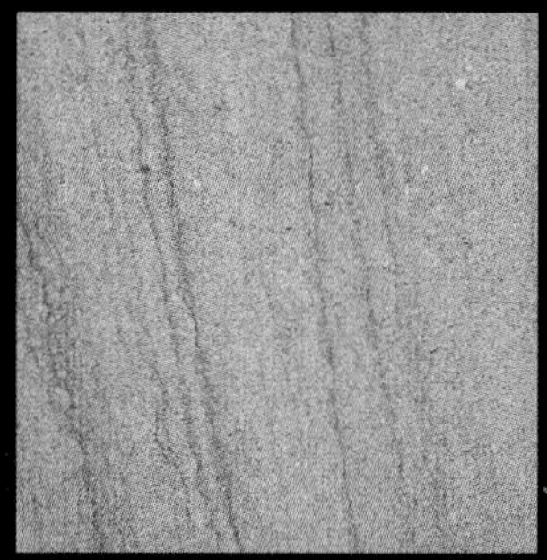

Pietra Dorata

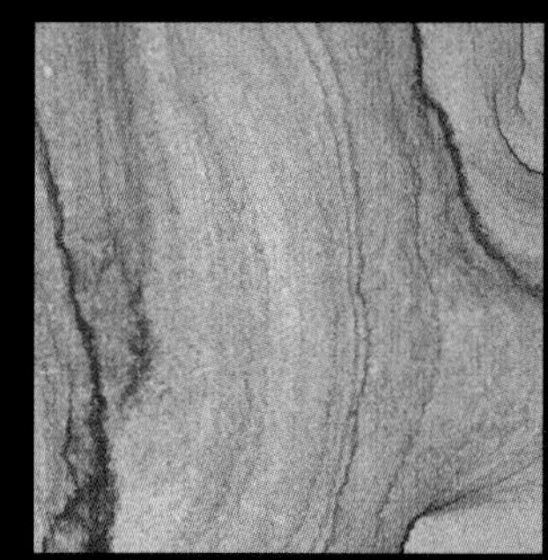

Pietra Dorata Venata

STONE SAMPLER INDEX

MARBLE

TRAVERTINE

ONYX

GRANITE

QUARTZITE

LIMESTONE

STONE SAMPLER
CD ROM

ABOUT THE CD-ROM

The accompanying CD-ROM
contains printable screen resolution
files of all the samples in the book.
With the appropriate graphics
software, the CD images can be
used by designers in developing
concepts, preparing presentations
for clients, and communicating visual
information to others.
Although the images are primarily
intended for on-screen display, they
can also be printed on either a
black and white or color printer.
Further information about the
image formats can be found on the
readme.txt file on the CD.
The images found in this CD-Rom
may not be reproduced
for commercial use without the
written authorization
of Studio Marmo.
Original images can be obtained
from Studio Marmo,
6663 Sedgwick Place,
Brooklyn, NY, 11220.
Email: studiomarmo@firenze.net